Net Crimes & Misdemeanors

Outmaneuvering the Spammers, Swindlers, and Stalkers who are Targeting You Online

By J. A. Hitchcock

Edited by Loraine Page

📖 **Information Today, Inc.**

Medford, New Jersey

First printing, 2002

Net Crimes & Misdemeanors: Outmaneuvering the Spammers, Swindlers, and Stalkers Who Are Targeting You Online

Library of Congress Cataloging-in-Publication Data

Hitchcock, Jayne A.
   Net crimes & misdemeanors : outmaneuvering the spammers, swindlers, and stalkers who are targeting you online / by J. A. Hitchcock ; edited by Loraine Page.
      p. cm.
   Includes bibliographical references and index.
   ISBN 0-910965-57-9 (pbk.)
    1. Computer crimes. 2. Computer crimes--Prevention. I. Title: Net crimes and misdemeanors. II. Page, Loraine, 1952- III. Title.

HV6773 .H575 2002
364.16'8--dc21

                      2002004686

Printed and bound in the United States of America.

Publisher: Thomas H. Hogan, Sr.
Editor-in-Chief: John B. Bryans
Managing Editor: Deborah R. Poulson
Copy Editor: Pat Hadley-Miller
Cover Design: Victoria Stover
Book Design: Kara Mia Jalkowski
Proofreader: Dorothy Pike
Indexer: Robert Saigh

Dedication

To my husband, Chris, who has never wavered in his support for me during the ups and downs of my cyberstalking case, who has been my biggest cheerleader when the going got tough, who has put up with my getting laws passed, traveling the country training law enforcement, being interviewed by the media many, many times, and who has endured my writing of this book past dinnertime more often than not. You're the best, hon!

Table of Contents

Chapter 12

Chapter 13

Chapter 14

Chapter 15

Figures

Sidebars

Acknowledgments

Thank yous go to many people, and I know I'll probably forget someone:

My "Internet Posse"—especially the ones who stuck it out to the end, namely Cyber-Sheriff Chris Lewis, Jack Mingo, Stan Kid, Curt Akin, James Charles Rau, Mary Kay Klim, Bob Pastorio, Dick Harper, Erin Barrett, Colin Hatcher, Wayne Lutz, Crusader Rabbit, and Mary Jo Place aka "Kiki"; also Marty, Sal, Bjorn, Ellie, Marjike, Kye, and Katy Munger; and the newsgroup misc.writing. Without all of you, I never would have learned so much about the Net and how to educate others about it.

My lawyer, John Young, who took my cyberstalking case on contingency—you truly are a blessing.

My "big brother" Raymond E. Feist. He kept me sane when I was depressed about my cyberstalking case and encouraged me to keep at it when my book proposal was rejected numerous times.

My editor Loraine Page. When I groused to her that my book proposal was rejected by just about every publisher and I'd gone through three literary agents, she suggested sending the proposal to the book division of the publishing company that produces *Link-Up,* a print Internet magazine I contribute to and she edits. I slapped myself on the forehead for not thinking of it myself. If it hadn't been for Loraine, this book might never have come to fruition—and she's one of the best editors I've ever worked with.

All the people interviewed for this book—victims and experts. There are too many to mention by name, but you know who you are, and you were all wonderful to share your experiences and expertise.

My fellow volunteers at WHOA (Working to Halt Online Abuse). I couldn't ask for a better group of people to work with, and a special thank you to Lynda Hinkle, who founded WHOA in 1997 and handed over the reins to me in 1999.

The University of Maryland University College and my boss (and friend) Art Huseonica. UMUC became one of the first universities to deal with a cyberstalking case—mine—and they handled it well (especially Rocky). I'm glad I didn't "quit teachering" after all!

Foreword

It is my happy privilege to write a foreword for a book about protecting your privacy and personal security in the Internet age. More than that, I am especially happy to write it for my longtime friend Jayne Hitchcock. Still, it disturbs me that such a book is necessary, and as I think readers will come to agree, the environment that has led to the need for such a timely book is something that should concern us all deeply.

The problems of stalking, harassment, identity theft, and the other topics covered herein are not at all unique to the Internet. For a thousand years, paupers have paraded around passing themselves off as princes, and even a few princes have skulked around in paupers' guise. But with modern technology, what was once the province of a few flim-flam artists is now available to millions.

The ease with which people—be they criminals, the news media, or just nosey neighbors—have been able to access the personal information of others, both off-line and online, has been a source of increasing concern for privacy advocates for some years now. In fact, an entire industry has grown up around the construction of massive databases filled with every shred of data about your life, your health, your finances, your buying habits, and your desires.

These databases are carefully guarded, except of course if you are willing to pay the right price; then the doors are flung open so the data can be massaged and manipulated for purposes of sending you junk mail and calling you at dinnertime. If you ask these new merchants of data why they gather and sell the personal information of consumers, they cheerfully answer that it is so that businesses can better serve consumers. This is the "just think what terrible offers we'd call you with at dinnertime if we didn't know you so well" argument.

The depressing news is that calls at dinnertime are surprisingly the happy side of this story.

There is a much darker and more sinister side to this new market-place of personal information, a side that we are reminded about all too frequently. In recent years we have seen an explosion of news reports about stalkers and identity thieves who have bought or stolen personal information and used that data to destroy their victims' lives, both figuratively and literally.

As a law student studying under the great trial lawyer Jonathan Turley, I learned that problems are often best solved by those for whom the cost and complexity of the solution is the least. Carrying that lesson into a career in the privacy arena, I have long argued that when the practices of data collectors become a problem, those best suited to solving the problem are the ones whose activities have helped create the problem.

I do not dispute that some uses of personal information are helpful, such as credit services that help consumers get loans more promptly than in years past. Yet where more menacing uses of personal data are occurring, the data brokers have largely thrown up their hands and declared that there is nothing to be done about the many personal disasters their services have made possible. For businesses whose stock in trade is keeping tabs on people whose car payments are a few weeks past due, their apathy toward promptly fixing the destroyed credit of an identity theft victim borders on criminal negligence. As a result it can take years to fix what identity thieves can do in days.

What gives me such mixed feelings about the reasons for this book is that, as critical as it is for everyday people to understand how desperately important it is to protect themselves and their private information from misuse and abuse, the need for such a book reminds me that things are getting worse. The negligence of the data brokers in today's information age, coupled with ways new technologies are being employed to gather even more information, evokes the image of a new Wild West kind of frontier, where all men, women, and children are forced to fend for themselves.

For these reasons, books like *Net Crimes & Misdemeanors* have become urgently necessary. If our privacy is up to us to protect, we need resources like this book to teach us how to assert our right to be left alone. We should all be thankful that Jayne has assembled a balanced and thoughtful resource for teaching us all how to sail through our lives in the information age, leaving fewer broken bits of our privacy floating in our wake.

When I think about why Jayne Hitchcock is such a perfect person to help average folks learn to protect themselves, I am reminded of an illustration from a political event many years ago. In 1987, I had the privilege of working for then-Senator Al Gore on his first campaign for president. At a fundraising breakfast he thanked everyone for coming to the event and expressed his appreciation for their involvement in his fledgling campaign. But, he exhorted the crowd, it was now time for each of them go a step farther, to move from just being involved to being fully committed to the campaign.

To illustrate the difference between involvement and commitment, he pointed to a plate sitting on the head table, still piled high with scrambled eggs and country ham. "Just looking at this fine breakfast, the difference between involvement and commitment is clear," he continued. "The chicken was involved. But the hog is committed!"

There are a growing number of very excellent books on the market discussing the perils of privacy invasion and threats to personal safety coming both online and off-line. But for the vast majority of those authors, their relation to the issue is much more akin to the relationship between the chicken and that breakfast plate: they have an expertise and interest sufficient to inspire them to take on the task of writing a book. For Jayne, it is something much deeper than that. This book is evidence of her passionate commitment to make sure that others are not forced to live through the nightmares.

Unfortunately, it is a commitment that was forced upon her in an especially awful way.

It was while doing some consulting work for America Online (AOL) that I first met Jayne. AOL had asked me to help them develop and enforce policies regarding Internet abuse, including "spam" and other inappropriate uses of network resources. In the course of that work, I spent a lot of time working on problems related to the Internet discussion boards called Usenet newsgroups.

In culling through piles of complaints and abuse reports, I noticed a sizeable number of complaints relating to a few newsgroups devoted to creative writing. The more I delved into those reports, the more complicated and sordid the tale became. Before I realized it, I was smack in the middle of Jayne's protracted battle with cyberstalkers. I will not steal her thunder except to say that it was, at the time, both gripping and deeply disturbing to see the harassment, abuse, threats, and intimidation heaped upon Jayne by a band of thugs.

Reflecting upon the circumstances that give Jayne such intimate knowledge of these issues, the old adage "that which does not kill us makes us stronger" comes to mind. I must admit however that I use that phrase with some trepidation. For me, that phrase has always seemed particularly infuriating, offered up as consolation from bystanders to the struggle, as if it actually helped to soothe a wound. As maddening as that saying can be, it is nevertheless apt. The horrific circumstances through which Jayne passed not only made her stronger, but made her something more: a passionate and articulate advocate for those who, like her, have landed in the sights of the deranged and disturbed.

It is so very understandable that many who have experienced a loss of privacy and security would seek to return to an anonymous life as quickly as possible. That is why I am amazed at how often people choose to turn the trauma of such events into action. But I am happy to report that Jayne Hitchcock is no shrinking violet—not by any means! She chose to see her struggles as a challenge laid, a gauntlet thrown. That which did not kill her did indeed make her stronger, turning her into a fierce advocate for victims of abuse.

The encouraging irony is that such ghastly incidents often turn victims into some of the world's most effective advocates for change. One would never wish hardship on anyone, yet if there was an easier and more pleasant way to inspire good people to draw such strength from deep within themselves, I wish we could reproduce it and put it in the drinking water. Until that day, we have books like this and people like Jayne to show us not just how to survive, but to reassert control over our lives so we can thrive and prosper in this new frontier.

I urge you to read carefully and let these lessons help you to assert your right to privacy and take charge of your own life again. And who knows? Some day, you might even get to finish your dinner without being called to the phone.

Ray Everett-Church, Esq.
San Jose, CA

Ray Everett-Church, a senior privacy strategist at ePrivacy Group, is an internationally recognized expert on privacy law and Internet-related public policy. He is an advisor to the Privacy Officers Association and a member of the National Advisory Council of The George Washington University School of Engineering and Applied Science. A graduate of George Mason University, he received a law degree from the National Law Center at The George Washington University.

About the Web Page:
netcrimes.net

The world of online information changes with each blink of the eye, and the limitations of any print volume covering Internet resources are obvious: New sites and resources appear every day, other sites are expanded to include new or enhanced features, and still other sites disappear without a trace.

At netcrimes.net, the author is maintaining a regularly updated directory of key Internet resources—including, wherever possible, active links to sites (you must have an Internet connection and WWW browser to utilize these links). This directory is designed to help you pinpoint sites offering specific types of help and information, and to keep you up-to-date on the trends and issues. It is being made available as a bonus to readers of *Net Crimes & Misdemeanors*. Please take advantage of the feedback feature at the site to let us know what you think, and to recommend additional sites that readers may find useful.

Safe surfing!

Disclaimer

Neither publisher nor author make any claim as to the results that may be obtained through the use of the above mentioned links to Internet sites and resources, which are maintained by third parties. Neither publisher nor author will be held liable for any results, or lack thereof, obtained by the use of any links, for any third party charges, or for any hardware, software, or other problems that may occur as a result of using netcrimes.net. This program of Internet resources and links is subject to change or discontinuation without notice at the discretion of the publisher.

Introduction

You Can Be Safe Online

You wouldn't walk down a dark street in an unfamiliar neighborhood alone, would you? You wouldn't divulge where you live or work to a stranger in an elevator, would you? Surprisingly, many otherwise sensible people throw caution to the wind when they're online, assuming, apparently, that they're completely safe. They're not, no matter how computer savvy they think they are.

Danger lurks on the Internet.

Consider these scenarios:

- You purchase bath products from an online shopping site. When you receive your credit card bill, you find there are several more charges on it...and you didn't buy anything else.

- You go to an online auction, bid on a photograph "signed" by a celebrity, and win. You send in your payment and wait. And wait some more. You do some investigating and find that not only are you not going to get the photograph you paid for, but there are serious doubts about the authenticity of the autograph.

- You receive phone calls and knocks on your door from strangers—all in response to a message "you" placed online. Only you don't own a computer.

- You're on a newsgroup called alt.business.home and someone gets angry at an innocent question you've asked. Messages begin to appear from "you" insulting other people in the group. This results in a barrage of e-mails to you from the

1

people "you" offended. Your e-mail account is canceled, and your employer receives phone calls from people complaining that "you" are harassing them online.

You may think you know better than to get caught up in a scam or a harassment situation. But I will show that it can happen to even the most experienced online user. It happened to me. In 1996, I thought I knew everything about the Internet. I'd already been online a number of years, was a teaching assistant for basic and advanced Internet courses at a university, wrote hardware and software reviews for magazines, participated in newsgroups and forums, and surfed like a pro. Then I unwittingly became the victim of Internet harassment so threatening that it changed my life. Read my story in Chapter 1.

Net crimes and misdemeanors are committed against more than 60,000 people a year, and the number is growing every day, according to statistics from the FBI and victim advocate organizations. NUA Internet Surveys (www.nua.com) estimates there are more than 500 million people online worldwide. If only 1 percent become online victims, that is still over five million people—a drop in the bucket as more people go online for the first time every day.

When my harassment occurred, I didn't know where to go for help. There certainly was no book available to explain things to me, and there were no laws to protect me. Because what happened to me was so extreme, and because I saw such a lack of understanding of cybercrime, I have since become one of the nation's leading cybercrimes experts, giving lectures nationwide and appearing on TV programs to get the word out about Internet crimes. I serve as president of Working to Halt Online Abuse (WHOA), a group that works with more than 100 online victims a week.

The media has given some coverage to this growing problem, but not enough. It tends to emphasize sensational cases without imparting safety information to the public. I give lectures and training workshops to law enforcement personnel around the country, and am always surprised at how few of those in attendance are up-to-date on online harassment and cyberstalking issues. I've been told time and again that a book explaining what can occur and offering preventative measures would be welcome.

That's why I decided to write this book.

Net Crimes & Misdemeanors is written in language that is easy to understand if you are not familiar with the online world, but it is not written so simply that experienced Internet users will find it too basic. Each chapter begins with an explanation of the chapter's focus—and sometimes a definition or two of online harassment terms—and includes one sample case or more to show that even smart folks can have bad experiences. This is followed by tips and advice from experts. If, as you're reading, you come across a computer term you're unfamiliar with, check the Glossary in the back of the book. If you see an organization or a product you want to know more about, check the Resources section for the Web site address. In addition, there is an official Web site for the book at www.netcrimes.net, where you will find an updated list of links from the book and other links that may be of interest.

This book is only a first step in learning how to be safe online. To be truly Net-savvy, you'll have to keep vigilant long after you've read these chapters. Though I am known as a cyberstalking expert, I always keep an eye open for the latest developments in the world of online safety. If you and I don't remain alert, danger could strike. I don't know about you, but I don't intend to let it happen to me—not again.

A note on the case histories: Some of the victims I describe are actually composites of people from cases I've worked on through WHOA; I have done this to keep those victims anonymous. Some victims allowed me to use their real names, and others allowed me to use their stories verbatim but asked me to use pseudonyms. When recounting case histories, sample e-mail messages, posts, or chat room transcripts, they are exactly as they appeared online—with grammatical and spelling errors intact. Profanities are not spelled out, however, because I wanted parents to be able to share the information in this book with their children.

Don't let trolls, spoofers, spammers, e-mailbombers, cyberstalkers, and other online miscreants make you live in fear or give up the many advantages of Internet use. In reading this book, you've already taken the first step to arm yourself.

You're on your way toward becoming safe online.

Cyberstalking
Happened to Me

We'd been living in Maryland for just over a year in a nice, quiet neighborhood near Annapolis. On Saturday, December 21, 1996, a nasty cold I had quickly developed into bronchitis. We canceled plans to visit relatives on Christmas, had no tree or decorations up, and I was miserable. That night I went to bed early after taking some nighttime cold medicine. My husband, Chris, went upstairs to his office about 10 P.M. to get our e-mail. All of a sudden I heard his voice—very angry.

"What the hell?" he yelled.

I bolted upright, got out of bed, and went upstairs.

"What's the matter?"

"Who do you know named Sfon@aol.com?" Chris was furiously pounding keys on the keyboard.

"I don't know anyone by that name." I walked over to his desk and looked at the computer monitor.

Our e-mail messages were being downloaded. Hundreds of them. We usually averaged 30 messages a day.

"Can you stop it?"

"I'm trying." Chris repeatedly clicked the Cancel button and the messages finally stopped downloading.

Chris opened one message. Then another. And another. They were all the same. Someone had taken my reply to a message that had been posted on the "misc.writing" newsgroup and added an extra-long "Happy New Yearrrrrrrrrrrrrrrrrrrrrrr" at the end of my signature file.[1] The "rrrrrrr's" went on for two pages when we printed out the message.

I was stunned. I had no idea who did this. Maybe someone didn't like my reply, which was intended to be humorous. No one I knew on misc.writing would stoop to something this low.

Chris downloaded the rest of the messages, weeded through the e-mail bombs to get our real messages, then deleted all but a couple of the e-mail bombs—just in case we needed them. For the rest of the time he was online that night no more e-mail bombs arrived.

The next night at about the same time, it happened again. Chris yelled again. I raced upstairs. His face was red.

"I can't believe this jerk," he muttered angrily, jabbing his finger in the direction of the computer monitor.

Hundreds of messages were being downloaded. This time it was a different message, but the same return address: Sfon@aol.com.

I hadn't told Chris that earlier in the day I went online and posted a message to the misc.writing newsgroup. I asked if anyone else had been e-mail bombed. No one had, but some of the people on the newsgroup asked me to send them one of the e-mail bombs we'd received. We discovered that the e-mails were coming from an ISP called IDT out of New York and not AOL.[2] Just about everyone on misc.writing knew one particular group of people in New York who were the most likely candidates for the e-mail bombs—the Woodside Literary Agency.

● ● ● ● ●

Earlier that year, I had read a post on Usenet from the Woodside Literary Agency:

```
Subject: WRITERS SEEKING PUBLICATION
From: CFSQ98A@prodigy.com (James Leonard)
Date: 1996/01/24
Newsgroups: rec.arts.books.childrens

The Woodside Literary Agency is now
accepting new authors, re: fiction and non-
fiction: children's books. Advances from
publishers can be high. You must have a
completed manuscript. We have offices from
New York to Florida. E-mail for informa-
tion: CFSQ98A@prodigy.com. If you respond
during the month of February, call my new
```

Florida agency at: 813-642-9660. I will be
there in February.

James

I called the phone number listed and spoke with James Leonard. He sounded professional and courteous and answered all of my questions. Then he asked me to submit a book proposal. Shortly after I mailed the proposal to Woodside, I received a letter from the company claiming it was the most professional proposal they'd ever read and they wanted to see the full manuscript. One paragraph down was a request for a $75 reading fee. Since I'd already published six books, I knew the majority of agents don't charge reading or editing fees. Red warning flags appeared in my mind.

I visited a discussion group called misc.writing and asked if anyone had heard of Woodside, and then I recounted my experience. I soon found that Woodside was infamous for spamming[3] its "Writers Wanted" message ad in any newsgroup it could find. It was obvious that Woodside hoped to entice aspiring writers or others unfamiliar with the business of writing and hit them with a reading fee. Woodside could find a lot of prey; wannabe writers are desperate to see their work published. Along with several writer friends, I began to search for Woodside's posts in various newsgroups. We left warnings about the agency as an act of kindness.

I began to receive e-mail from people who had sent Woodside their manuscripts or proposals and paid the requested reading fee. Some paid more than that—a contract fee and other miscellaneous fees—but never received anything in return except requests for more money. One woman lost about $1,000. Some of these people asked me for help. I contacted the New York State Attorney Generals (NYSAG) office. I was told if I could find more victims, they would begin an investigation into Woodside's activities. So I posted messages on writing newsgroups asking if anyone who had given money to Woodside would be willing to join this investigation.

What I considered a helpful warning to fellow writers was seen by Woodside as a call to war.

• • • • •

Chris waited while the messages downloaded. He deleted all but one—again, just in case it was needed later—and there were no more e-mail bombs for the rest of the night.

Although I was pretty sure this was the work of Woodside, I had to be positive before making accusations.

The next day I began receiving e-mail messages from mailing lists[4] claiming I had subscribed to them. I hadn't. Luckily, most of the lists asked for confirmation before adding me, so I was able to stop most of the subscriptions before they got started. For the others, I had to make the effort to contact them and get the subscriptions cancelled.

I found out that the University of Maryland University College (UMUC), where I was employed, was also e-mail bombed with messages from "me." It was obvious that this was an attempt to get me fired. Here is one of the messages, dated December 29, 1996, verbatim:

> I'm an assistant teacher at UMUC and I think you and the whole of UMUC are a bunch of morons insidiously festering away your small brains. I may or I may not resign. I may stay to awaken you idiots. I'm an international author and I know what I'm talking about. I am also very powerful and wealthy, so don't even think of messing with me.
>
> J.A.Hitchcock—Teaching computer cources at stinking UMUC.

• • • • •

The next night, at 10 P.M., the e-mail bombs hit again. Chris had installed "kill filters"[5] so that this time any e-mail from Sfon@aol.com would be deleted automatically. But our e-mailbox began to fill up anyway. It was Sfon@aol.com again, but with a new twist—he or she had added the letter "a" or "b" so that the return e-mail addresses read either Sfona@aol.com or Sfonb@aol.com. The kill filters Chris created were useless.

"That's it!" Chris yelled. "Call Netcom." Netcom was our ISP.

By this time it was midnight. Not only was I still sick, I was ready to burst into tears. If it was Woodside, why was I being targeted and not the other writers from misc.writing?

I called Netcom. The tech support representative who answered was very understanding and quickly gave us a new e-mail address and proceeded to weed out our real e-mail from the e-mail bombs.

Chris decided it was time to separate our e-mail into "his" and "mine." We had a free e-mail account with Geocities,[6] where our Web pages were located. Chris began using the hitchcocks@geocities.com e-mail address and I used our new e-mail address from Netcom. Even with the new address, I knew I couldn't take the chance of posting messages on newsgroups for fear of being e-mail bombed again. I contented myself with just reading the messages even though I longed to join in on many of the discussions.

The change in e-mail addresses didn't stop the cyberharasser.

Messages forged in my name began appearing on newsgroups—hundreds of newsgroups, from alt.fan.harrison-ford to rec.climbing to alt.abortion. Some of the messages used my old e-mail address, latakia@ix.netcom.com, while others used sock puppets.[7] One message appeared in all caps on the alt.atheism newsgroup:

> ATHEISTS ARE MORONS:
> AS A DAILY SPOKESPERSON FOR THE NEWSGROUP MISC.WRITING, I FIND THAT ATHEISM IS FOR UNINFORMED BRAINDEAD IMBECILS. TO LEARN ABOUT CREATIVE THINKING CONTACT ME AT MISC.WRITING AND MAYBE I WILL SEND YOU ONE OF MY BOOKS. AFTER ALL, I AM AN INTERNATIONAL AUTHOR AND KNOW WHAT I AM TALKING ABOUT. HITCHCOCK.

Another appeared, also in all caps, on the alt.beer newsgroup with the subject heading "Beer drinkers are morons."

> BEER DRINKERS ARE MORONS:
> BEER DRINKING MOST CERTAINLY CREATS AN ENORMOUS POPULATION OF DRUNKS WHO NEVER CONTRIBUTE ANYTHING TO SOCIETY, THEIR FAMILIES OR ANYTHING LIVING. I AM AN INTERNATIONAL AUTHOR AND KNOW WHAT I AM TALKING ABOUT AND CAN BE REACHED AT MISC.WRITING. I'LL BE HAPPY TO GIVE YOU ONE OF MY BOOKS TO GET ALL YOU DRUNKS ON THE RIGHT PATH WHERE IT IS ONLY AN ARM'S REACH AWAY. HITCHCOCK.

Online friends from the misc.writing newsgroup went about canceling these messages whenever and wherever they popped up.

Then the cyberharasser discovered Chris's Geocities e-mail address and began e-mail bombing it with a vengeance. One of the e-mail bombs consisted of a single word repeated over and over—

the name of our dog, Bandit. Chris was very upset at this new blow, and I was at a loss as to how to handle the whole thing.

Just when I thought it couldn't get worse, more forged posts appeared in newsgroups. The messages were still on the same "morons" theme but had a new twist: They now included my home phone number and dared the morons to call me. No one did, thankfully.

As if this weren't enough, problems began to appear in my off-line life as well. Magazines I hadn't subscribed to arrived in my mailbox, as did memberships to music and book clubs I hadn't ordered. And I received notification of pending deliveries of porcelain figurines I never ordered. I had to call to cancel all of these. I realized someone was subscribing me to everything and anything.

We had company for dinner a week later, just after New Year's Day. We sat in the living room eating appetizers and chatting. Chris finished cooking dinner and I helped him serve it. It was a nice, relaxed evening with good friends, a relief after all the problems online.

A phone call came at the end of dinner. Chris answered and handed the receiver to me with a quizzical look on his face.

"It's some woman from California. She says it's about the Internet."

I shrugged my shoulders and took the phone from him.

"Hello?"

"Hi, my name is Cindy. I saw those posts on the newsgroups. I had the same thing happen to me and I thought you might want to know about them."

"I already know about the 'morons' posts and I have some people helping me cancel them," I replied.

She paused. "I don't think you've seen these. They're new messages posted on sex-related newsgroups."

"What?"

Everyone at the dining room table stopped talking.

"It's something called Hot For Lovebites," Cindy went on. "Your home phone number and address are in it. You'd better get online and see what I'm talking about. Then you might want to call the police."

"Thank you," I said and hung up the phone.

I excused myself from my guests, ran into my office, and turned on the computer. I quickly got online and discovered "I" had posted messages to hundreds of newsgroups—all of them sex-related or controversial, such as alt.skinheads or alt.sex.bestiality, and most of them with the subject heading Hot For Lovebites. I cringed as I read this post, which is verbatim except that I have substituted XXX's for my real address and phone number at that time:

```
From: Jayne Hitchcock
      <FunGirl@netcom.com>
Newsgroups: alt.sex.bondage
Subject: Hot Lovebites
Date: Sat, 04 Jan 1997 22:59:13 -0800
Female International Author, no limits to
imagination and fantasies, prefers group
macho/sadistic interaction, including love-
bites and indiscriminate scratches. Invites
you to write or call to exchange exciting
phantasies with her which will be the topic
of her next book. No fee for talented
University of Maryland students. Contact me
at misc.writing or stop by my house at XXX
XXXXX XXXXX, MD. Will take your calls day
or night at (410) XXX-XXXX. I promise you
everything you've ever dreamt about.
Serious responses only.
```

Not only was the fungirl@netcom.com address fake, but my employer, UMUC, was being dragged into this. And I was scared to death because the harasser and untold others now had my address and phone number.

I swallowed hard, fired off a quick e-mail to my cyberfriends asking for help again, then went back to my dinner guests and very calmly told them what was happening. They were appalled.

The phone rang continually. I answered it only once—when I received a collect call. I thought it was from my mother or sister. But when the prompt came for the caller to identify himself, a man's guttural voice announced, "It's Loverboy."

I didn't get much sleep that night. I was online most of the time and kept finding more and more of the Hot For Lovebites posts. Every time the phone rang, I cringed.

The next morning I checked the answering machine for messages. There was only one. I heaved a sigh of relief. I played the message and a man's scary-sounding voice said, "This is a serious phone call. Do you know your phone number is on the Internet at Fungirl dot-com? I live nearby and you should go to the police before someone knocks on your door."

I knew this, and inwardly thanked him for being nice enough to warn me even though I felt it was a somewhat crude phone call.

I called the local police and they told me they weren't computer literate—they didn't know what a newsgroup was. They said they'd be happy to send a patrol car over, but I told them that if they didn't understand what I was talking about, they couldn't help me. They referred me to the police commissioner's office in Annapolis. When speaking with a representative there, the dismissal was swift: "I don't know what to tell ya, lady."

Frustrated and afraid, and not knowing how far the harassment would go, I contacted the FBI Computer Crimes Unit in Baltimore, Maryland. I was informed that unless a death threat or threat of physical harm had been directed at me or I'd actually been physically assaulted, there wasn't much they could do. But they said they would send an agent to look into it. When an agent finally arrived to interview me it was almost a month later.

The phone calls continued. One came from Germany, and the message lasted for five minutes. This caller assured me I could call or fax him 24 hours a day if I was interested; he left both numbers with the country code. Another person who'd seen a Hot For Lovebites post left this message for me online:

```
You must be one DIM writer. I'm about 20
miles away from you {along with a goodly
amount of rapists, murderers,& crack-heads}
Good Luck, you are going to NEED it. By the
way, if you don't already own a gun; I sug-
gest you go down to West street in Parole
and buy one.
```

I began to fear that someone would actually come to the door looking for sex. I feared for my life. We bought a gun. I learned how to use it, and I learned well.

In cyberspace I had to fend for myself. So I did the only thing I could think of: I turned again to my fellow writers on the misc.writing newsgroup. Angered by the harassment and lack of help from law enforcement, we, as a group, decided to take control of the situation ourselves. I dubbed them my Internet Posse.

Control it we did. We dug into old files and records online. We made phone calls, took photos, and e-mailed anyone we thought would be able to help.

We finally found the proof we needed that the harasser was indeed the Woodside Literary Agency. They posted their "Writers Wanted" ad (similar to the one I had replied to) to several newsgroups on January 5, 1997. But they forgot to remove my name and fake e-mail address from the "From:" line on the message. This same fake e-mail address had been used earlier that day to forge the Hot For Lovebites posts and e-mailbombs in my name. This, along with other important information discovered soon after, encouraged me to file a civil suit against Woodside et al. in January 1997 in Eastern District Court, New York, for $10 million.

In the civil suit, my lawyer named the Woodside Literary Agency and any of the names attributed to it, plus 10 John Does and Richard Roes[8] in case we missed anyone.

Two of the people named in the suit, Ursula Sprachman and James Leonard, soon came forward with a lawyer. A third, John Lawrence, made himself known to my lawyer a week after I appeared on the TV program *Unsolved Mysteries* in May 1997.

The ISP used for the harassment, IDT, cooperated fully with my lawyer. We soon found there were several accounts opened at IDT by the Woodside Literary Agency, but with different credit card numbers and different names so that when one account was canceled Woodside would jump to a new one and continue the harassment. IDT notified us that they found all of the accounts and canceled them. I began to breathe easier.

But the people at Woodside weren't done with me yet. My lawyer received a death threat over the phone. An employee of one of the ISPs Woodside spammed from also received a death threat. Woodside continued to harass me, online and off, including going to a great deal of trouble to find our new unpublished phone number. They went so far as to call neighbors I'd never met and ask if they knew our phone number. One neighbor was so rattled he knocked on our door to tell us about it.

Fellow writers formed a legal fund for me called H.E.L.P. (Hitchcock Expenses for Legal Proceedings). Contributions were put in a savings account and used for any legal expenses I incurred for my case against Woodside. I soon found out that Ursula Sprachman called and wrote the Maryland State Police, Maryland State Attorney General, and the FBI in Baltimore to file a complaint about me, claiming that the H.E.L.P. fund was illegal and something should be done to stop me. I was notified of the complaint by each organization, which added it to their files on me. I'm pretty sure Ursula wanted me arrested. That was very disturbing and it frightened me.

A year to the day after the harassment began, December 21, 1997, the phone rang at 7:15 A.M. I sleepily picked it up, heard someone breathing on the other end, and said hello a few times. No answer, so I hung up. When I awoke an hour later, I remembered the phone call and dialed *69. The phone call had come from the Woodside Literary Agency. I called the police to file a report and then called the telephone company to install Caller ID. I wondered what would happen next.

I didn't have to wait long. It came in the form of a letter titled "For Employment Purposes," which was sent to UMUC inquiring about my position there, how much money I made, what I did, and so on. The letter made it look like the company was planning to hire me and was doing a background check. It wasn't signed but the letterhead said WILA, which are the initials for Woodside International Literary Agency—their latest "new" name.

A secretary at UMUC told me she called the phone number listed and was yelled at by a woman with a German accent. This woman, who gave her name as Rita Maldonado, was angry that the secretary refused to give out any information about me. Ursula Sprachman, one of the known defendants, has a German accent. The letter was sent to my lawyer as evidence.

At a speaking engagement soon after this latest incident, a car followed me in the parking lot. The security guard on duty chased after the car but couldn't get the license plate number. Although I can't prove that Woodside people were in that car, I felt that this incident was too much of a coincidence.

It seemed as though Woodside et al. had become obsessed with me. Every time I turned around, they did something else. Much of what they did made no sense, and at times was actually humorous. But it seemed they were determined to make my life so miserable that I would drop the suit against them.

I became so paranoid at one point that I would get down on the ground and check under my car before going anywhere. If anyone drove too closely behind me or seemed to be following me, I changed directions, changed lanes, or took a different exit—whatever it took to make sure I wasn't being followed.

I got a cell phone and carried it with me everywhere. The mental stress of the whole thing got to be too much and I began to see a psychotherapist. She helped me put things in perspective, calmed me down, and gave me a chance to talk it out. If I hadn't gone to see her, I don't know how I would have coped. I know I was on the verge of a mental collapse.

I came to realize that I should turn the "negative" of this situation into a "positive." So I got busy. I contacted the writers who'd been scammed by Woodside, got copies of letters and cashed checks from them, and then sent all of it to the NYSAG. On November 14, 1997, NYSAG filed a civil suit against the Woodside Literary Agency et al. on four counts: false advertising, deceptive business practices, fraud, and harassment (the last for what they did to me). On February 17, 1999, NYSAG won a default judgment against Woodside. In July and August 2001, victims who paid Woodside money received restitution checks as part of that judgment.

After I testified before three Maryland legislative sessions, a bill that would make e-mail harassment a crime passed in April 1998. It is now a misdemeanor to harass anyone via e-mail in the state of Maryland, with penalties of $500 and/or jail time.

I provided written testimony to the California legislature for a proposed cyberstalking bill. An amendment of the civil and penal codes related to stalking, this bill added the Internet and other forms of electronic communication as another method of harassment and stalking. It passed and became a law on January 1, 1999.

New Hampshire quickly approved a bill that made Internet harassment a Class A misdemeanor, punishable by up to a year in jail and/or up to a $2,500 fine. I testified before the State House, helped amend the bill, then testified before the State Senate, where the bill was unanimously passed and put into law immediately after Governor Jeanne Shaheen signed it on June 25, 1999. Other states soon followed, with either written or in-person testimony from me: Maine, Rhode Island, Minnesota, and Illinois. I'm working on similar legislation in other states. I don't want to see anyone else go through what I've gone through.

I volunteer my services to various organizations and law enforcement agencies nationwide, including the Department of Justice Victims of Crime, National Center for Victims of Crimes, Maryland State Police Computer Crimes Unit, various other law enforcement agencies, and Working to Halt Online Abuse (WHOA), of which I'm president.

I've become known as a cybercrimes expert, specializing in cyberstalking. I speak about the subject nationwide, appear on TV and radio, and am mentioned in magazine and newspaper articles. I travel the country to train law enforcement professionals how to track down cyberstalkers and work with victims. I want to get the word out to the public as much as possible to make them as cyber-streetsmart as I am now.

As a result of everything that's happened, my husband and I have moved to an undisclosed location in New England and have taken extreme caution to keep our new residence private. Although it's worked to a certain degree, we know we're never going to be safe and that scares me. The good news is that in January 2000, I received a phone call from the U.S. Postal Inspection Service. They arrested Ursula Sprachman and James Leonard on federal charges of mail fraud and perjury. It turns out the third person, John Lawrence, was fictitious. James Leonard made up this persona, complete with social security number, driver's license, credit cards, bank accounts, and more, to do the majority of the harassment and cyberstalking. To become so obsessed with me to create this persona scared me more than anything else they'd done so far.

Instead of facing a trial, the two decided to plead guilty. The federal sentencing hearing concluded on December 6, 2001. James Leonard received eight months in prison, which is the maximum sentence, and three years probation; Ursula Sprachman received three years probation, as she had no prior criminal record and because of her age and poor health. My lawyer made a handshake agreement for a settlement in my civil suit, the amount of which I could not disclose when this book went to print.

I saw this situation to the end, and I prevailed and won—not only for me, but for all writers and for all online victims.

There is justice, after all.

Endnotes

1. Signature File: A line or two of words, usually a user's name and contact information or favorite Web site URL, automatically added to the end of every e-mail or Usenet message sent out.
2. AOL: America OnLine, a popular Internet service provider.
3. Spamming: When someone posts a message to more than 20 newsgroups at a time.
4. Mailing List: Similar to a newsgroup except that all messages and replies are sent to your e-mail inbox. Most mailing lists are moderated; someone reads the messages before sending them to the list, eliminating most of the spam and unwanted clutter. However, some mailing lists are so busy that members can receive 100 or more messages per day.

5. Kill Filter: Many e-mail programs offer this feature so that the e-mail program can automatically delete any e-mail the user doesn't want. Most people use this for spam.
6. Geocities: An online "homestead" where people can get free Web page space, free e-mail, and other online extras. Located at www.geocities.com.
7. Sock puppet: An e-mail address that goes nowhere when someone tries to send a message to it.
8. John Does and Richard Roes are often used in cases where the plaintiff does not know all the names of the defendants.

Words Can Hurt

E-Mail Bomb

When hundreds of e-mail messages are sent to one e-mail address in an effort to overload the account and shut that e-mailbox down.

E-Mail Threats

Threats and/or harassment sent via e-mail.

In August 1999 an Australian student was convicted for sending an e-mail threat to American tennis player Chanda Rubin while she was competing in the Australian Open. The student's message to Rubin included expletives, a racial slur, and a threat: "I'm going to assassinate you on the court."

Rubin almost backed out of the tournament, but finally decided to play. When the student was arrested, he pleaded guilty to making a threat to kill and using telecommunications to menace another person. He was fined $250 (Australian) and ordered to perform 100 hours of community service over six months.

In recent years, other sports celebrities and famous names in politics and Hollywood were also targets of e-mailbombs and threats. The incidents were reported in the media and the perpetrators were dealt with swiftly and severely. But what happens when you're not a celebrity or well-known? When the police won't help, you have to rely on your own resources, as one Australian woman discovered.

Nina's Story

Nina liked to visit a newsgroup called soc.support.fat-acceptance. She was overweight and found solace in the camaraderie on the newsgroup. But someone calling himself "Mike" took a distinct dislike to her newsgroup messages and began filling her e-mailbox with harassment and threats in all caps, such as the following (note: the expletives were fully spelled out in his message):

> YOU'RE A REVOLTING FREAK WHO SHOULD BE TAKEN OUT BACK AND SHOT.
> ALL YOU FAT HIDEOUS BITCHES HAVE NO REA-SON TO LIVE! END IT ALL!
> THE SOONER THE BETTER, FAT MESS! F---OFF, FATS!"
> STOP EATING YOU FAT C--T SMEAR!

Some of his e-mails had a forged[1] return address of FAT_BITCHES_MUST_DIE@JENNYCRAIG.COM. Others seemed to come from a Yahoo! e-mail address. Nina did the right thing and contacted Yahoo! and the other online mail services she thought Mike was using for his messages.

"But I was getting absolutely no response," says Nina, recalling the unpleasant incident. "I even brought it to the notice of the local branch of the Australian Federal Police, who basically said there wasn't much they could do. The system administrator at my ISP was a friend of mine and dealt swiftly with the one and only threat of an e-mailbombing I received."

Even though the e-mailbombs never made it to her inbox and she stopped posting to the newsgroup, Mike kept sending her e-mail messages. She tried to filter them out, but he would just change the return e-mail address to something else and the messages would come through, getting worse with each one.

Nina began to wonder where Mike was located. Since the Web is international, he could be on another continent and just trying to scare her into thinking she was in imminent danger, or he could be in Australia living near her.

With no help from the local police or online mail services, she turned to Working to Halt Online Abuse (WHOA). After examining the full headers (explained later in this chapter) of the e-mail messages, the staff at WHOA found that the messages were going through several remailers[2] but originated from an ISP in Chicago. WHOA sent complaints to the appropriate ISP and remailers on Nina's behalf. Within three hours, all the parties involved had canceled Mike's accounts, including his ISP.

"WHOA not only got a response, but solid results," Nina says. "It's nice to know that I can now open my e-mailbox without having to worry."

Andy's Houseguest

Male victims of e-mail harassment are often embarrassed to go to the police or ISPs with complaints and usually wait until something really scares them before doing anything. That's how it went with Andy from California.

"Someone set up a Yahoo! e-mail account using my name," Andy says. "They created the account so that when anyone replied to an e-mail from the Yahoo! account, a copy would be sent to my real AOL e-mail address."

When Andy got an acknowledgment from Yahoo! for the e-mail address "he" set up, he followed their procedures for canceling it. Two days later, he found another account had been created, but this time an e-mail had been sent to everyone listed in his personal AOL address book. The message was titled "The Biggest Clown" and it contained no text. The same message was sent several times and each time Andy got a copy of it.

Some of the people listed as recipients e-mailed or called Andy to ask what was going on, and some thought it was funny. Andy found it disturbing and definitely not funny. But he decided to ignore it. Then a message titled "Meatloaf" was sent out. This time a photo was attached: a naked, obese man with Andy's head. It was an obvious forgery, but the people receiving this were the employees and managers he worked with at a Hollywood film studio. This was not good.

Andy got more reaction this time, with recipients asking if the photo was a joke. He was humiliated. He didn't want to go to the police. He was a man, after all, and could take care of this himself. Besides, they'd probably just laugh at him. So he did some digging and discovered that the messages originated from Spain. Then it clicked. About six months earlier, he'd let a male friend from Spain,

Antonio, stay with him. Antonio had brought along a friend, Marcel. The three men got along fine, along with Andy's roommate and dog.

One day, Marcel asked Andy if he could check his e-mail. Andy agreed and signed onto his AOL account. Although Andy noticed later that Marcel had forwarded a message with all the addresses from his address book, Andy dismissed it as a mistake since Marcel didn't speak English very well.

Then he remembered something that happened when Antonio and Marcel were visiting. Antonio had gone to the store and Andy took his dog for a walk. Marcel followed him out and began yelling at him for no reason.

"We were standing in front of my apartment building, so I said we need to walk to a quieter place," Andy says. "Marcel refused and when I started to walk away, he grabbed me by the shoulders, then put one hand over my mouth. Luckily, my roommate came out and Marcel pulled away. Marcel was crying later, saying he almost killed me and then said he had almost killed his sister once. I don't know if he was overdramatizing, but it was scary at the time. It was at that point that I decided I did not want further contact with him when he went back to Spain. I just never put two-and-two together when the e-mails were sent to people in my address book."

Andy contacted Yahoo! again about the second e-mail account created in his name and they canceled it. He also did some more investigative work and found the forged e-mail messages were routed through two remailers in Canada but originated in Spain. Andy sent an e-mail to the remailers and ISP in Spain explaining the situation. Although he didn't hear anything from any of them, he did receive a postcard from Marcel begging for forgiveness. He didn't reply to Marcel and hasn't heard from him since.

Andy feels vindicated, and he's much more careful online now.

"I pretty much stay away from e-mails from strangers since the incident," he says. "I only use the Internet to shop, do research for work, or do some selling on eBay. I also learned a valuable lesson: Do *not* let anyone have access to my e-mail account, even if all they want to do is check their e-mail. Now I send people to our local library."

"I'm Your Worst Nightmare"

A Minnesota teenager found she was the target of an e-mail harassment campaign that she couldn't stop. Taryn was 15 years old in May 1998 and a popular, straight-A student. Like many others at her school, she was "wired" and spent time after school e-mailing and IMing[3] friends. Then she began to receive messages from an e-mail address she didn't recognize. The first one read:

```
I'm your worst nightmare. Your troubles
are just beginning.
```

The messages got worse from there, and eventually included pornography. They continued for three weeks.

"I locked all the windows and doors in the house, even if my whole family was home," Taryn says. "We were all so upset about it."

Taryn's grades began to fall, and she spent more and more time at home. She did the right thing by going to her local police, but they told her they couldn't tell where the messages originated; they didn't have the online expertise to do this at the time. She turned to her ISP who then worked with the police and finally figured out that the perpetrator was a high school friend of Taryn's. He had sent the messages on a dare and promised to never do it again. His sentence was 100 hours of community service; if he'd been 18, he would have gone to prison.

"That was the most terrifying thing I had ever been through," says Taryn. "So I decided I needed to make others aware of what they could do if they got threatening e-mails."

Taryn put together an online safety brochure called *Shut the Door.* She hands this out when she speaks at schools and to law enforcement personnel throughout Minnesota; she has distributed over 100,000 copies since 1999. The brochure is available online at www.trf.k12.mn.us/lhs/shutthedoor.html.

"When I hear from other people that they feel better because they learned from my experience, it makes all the work I've put into my brochure worthwhile," Taryn says.

Taryn didn't stop there. Together with help from WHOA and Minnesota Senator LeRoy Stumpf (D), she helped introduce a bill in February 2000 that would amend the current harassment law and make online harassment like hers a crime in Minnesota.

"I was really, really nervous when I gave my testimony to the House of Representatives," Taryn recalls. "I've spoken to adults before, but this was such a formal setting it made me really nervous. But it went well. They decided to take the bill and fold it into a larger Crime Prevention/Sex Offenders Act."

The bill passed and went into effect March 23, 2000, when Governor Jesse Ventura signed it.

Taryn has received many awards—the Minnesota Governor's Acts of Kindness Award and the Prudential Spirit of Community Award, to name just two. These honors have been bestowed on her in recognition of the work she's done in online safety. She truly turned a negative experience—her harassment—into a positive one.

What You Should Do

This section will tell you explicitly what to do if faced with an e-mail harassment situation.

Nina, Andy, and Taryn were correct when they looked for help from their own ISP first and then with the ISPs of the person harassing them. But they might have been able to stop the unpleasantness even sooner if they had contacted their harassers directly.

An e-mail to your harasser stating you are uncomfortable with the communications and want an immediate end to them might work. It's worth a try. In your e-mail message to them, don't go into detail and don't act defensive. Keep it simple and clear. If the harassment continues after you've made this effort, then contact the ISP(s) involved.

What the above three victims also did correctly was approach the ISPs with the full headers of the messages they'd received. What's a full header? An example appears below. Each e-mail program has a different way to show full headers. A list of the more popular programs and instructions on showing full headers are available at www.haltabuse.org/help/headers.

Here is an example of what you usually see when receiving an e-mail. We'll look at one of the messages sent to Nina:

```
From: "-MIKE-" <-mike-@yahoo.com>
To: <nina@vom.tm>
Subject: Thank you all
Date: Sun, 23 Jan 2000 125551 -0600
```

In this instance, the "From:" address is not where it originated. How can you tell? After activating the full headers, the message will look like this:

```
Return-Path: <-mike-@yahoo.com>
Received: from dynamite.com.au (m2.
          dynamite.com.au
          [203.17.154.20])
          by m0.dynamite.com.au
          (8.8.5/8.8.5) with ESMTP id
```

```
      EAA04193 for <nina@m0.vom.tm>;
      Mon, 24 Jan 2000 045827 +1100
  Received: from flyhmstr.vom.tm
(mail.vom.tm [212.32.5.2]) by
dynamite.com.au (8.9.3/8.9.3) with ESMTP
id EAA03011 for <nina@vom.tm>; Mon, 24 Jan
2000 045621 +1100
  Received: from millenicom.millenicom.com
([209.150.128.197] ident=root) by flyhm-
str.vom.tm with esmtp (Exim 3.11 #1
(Debian)) id 12CRF6-0007CS-00 for
<nina@vom.tm>; Sun, 23 Jan 2000 175604
+0000
  Received: from default (01-023.024.pop-
site.net [216.126.160.23]) by
millenicom.millenicom.com (8.8.5/8.8.5)
with SMTP id LAA16204 for <nina@vom.tm>;
Sun, 23 Jan 2000 115437 -0600
  Message-ID: <00670cdd2a017a078@default>
  From "-MIKE-" <-mike-@yahoo.com>
  To:    <nina@vom.tm>
  Subject:    Thank you all
  Date: Sun, 23 Jan 2000 125551 -0600
```

First, we know that dynamite.com.au is Nina's ISP, so we ignore it. We go down to the second "Received: from" line and find:

```
mail.vom.tm [212.32.5.2]
```

The group of four numbers in brackets makes up the Internet Protocol[4] (IP) address, the official address for vom.tm. You and I may "see" vom.tm if we went to their Web site, but their actual "comput-erese" address would be 212.32.5.2.

An IP address is always made up of four sets of numbers with a dot (period) between them. Each set consists of one to three numerals. With this example, you can see the first set has three numerals, the second set has two, the third set has one, and the fourth set has one. No two IP addresses are alike.

How does an IP address work? Every time you visit a Web site, your computer has to go through a server—through your ISP—called a Domain Name System (DNS) server.

So if you wanted to visit www.disney.com, your computer sends that information to the DNS, which translates it into computerese— an IP address—so that you're taken to the correct host (Web site).

A little more about that DNS. An ISP will have one or more servers that automatically assigns itself for customers to go through to get online. Every one of these servers has a similar IP address, except for the last set of numbers. The first three sets of numbers comprise the primary DNS info and the last set designates which server it came from. So, if you went online one day, you might be on server 208.14.24.176, and the next day you'd be on 208.14.24.12; it all depends on how many servers that ISP uses—the larger the ISP, the more servers it will have to accommodate its customers.

In this e-mail example, though, there is a free e-mail service, Yahoo!, and a remailer involved. A remailer is a service that takes a message you send, reroutes it so the message looks like it came from somewhere else, and sends it to the intended recipient. By using Yahoo! and a remailer, Mike was hoping to confuse Nina. The third "Received: from" line is the remailer IP address:

```
millenicom.millenicom.com
[209.150.128.197]
```

And the fourth "Received: from" line finds the originating ISP:

```
popsite.net [216.126.160.23]
```

Sometimes, as in the above examples, you will get the name of the originating ISP/Web site along with the IP address. Sometimes you will get just the IP address. What do you do if the IP address is all you have? A good resource is called WHOIS (see Figure 2.1), available through Network Solutions at www.networksolutions.com/cgi-bin/whois/whois. This is a list of just about every domain that's been registered, including who owns it and their contact information.

If we take the IP address of 216.126.160.23, put it in the WHOIS text box, and click on the search button, the result would be:

```
StarNet, Inc. (POPSITE5-DOM)
  473 W. Northwest Hwy., Suite 1A
  Palatine, IL 60067
  Administrative Contact
  Doe, Jane (IS168-ORG) janedoe@
STARNETUSA.NET (847)963-0116
  Technical Contact, Zone Contact
```

Figure 2.1 Whois.com.

```
Technical, Support (TS548-ORG) postmas-
ter@STARNETUSA.NET
    (847) 963-0116
    Fax: (847) 963-1302
```

You would then forward the harassing e-mail message, with the full headers, to the technical contact. Before you forward the message, visit the Web site of the ISP/remailer/Web service involved and see if there is a specific e-mail address to send complaints to. Many services have specific addresses. Sometimes you can just put a simple "www" in front of the ISP name, for example, www.starnetusa. net. You might have to dig around on the site to find the correct e-mail address, but look for something like "Privacy Policy," "Terms and Conditions of Use," or "About Us." If you can't find an appropriate e-mail address, then use the one you find in WHOIS.

For the e-mail Nina received, the full header message was sent to postmaster@starnetusa.net, castle@millenicom.com, and abuse@ yahoo.com.

Why wasn't the harassment complaint sent to the first IP address we found, vom.tm? If you look at Nina's e-mail address, you'll see she was using a free e-mail service (similar to Yahoo!) through vom.tm that then went through her ISP, dynamite.com.au.

Will It Stop?

Usually, a complaint to the ISP/remailer/Web service is all it takes to get the e-mail harassment or e-mailbombing to stop. There's a good chance it won't happen again—many harassers are not typical criminals or hackers, but once they know they can't get away with the harassment, they usually stop.

Sometimes people harass because of a dare, like the teenager who threatened Taryn, or because of a simple disagreement that blew out of proportion. If an ISP cancels the harasser's account or warns him or her to stop the harassment, they stop.

It's the harassers who aren't stopped at these beginning stages who are worrisome. They feel that if they can get away with e-mail harassment, how much further can they go?

The following chapters show what other kinds of online negatives there are, how other victims turned their experiences into positives as Taryn did, and how the harassers didn't get away with it—most of the time.

Endnotes

1. Forged: A term used when someone uses an e-mail address that is obviously a fake.
2. Remailer: An online service that allows you to send e-mail messages through their Web site instead of through your e-mail program so that you retain a bit of anonymity.
3. IMing: To send an Instant Message through a program such as AOL Instant Messenger, ICQ, or MSN Messenger; an Instant Message from the sender pops up on the recipient's computer screen. The two can then engage in live chat one-on-one as opposed to a regular chat room where many people can chat at once.
4. IP (Internet Protocol): How data is sent from one computer (aka "host") to another on the Internet. This is the most popular protocol on which the Internet is based. Each host has at least one IP address that uniquely identifies it from all other hosts on the Internet.

Spam Not in a Can

*I realize now that I was one of the first computer profes-
sionals to experience the feeling of dread evoked by a
flood of spam complaints.*

—Ray Everett-Church

Spam

Unsolicited electronic junk mail, usually advertisements or offers, and,
more often than not, unwanted by the receiver; sometimes used as a
revenge tactic by pretending to be someone, then spamming messages to hundreds, sometimes thousands of people.

In the early 1990s, as the Internet became accessible to more people, junk mail found its way online in the form of e-mail advertisements. Almost always unsolicited, these messages began appearing
in e-mailboxes, mailing lists, and newsgroups a handful at a time,
and were seen as more of a minor annoyance than anything.

But back in 1975 someone had seen the potential for a problem
with online junk mail. Jon Postel wrote in November 1975[1] that host
computers had to read every e-mail message coming in, but if there
was a malfunctioning host that began sending too many or unwanted
messages, there could be a problem. "It would be useful for a host to
be able to decline messages from sources it believes are misbehaving
or are simply annoying," he wrote.

Prophetic words.

What's in a Name?

Wait a minute, isn't SPAM the luncheon meat in the familiar blue can?

Meri Harris, spokesperson for Hormel Foods, the makers of SPAM, admits the company wasn't too thrilled when the term "spam" started being used to describe junk e-mail.

"But what can you do?" Harris says. "It's become so much a part of the Internet culture that as long as people don't come to *us* complaining about online spam and it's not spelled out in capital letters, like our trademark name, then we can live with it. We did get some people e-mailing us, thinking online spam came from us, and it got to a point where we put up a page on our site explaining the difference." Visit www.spam.com/ci/ci_in.htm.

So, why is the junk mail called spam? According to the narrative at the SPAM Web site, "Use of the term spam was adopted as a result of the Monty Python skit in which a group of Vikings sang a chorus of 'spam, spam, spam . . .' in an increasing crescendo, drowning out other conversation. Hence, the analogy applied because UCE was drowning out normal discourse on the Internet."

Although most people called it junk e-mail and promptly tossed it in their "trash,"[2] in 1994 a new term was coined for this problem: Unsolicited Commercial E-mail, or UCE. This was due to the following infamous story.

The Green Card Spam

Ray Everett-Church was working as an information specialist with the Washington-based American Immigration Lawyers Association (AILA). His job was to look for any news items related to U.S. government immigration policies. As their resident techno-geek, he began putting together an online newswire of the information he found. Occasionally, he also answered any technical questions.

"When I arrived in the office on the morning of April 13, 1994, the receptionist handed me a stack of angry faxes and forwarded a voice mailbox full of furious calls," he recalls. "By the time I stumbled to my cubicle, I had met the enemy. Their names were Laurence Canter and Martha Siegel."

A little background: In the early 1990s, Congress created the Green Card Lottery program. Although the program offered a great opportunity to immigrants, it also provided an opportunity for scammers to make money by charging hopeful immigrants high fees to file lottery entries when all that was required was a postcard, a stamp, and the person's name and address.

Canter and Siegel were a husband-and-wife law firm that saw dollar signs and wanted to jump on this potential moneymaking bandwagon. They were also technically savvy and began sending hundreds of messages to newsgroups.

"The faxes and phone calls I fielded asked what could be done to stop them and to sanction them for their activities," Everett-Church says. "As a voluntary association, AILA's only recourse was to throw them out of the association. However, when I went to AILA's senior staff to ask what that procedure entailed, a director of the organization said, 'Canter and Siegel? What did they do this time?'"

It turns out the pair were notorious for this sort of thing and had been disciplined many times. And now they were the initiators of the Green Card Spam, which is the term the media gave to it.

"They effectively were the ones that I consider 'the spam that started it all,'" says Everett-Church with a laugh. "I went on to get my license to practice law. They lost theirs. I realize now that I was one of the first computer professionals to experience the feeling of dread evoked by a flood of spam complaints. I've never quite forgotten that feeling, and it's part of the reason I've spent so much time combating Internet abuse."

Figure 3.1 CAUCE.

As Counsel for the Coalition Against Unsolicited Commercial E-mail (CAUCE) at www.cauce.org (see Figure 3.1), Everett-Church now helps address legal problems related to spam and spammers.

"We're focused on lobbying in favor of federal legislation to combat spam," Everett-Church notes. "We're also educating companies on how to use e-mail for marketing in a responsible manner as well as working with state legislators to teach them about anti-spam laws—what makes good ones, how to avoid constitutional issues, and why not to accept marketers' whining at face value."

This is valuable work, and Russell Allyn, whom you'll read about next, probably wishes it had started prior to the summer of 1997.

Samsung's Sad Song

No one knows the exact number, but it's estimated that more than 12 million people accessed their e-mailboxes on August 9, 1997, to find the following message:

```
From:     webmaster@compuserve.com
Date:     Sat, 09 Aug 97 10:47:22 EST
To:       suspected_flamer@somewhereincyber
          space.com
Subject:  Cease And Desist Flaming
Reply-to: khskllp@aol.com

    On behalf of our client, Samsung America
Inc., ("Samsung") we hereby request that
you cease and desist all inflammatory
internet hacking, telephone hacking, flam-
ing, jamming, and other illegal activities.
```

If you have responded aversely to a recent bulk e-mail message from our client, Samsung America, Inc., or from any of its subsidiary companies, then you may be one of the people who has performed fraudulent and actionable transgressions, thereby causing severe harm to our client.

Your e-mail name was provided as being suspected of connection to various acts of internet terrorism. Your acts are illegal.

Several messages have suggested that Samsung and/or its subsidiaries, including but not limited to Sailahead Global Emporium, www.sailahead.com, and Samsung Electronics, www.sosimple.com, violated US Federal Laws through activities commonly called "spamming." This allegation is unfounded in the law, as spamming is a protected activity under the laws of free speech.

Our client has asked us to inform you that all of your future correspondences should be directed to their counsel:

> Russell L. Allyn, Attorney at Law
> California Sate Bar Number (SBN) 143531
> Katz, Hoyt, Seigel & Kapor LLP
> Los Angeles, CA
> khskllp@aol.com
> 310-555-1212
> 310-555-1212 (fax)

All incidents of internet terrorism will be prosecuted where possible, and reported to appropriate law enforcement authorities as warranted. Please consider this as your notice to cease all attempts to harm multinational corporations who conduct legitimate commerce on the internet.

Russell L. Allyn, Attorney at Law

To put it mildly, those affected by this were not amused. Russell was inundated with angry e-mails, phone calls, and faxes from around the world. His superiors were contacted and told to fire him. Some people even contacted the American Bar Association to file complaints. The media began bombarding Russell's office for comments. He was overwhelmed by them and by the complaints. "It's not from our office; it's not from me," he said over and over.

Russell was trying to think of who might have done this. Though he couldn't name a specific person, he thought it might be someone dissatisfied with the settlement in a case in which Russell represented Samsung, and now this was that person's way of achieving retribution.

Russell and the law firm he worked for weren't the only ones getting complaints. Samsung was receiving 6,000 to 10,000 e-mail complaints a day, as well as hundreds of phone calls. It wasn't only as a result of this spam either. Since mid-July, Samsung had been dealing with angry people who were receiving forged messages from Samsung's newly established Internet service provider, Sailahead Global Emporium. There were more than a dozen different forged spams being sent out.

"We've spent millions and millions to maintain our reputation and our brand image," said Sang Cho, the in-house counsel for Samsung of America. "We don't care about retaliatory action, we just want it to stop."

Samsung officials thought they knew who was doing it. They'd recently had a conflict with a Southern California man who ran a religious Web site using Samsung's Internet service and who was behind in payments by $2,400. Company officials tried to collect, but the man told them that if they didn't pay him $1.2 million, he was going to ruin their business.

When the spam first started, Samsung contacted UUNET Technologies, the originating ISP, but they refused to give out any information about the account without a subpoena. Samsung hoped things would die down. Then, on August 9th, the Russell Allyn spam was sent out, again through UUNET. Subpoenas were issued this time, but it was found that fake names, addresses, and other information were used to open the accounts.

Samsung was so inundated with angry e-mail that they set up all of their public e-mail accounts to respond automatically with the following message:

This is an Auto-Response message:

If you are responding to the e-mail SPAM-
MING, please accept our apologies. I want
to assure you that SAILAhead/Samsung IS NOT
the originator of this spam. This is not
the type of activity Samsung condones.

Please help us remove Spamming from the
Internet. DO NOT SPAM US. I know you are
angry. So are we. We need everyone's
cooperation to catch the perpetrator of
this fraud. Spamming us back just makes it
harder to isolate the source.

If you have any information which may
help in identifying and apprehending this
offender, please contact me at 800-943-4252
ext. 4. We are offering a reward.

Thank you,
Avram Grossman
Manager, SAILAhead Internet Services

Eventually, the furor died down, and the spam stopped. But the person responsible was never found. Russell's life was turned upside down—rumors swirled that he almost lost his license to practice law because of the spam. He now works for a different law firm in Los Angeles.

On the Other Hand ...

If you want to receive spam, go to IWantSpam at www.iwantspam.com. This site lets you receive all the spam you want. Really. Advertisers can submit one ad (spam) per day and recipients who sign up for the free service will receive one message in their e-mailbox each day, not exceeding 100K in size.

In Defense of Unsolicited Bulk E-mail (spam) at www.
provider.com/framesbulke.htm provides news and information from the marketing—spammers'—perspective.

A little humor goes a long way at www.cspam.com, a
site that lets you listen to your choice of classical music
while you view a scrolling list of (real) spam. If this doesn't
make you laugh, nothing will.

Get all the latest news about spam sent to your e-mailbox with the Petemoss.com SpamNews digest at
http://petemoss.com/spam. It's free.

Finally, 101 Things To Do With A Spammer is at
www.studio42.com/kill-the-spam/pages/101.html. Don't try
these at home. My favorite is #32, "See how many spammers you can stuff into a phone booth."

Usenet Spammers

Usenet, also known as newsgroups, discussion groups, and forums, has
a similar problem with spam. Since there are literally tens of thousands of
newsgroups that cover possibly any subject you can think of (from
Harrison Ford to writing to bicycling to sex), spammers have an easy way
to send their messages. More likely than not, these spams contain fake
return e-mail addresses, which makes it harder to track them down but not
impossible. However, what's considered spam in e-mail isn't the same
definition for spam on Usenet. On Usenet, spam is when the same message is posted an unacceptably high number of times to one or more newsgroups, whether or not the content of the message is relevant to the
newsgroup(s). Although no specific number has been agreed on, if a message is posted 20 times to the same newsgroup or to 20 different newsgroups, it is considered spam. Some ISPs consider as little as five postings
of the same message to be spam, and may cancel the offender's account.
The message here is to be careful when posting messages to newsgroups.

Usenet spam is primarily aimed at lurkers—people who read
newsgroups but rarely or never post or give their e-mail addresses.

The spammers are hoping one of the lurkers will actually read their spam and maybe even visit their Web site or reply to the spam (some people do). Usenet spam makes it difficult for regulars to navigate their favorite newsgroup(s). Some newsgroup members are sick and tired of spam, which leads this discussion to "spamhunters."

Spamhunters on Usenet eagerly send copies of spam to newsgroups devoted to spam, such as news.admin.net-abuse.sightings. Usenet management then makes sure the right ISPs are notified of the spammers. Sometimes the accounts of the spammers are canceled, but if they are persistent they'll get a new account and begin spamming again.

If an ISP seems to be harboring spammers, a Usenet Death Penalty (UDP) will be set by Usenet administrators. A UDP effectively blocks all messages posted from the offending ISP, not just the spam. This means that if someone has a legitimate e-mail account with that ISP, they won't be able to post to any newsgroups. This usually gets a quick reaction from the ISP, which either works to identify the spammers or readjusts its services to prevent spamming.

Luckily, Microsoft Internet Explorer, Netscape Navigator/ Communicator, Forte Agent, and other newsreader programs offer a killfile feature, which can be used to filter out Usenet spam so that it almost never shows up when reading your newsgroups. Each program has a different way to set up killfiles (which are also available in most e-mail programs), so it's best to consult the HELP files in your program(s) for instructions on how to use killfiling.

When setting up a killfile, you can input an e-mail address or specific words found in the subject line of common spam, such as Make Money Fast, Free Software, Lose Pounds Quickly, etc. Some people put dollar signs ($$$) in a killfile, as many spams include them in the subject line to try to entice you to read the spam. Other commonalities includes sexx (with two x's), penis (because the subject line usually reads Grow Your Penis Larger or Bigger Penis Guaranteed), two or more exclamation marks (!!!!), or question marks. Once the killfiles are set, you'll see a dramatic drop in Usenet spam.

How to Avoid Spam

You can't avoid it entirely, just like the junk mail that comes to your mailbox at home. But there are some things you can do to combat it. (Thanks go to Ray Everett-Church for some of these tips):

1. Know where your e-mail address can be found (white pages, Web pages). Do you know who has your e-mail address? Do you participate in chat rooms? Message boards? Newsgroups? Do you have your e-mail address posted on your Web page? Spammers look for legitimate e-mail addresses everywhere on the Web.

2. Guard your primary e-mail address. When somebody asks for it, think twice before giving it out.

3. Choose an ISP that actively blocks spam.

4. Learn to filter your e-mail. Some e-mail software has pretty decent filtering features that, if you take the time to read the instructions, can be useful in helping you manage your mailbox, and may even help you filter spam into the trash. It won't save you money, but it might save your sanity.

5. Don't hit Reply! Most of the return addresses in spam are false in order to deflect complaints. However, some spammers use real addresses because they really do want to hear from you. Why would they want to hear your angry diatribe? Because then they know that your e-mail address is functioning and that there's a real live body on the other end of that connection. By replying, you wave a big red flag that says, "Spam me some more!" So, don't hit Reply.

6. In newsgroups or forums where spam appears, again, don't reply to a spam. If you want a good laugh, read some of the responses to spam on various newsgroups; they can be quite humorous. (For example, someone posted the following reply in response to an "enlarge your penis" spam: "Hey, I'm a woman— if it works, I can get rich!")

7. Establish secondary "screen names" for chat rooms/ boards, which are among the most appealing places for spammers to gather e-mail addresses. Many ISPs like AOL, AT&T, and CompuServe allow you to create secondary screen names or additional e-mail

addresses at little or no cost, shielding your main address from the flood.

8. Give/use false e-mail addresses. Many people know that spammers troll through chat rooms and message boards looking for e-mail addresses, so they use fake or altered (sometimes called "munged") e-mail addresses. For example, "JohnDoe123@ hotmail.com" might give out his address as "JohnDoe123@I-hate-spam.hotmail.com" and then give instructions to remove the "I-hate-spam" part before sending him e-mail. This tends to confound many spammers, particularly those who use automated e-mail "harvesting" programs that gather anything with an @ sign in the middle. Spammers are usually too lazy to sort the millions of addresses by hand, so they end up sending to the altered address.

9. Establish valid secondary e-mail accounts at free e-mail services (such as Hotmail or Yahoo!). This is useful if your ISP doesn't let you create secondary accounts easily or cheaply.

10. Use unique e-mail account names not found in a dictionary. A growing number of spammers are grabbing names out of dictionaries, randomly sticking numbers in there, and then pasting on an @hotmail.com or @aol.com, or @wherever.com. This way they don't have to gather addresses. Thus was born the "dictionary" spamming attack, and this is why you might want to pick an e-mail address that is less predictable.

11. Learn how and where to complain to get spammers shut down, such as using SpamCop or other programs or Web sites listed in the Resources section at the back of this book.

Fighting Spam

CAUCE is an ad hoc, all-volunteer organization created by Netizens[3] and is a good first stop for everything you want to know about online spam, anti-spam legislation, and what to do about spam (go to www.cauce.org). It costs nothing to join CAUCE, and each person who joins makes CAUCE's "voice" stronger on Capitol Hill (Washington, DC) and in member states—and better able to get anti-spam legislation passed and enforced.

SpamCop puts you in control of the spam you receive. Register for free at www.spamcop.net. When you receive a spam, activate the full headers (see Chapter 2 for instructions) and copy and paste the spam into the text box. SpamCop then does the work, figuring out where to report the spam. All you need to do is click on SEND and it's taken care of. Figure 3.2 is an example of SpamCop's reporting page.

Julian Haight created SpamCop in 1998 to deal with spam he was getting in his personal e-mailbox. Haight's first SpamCop program was a simple, 100-line script he put up on his personal Web page. "When it was released, there was a lot of skepticism in the spam-fighting community," says Haight. "I received a lot of criticism but also a lot of feedback, which helped make it what it is today."

SpamCop works by using a combination of Unix utilities such as nslookup[4] and finger[5] to cross-check all the information in an e-mail header to find the correct e-mail address of the administrator on the network where the message originated. It then formulates a polite request

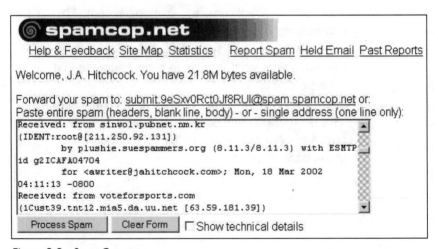

Figure 3.2   SpamCop.net.

Figure 3.3   SpamCon.

for discipline, including all the information needed to track down the user responsible for the spam. Sometimes the person reporting the spam through SpamCop will receive a reply from the ISP involved thanking them for reporting the spam, and sometimes the account involved is canceled.

"SpamCop gets about 100,000 reports a day, if that gives you an idea of the scope of the problem with spam," says Haight. "There are some spammers who aren't too happy with my site. A couple of years ago someone sent out a spam 'advertising' SpamCop, which caused a problem. Thankfully, it has always been hosted on my own server, so there has never been a real threat of getting it shut down. Now I co-locate my server with nyi.net, a company who approached me specifically because they wanted to host SpamCop."

The SpamCon Foundation (www.spamcon.org, see Figure 3.3), founded by Tom Geller in January 1999, is for those who have been damaged by spam, or "e-mail vandalism," as Geller calls it. This site provides a list of states with anti-spam laws, the status of any state or federal legislation, information on how to sue spammers in states where there are current laws, a forum to discuss spam and spammers, and resources.

If you're really angry about spam, go to www.madaboutspam.org, sign the online petition, and join their boycott.

If you want all the technical details of spam, go to http://spam.abuse.net, where you'll find tutorials on filtering, blocking, and more.

Sometimes the war against spam can be won, if you take the initiative to fight it.

Endnotes

1. Full comments on this can be found at www.ietf.org/rfc/rfc0706.txt.

2. Trash: Usually a function in e-mail programs that allows the user to delete unwanted e-mail, thus putting it in the trash; usually the trash empties when the user exits or ends use of the e-mail program.

3. Netizens: Common nickname for online users.

4. NSLookup: A software program where you enter a host name (for example, "disney.com") and see the corresponding IP address. NSLookup also does reverse name lookup to find the host name for an IP address you specify.

5. Finger: A program that reports the name associated with an e-mail address and may also show the most recent logon information or even whether the person is currently connected to the Internet.

4

Urban Legends and Hoaxes: Can They Possibly Be True?

Urban Legends

Online, they're much like the ones you've heard off-line—stories so incredibly unreal they're, well, unreal. Online legends keep popping up in e-mail, on Web sites, in newsgroups, and in chat rooms even after they've been debunked.

Hoaxes

Similar to urban legends, hoaxes are the messages and posts that try to convince people they can get something for nothing, or that a bad virus is coming their way, or some other nonsense. P.T. Barnum supposedly said, "There's a sucker born every minute"—online, there's no shortage of hoaxes aimed at proving the point.

You've seen them in your e-mailbox or heard about them in newsgroups and forums. Sometimes you've even wondered if they could be true. Your friends e-mail you warnings about viruses, and this time it's a REALLY BAD VIRUS. Or you get a message stating that if you send the message to eight of your friends, you'll have good luck, good health, or something else (but never money).

A boy sends you an e-mail about his quest to add as many business cards to his collection as he can, and he's dying of cancer. Another boy writes that if you forward your message, a $1 donation will be sent to him, and if he can get 50,000 people to do this, his operation will be paid for.

The list goes on and on.

These are Net urban legends and hoaxes, the modern version of myths and chain letters. There are so many that I can't list them all here. Instead, I'll mention the more common ones, explain how to tell if it's a hoax, and advise what to do if you get one.

The David Allen Legend

This started off as a real mission. David actually did ask friends to send e-mail prayers for him in 1997 when he thought he was dying. Here he recounts his experience:

> On 5 March 1997, we began our home leave, flying from Chiang Mai in northern Thailand to Los Angeles in the USA. In the plane, I suddenly started having such strong stomach pains that I seriously doubted that I would make it to Los Angeles. It was an unidentified infection: I lost weight, and it was clear that I was suffering from an infestation of microscopic parasites and was possibly in danger of dying.
>
> The American doctors could not discover the exact source of the illness. In May 1997 I had to be fed intra- venously. Shortly before my admission to hospital, I wrote an e-mail message to a mission team in Thailand, telling them that I did not yet feel ready to die. The thought of leaving my wife, newborn baby, and the new church in Thailand behind was unbearable.
>
> The reaction to my message was almost unbelievable, with Christians throughout the world praying, some so fer- vently that they cried, some fasted, others throwing them- selves on the floor before God. I received over 7,000 e-mails from around 80 countries, often from whole churches united in prayer for me.
>
> One church even called me and said that they had been divided before hearing of my illness, but decided to put their small differences aside when they received the news, and started to pray. My family received telephone calls from morning until evening for months. I must admit that I was overwhelmed.

Parasitologists from Washington's Walter Reed military hospital, doctors from England, Canada, Africa, Brazil, Mexico, Thailand, and other countries called to offer their help and advice. Then suddenly, probably in answer to prayer, the doctors were no longer needed. The tests became negative, the parasites had vanished and have not reappeared since.

People around the world began receiving requests in their e-mail boxes to pray for David. Here is one such request:

Dear Friends and Family,
The prayer for this Southern Baptist Missionary needs to be forwarded to everyone you know that can pray. Pray diligently and then send it along today!!!! Ezekiel David Allen is a young missionary on the Chiang Mai, Thailand mission team. He is critically ill with an unknown parasite and apparently WILL DIE WITHIN TWO MONTHS unless there is an intervention by the Lord. Please help create a global blanket of prayer for David, Michelle, and their four-month old daughter, Brianna.
From: David Allen

David's original e-mail to his mission team asking for prayers was pasted in this spot, followed by:

We are encouraging everyone we know to lift up David and his family before the Lord of Lords. Please forward this message to those you think will join us in this global chain of prayer.
Thanks,
INTERNATIONAL MISSION BOARD, SBC
Southern Africa Regional Office
PO Box A-614, Avondale
Life is good because God IS.
P.S. Please send this out to all your friends, sisters, brothers, and other relatives.

Nice sentiments. It worked, but as David noted, he recovered and is fine these days, even though this legend seems to pop up every few months. Then the cycle begins all over again with thousands of people forwarding the original message to everyone they know. Just do a search on his name and you'll find over 7,000 Web sites that mention this common legend as if it were happening right now.

The E-Mail Tax

This appears here and there, sometimes worded differently, but it's the same old message. Online users will be charged five cents for every e-mail they send. Each time this appears, the U.S. Postal Service and U.S. Government have to announce that it is a hoax. But many people fall for it and end up forwarding the message to not only everyone they know, but to newsgroups and forums like it's new news.

An interesting fact: Congress was so upset that they did pass a law—to stop the hoax. This is a sample of one of the hoax messages:

```
Dear Internet Subscriber:
Please read the following carefully if
you intend to stay online and continue
using email: The last few months have
revealed an alarming trend in the Govern-
ment of the United States attempting to
quietly push through legislation that will
affect your use of the Internet. Under pro-
posed legislation the U.S. Postal Service
will be attempting to bilk email users out
of "alternate postage fees". Bill 602P will
permit the Federal Govt to charge a 5 cent
surcharge on every email delivered, by
billing Internet Service Providers at
source. The consumer would then be billed
in turn by the ISP. Washington D.C. lawyer
Richard Stepp is working without pay to
prevent this legislation from becoming law.
    The U.S. Postal Service is claiming that
lost revenue due to the proliferation of
email is costing nearly $230,000,000 in rev-
enue per year. You may have noticed their
recent ad campaign "There is nothing like a
letter". Since the average citizen received
about 10 pieces of email per day in 1998,
the cost to the typical individual would be
```

an additional 50 cents per day, or over $180
dollars per year, above and beyond their
regular Internet costs. Note that this would
be money paid directly to the U.S. Postal
Service for a service they do not even provide. The whole point of the Internet is
democracy and non-interference. If the federal government is permitted to tamper with
our liberties by adding a surcharge to
email, who knows where it will end. You are
already paying an exorbitant price for snail
mail because of bureaucratic efficiency. It
currently takes up to 6 days for a letter to
be delivered from New York to Buffalo. If
the U.S. Postal Service is allowed to tin-
ker with email, it will mark the end of the
"free" Internet in the United States. One
congressman, Tony Schnell (R) has even suggested a "twenty to forty dollar per month
surcharge on all Internet service" above and
beyond the government's proposed email
charges. Note that most of the major newspapers have ignored the story, the only
exception being the Washingtonian which
called the idea of email surcharge "a useful concept who's time has come" March 6th
1999 Editorial) Don't sit by and watch your
freedoms erode away!

Send this email to all Americans on your
list and tell your friends and relatives to
write to their congressman and say "No!" to
Bill 602P.

The U.S. Postal Service offers this standard reply when concerned
citizens e-mail them (www.usps.com/news/2002/emailrumor.htm):

WASHINGTON - A completely false rumor
concerning the U.S. Postal Service is being
circulated on Internet e-mail. As a matter
of fact, the Postal Service has learned
that a similar hoax occurred recently in
Canada concerning Canada Post.

The e-mail message claims that a "Congressman Schnell" has introduced "Bill 602P" to allow the federal government to impose a 5-cent surcharge on each e-mail message delivered over the Internet. The money would be collected by Internet Service Providers and then turned over to the Postal Service. No such proposed legislation exists. In fact, no "Congressman Schnell" exists. The U.S. Postal Service has no authority to surcharge e-mail messages sent over the Internet, nor would it support such legislation.

Good Luck, Mr. Gorsky!

One of the funniest hoaxes on the Net has to be the one known as "Mr. Gorsky" (www.snopes2.com/quotes/mrgorsky.htm).

When Apollo 11 astronaut Neil Armstrong uttered the famous, "One small step for man, one giant leap for mankind," he also said, "Good luck, Mr. Gorsky!"

Or did he?

This rumor began on the Internet back in 1995 as a pretty obvious joke, but some media outlet picked it up and ran with it, causing it to become one of the Net's most famous (or infamous) legends.

What did this phrase mean? Supposedly, Mr. Gorsky was Armstrong's neighbor. When Armstrong was a kid, he overheard Mrs. Gorsky tell her husband in their backyard that he'd get oral sex when the kid next door walked on the moon. Armstrong was said to have divulged this 25 years after the moon landing, presumably when Mr. Gorsky died.

Guess what? There was no Mr. Gorsky (or Mrs. Gorsky) and the joke still floats around the Net, usually with minor changes, such as the name of the neighbor and how Mrs. Gorsky tells her husband when he'll get oral sex.

Armstrong publicly denied he ever made the statement and if you doubt it, check out the official NASA transcripts of what was said during the moon landing at www.hq.nasa.gov/office/pao/History/alsj/a11/a11.step.html.

Free Stuff

These e-mails claim that if you pass the message on to other people, you'll get free stuff. There's just one thing they forget to say: How are you supposed to receive the free stuff if the company supposedly giving it away doesn't have your contact information? Some of the chain letters claim the companies can tell where you're located with special e-mail tracking. This is—you got it—untrue.

I've received these chain e-mails myself. Here's one of them:

> Subject: Fw: Gap certificates free !!!!!!
> Hey guys,
> I finally found one that is TRUE! I went down to the Gap myself and redeemed my GIFT CERTIFICATES already!!! I sent enough e-mails to get over two hundred dollars worth of clothes from the GAP! You know, with all the crap sent over the mail, it is good to know that something finally rings true in this environment of virtual deception.
>
> Send it to everyone you know, and you too can have a whole new wardrobe, courtesy of THE GAP!
> Isn't it grand?
>
>   * * * * *
>
> Hi!
> My name is Janelle McCan, Founder of the Gap. I am offering thirty five dollar gift certificates to every seven people you send this to. When you have finished sending this letter to as many people as you wish, a screen will come up. It will tell you how much you have earned in Gap gift certificates. Print that screen out and bring it to your local Gap store. The sales clerk will give you your certificates and you can SHOP BABY!

```
    This is a sales promotion to get our name
    out to young people around the world. We
    believe this project can be a success, but
    with your help. Thank you for your support.
    Sincerely,
    Janelle McCan Founder of Gap
```

The person who sent this to me was extremely embarrassed when I pointed out that this was a chain letter, a hoax, and an urban legend all rolled into one.

But many people fell for it, hook, line, and sinker. The Gap wasn't pleased when it received complaints when no free gift certificates were forthcoming. But, they figured, publicity is publicity. And it certainly hasn't hurt sales.

The Top 10 Urban Legends/ Hoaxes/Chain Letters

It's hard to select the Top 10, but here are my personal favorites:

1. Kidney Theft: www.snopes2.com/horrors/robbery/kidney.htm

What's scary about this is that the media picked it up and ran with the story like it really happened. An e-mail made the rounds from a friend of a friend (FOAF) who supposedly knew someone this happened to. The deal was that while traveling to New Orleans (in this case), a businessman is approached by a stranger in a bar who buys him a drink. The drink is drugged and the last thing the businessman remembers before passing out is being in a bathtub submerged to his neck in ice. When the businessman wakes up, there is a note tacked near the tub instructing him to call 911, which he does. The 911 operator then asks the businessman to carefully feel behind him and see if there is a tube in his back. When he replies that there is, an ambulance is sent to the hotel, the businessman is taken to the hospital and finds out his kidney has been harvested. The e-mail then goes on to claim that this is really happening and is not science fiction.

The New Orleans Police Department was inundated by concerned citizens about this e-mail. It got so bad, they put up a page on their Web site, which stated, in part:

```
    Internet Subscribers:
    Over the past six months the New Orleans
    Police  Department  has  received  numerous
```

inquiries from corporations and organizations around the United States warning
travelers about a well organized crime ring
operating in New Orleans. This information
alleges that this ring steals kidneys from
travelers, after they have been provided
alcohol to the point of unconsciousness.

After an investigation into these alle-
gations, the New Orleans Police Department
has found them to be COMPLETELY WITHOUT
MERIT AND WITHOUT FOUNDATION. The warnings
that are being disseminated through the
Internet are FICTITIOUS and may be in violation of criminal statutes concerning the
issuance of erroneous and misleading
information.

The National Kidney Foundation was outraged. They asked that anyone who had his or her kidney stolen to contact them. Not surprisingly, no one has.

2. Rat Urine: www.snopes2.com/toxins/raturine.htm

This e-mail warns of a family friend of someone who knew a stock boy at a grocery store who opened a can of soda without washing the top of the can, or moved the cans and touched the top, then became seriously ill and died because of rat urine on the can. Even though it was thoroughly debunked and health officials proved that you won't die from unclean cans even if rat urine was on them, people freaked out about this one.

The moral of this story: Just clean the top of the darned cans anyway.

3. Klingerman Virus: www.snopes2.com/toxins/klinger.htm

This one appeared in e-mail boxes claiming that if you received a large blue envelope from the Klingerman Foundation and opened it, you'd find a virus-filled sponge inside, which would kill you. There is no Klingerman Foundation and there were no sponges being sent in the postal mail. However, this urban legend almost became real when people who did receive large blue envelopes in their mailbox called the police, thinking a virus-filled sponge was inside. In 2000, a man in Auburn, Maine, dialed 911 when he received a blue envelope that contained a free sanding sponge from a handyman company. While the dispatchers kept him on the phone, listening to his worries that this was a virus-filled sponge, he soon had ambulances, fire trucks, police cars, and curious neighbors in his yard. The FBI arrived in HAZMAT suits and made him strip, then hosed him down. When they realized there was no virus and it was based on the e-mail hoax, they were able to calm the man down.

Need more proof this isn't true? Go to www.cdc.gov/ncidod/ klingerman_hoax.htm

4. Needles in the Payphone: www.snopes2.com/horrors/mayhem/ payphone.htm

With the AIDS and HIV scare, this e-mail began appearing, claiming that someone (yes, another FOAF) went to a public payphone, put money in the phone, made a call, and then reached into the coin slot to get the change. The person felt a sharp prick and became infected with HIV, AIDS, hepatitis, or other infectious disease because someone left a hypodermic needle in the coin slot. Sometimes the e-mail claims the message came to the sender from a certified EMT.

This is one time when an urban legend did become real, but definitely after the fact. When newspapers began running articles about this new urban legend, real incidents began to happen. There were reports of hypodermic needles being found in mail deposit slots, night deposit slots at banks, and yes, payphone coin slots. But all the needles were uncontaminated.

This only gave the urban legend a longer life. In 2000, the legend resurfaced as an e-mail claiming that vending machines in Alberta, Canada, were now harboring those dangerous AIDS-infected needles. Not true. Another legend similar to this is about needles affixed to gas pump handles that then prick the user.

5. Jen's Embarrassment: www.snopes2.com/sex/mistaken/jen.htm

This is particularly sick. A girl named Jen meets a man in a chat room and they become better acquainted, to the point where they engage in cybersex. After a few weeks of this, they decide to meet in person and find they live in the same town. They arrange their real life tryst in a hotel and Jen arrives first, removes her clothes, hops in bed, shuts off the light, and waits. She hears the door open, whispers, "Jeremy?" He whispers back, "Katie?"—the fake name she used in the chat room—and then turns on the light. They both scream when they realize they're father and daughter.

Not only is this untrue, it comes in the form of several tales. Sometimes they are college students who turn out to be brother and sister. Sometimes it's a businessman on holiday who asks for a hooker to be sent to his room—yep, his daughter, or his wife; and so on. But this story does serve to warn you that you never know who you're really chatting with online.

6. Craig Shergold: www.legends.org.za/arthur/craig01b.htm

This legend has been around since the early 1990s, when it started as a postal mail legend and was picked up the media. Craig is a real person who really did have cancer and put out a plea for get-well cards to brighten his hospital room. He ended up recovering through surgery paid for by a wealthy philanthropist, but the legend has now moved to the Internet. Craig still receives thousands of cards a week in his postal mailbox, even though he has publicly announced his recovery and has asked that people stop sending him cards. It got so bad that the Make-A-Wish Foundation put up a page on their Web site about this at www.wish.org/home/frame_chainletters.htm.

7. E-mail Petition to Save PBS/NPR: www.urbanlegends.com/ulz/ pbs.html

E-mail petitions to save PBS and/or NPR began circulating in 1996 and continue to this day. Even though the U.S. Government considered cutting funding to these organizations in 1995, it never did. Other fake e-mail "petitions" include one to help mistreated Afghanistan women, women and children sold into slavery in Africa, and so on. If you get an e-mail petition, delete it.

8. Deadly Spiders in Public Toilets: www.urbanlegends.com/ulz/ tspiders.html

I heard about this one just before I was scheduled to take a lengthy business trip. A well-meaning friend e-mailed the warning to me and I got a good laugh out of it. Depending on the message, it always contains information about three women who went to the same restaurant, airport, movie theater, etc., used the restroom, then died three days later. A Dr. Beverly Clark, who published an article in the *Journal of the United Medical Association (JUMA),* is quoted in the e-mail saying that these deaths occurred because a deadly spider called a South American Bush Spider bit the women when they sat down on the toilet seat. It was hiding on the underside of the seat.

There is no such spider. There is no Dr. Beverly Clark. There is no *JUMA.*

9. Mel Gibson Was the Man Without a Face: www.urbanlegends. com/ulz/gibson.html

The movie Mel Gibson starred in was really about what happened to him. E-mails sent out in 2000 claimed Paul Harvey devoted one of his commentaries to this, although no one who sent the e-mail actually heard the commentary. Paul Harvey never wrote or broadcast this. Mel Gibson never was savagely beaten and almost killed, needing extensive plastic surgery to repair his face. In fact, the movie he starred in, *The Man Without a Face*, was based on Isabelle Holland's 1972 novel of the same name.

10. The *Blair Witch Project* Was Real!: www.urbanlegends.com/ ulz/blairwitchproject.html

This is my ultimate favorite: Before the movie came out, there was a Web site that convinced visitors that three students really did disappear, that the Blair Witch legend is a real legend (there's an oxymoron for you) and that the movie is really, really true.

Even though the stars of the movie, the producers, and the studio publicly announced the Web site was just a great marketing gimmick (and caused the *Blair Witch Project* to become a high-grossing movie), people still believe it really happened.

Suckers.

Educate Yourself

The U.S. Department of Energy in conjunction with Computer Incident Advisory Committee (CIAC) has a Web page devoted to chain letter hoaxes (http://HoaxBusters.ciac.org). At the site, they impart this advice:

> Users are requested to please not spread chain letters and hoaxes by sending copies to everyone you know. Sending a copy of a cute message to one or two friends is not a problem but sending an unconfirmed warning or plea to everyone you know with the request that they also send it to everyone they know simply adds to the clutter already filling our mailboxes. If you receive any of this kind of mail, please don't pass it to everyone you know, either delete it or pass it to your computer security manager to validate. Validated warnings from the incident response teams and anti-virus vendors have valid return

addresses and are usually PGP signed with the organization's key. Alternately, you can and should get the warnings directly from the web pages of the organizations that put them out to insure that the information you have is valid and up-to-date.

There is a host of other information available about the e-mail hoaxes, legends, and chain letters found on the Net. One such site is the well-known Urban Legends Reference Pages at www.snopes2. com, run by David and Barbara Mikkelson. David began reading and posting to a newsgroup about urban legends in 1989. Barbara joined the newsgroup in 1993 and found that David had quite the reputation as a researcher and debunker of false tales.

"I was thus deathly afraid of him," Barbara says laughing. "We began corresponding by e-mail and eventually met in real life and liked each other enough to get married. Our love of research is one of the things we have in common, and our love of the legends is another."

That love grew into a passion for finding out the stories behind these legends and hoaxes. How did they begin and where? What changes have they gone through over the years? They found that society tells tales, and has for centuries. The most popular legends tend to be what folks are apprehensive about, titillated or fascinated by, and morals and beliefs are held as the one true standard.

"Urban legends are our way of venting what we're concerned about, and in the process we pass along our prejudices and our view of how things are supposed to be," Barbara explains.

Their Web site was a natural progression of their research. It features not only Internet-based urban legends and hoaxes but also tall tales that have been spread for ages.

So, why do people fall for these deceptions over and over again?

"It doesn't occur to us to question what a friend tells us; we take what they say as gospel because we trust them to never lie to us," says Barbara. "It also never occurs to us that our friends could be honestly mistaken, having made the same error of wholeheartedly believing what a friend told them."

What do you say to a friend who has unwittingly sent you deceptive e-mail?

"I'm afraid there's no one right answer," Barbara says. "With some folks, it won't matter how gently you try to tell them what they're sending is false; they're going to feel hurt and upset anyway. People don't like being wrong, and we often fail to handle such a turn of events gracefully."

Some people just dump the hoax/legend/chain e-mail into their trash bin and forget about it. Some do e-mail their friends and let them know it's a well-known hoax and send them to a site such as Barbara and David's to prove it.

"I've heard including a little note that omits any implication of the other person being misinformed works best," Barbara says. "Something along the lines of 'Wow! I just read about that very thing on an urban legends site. Have a look at <insert relevant URL> and let me know what you think.'"

Is It Real?

1. If a message includes a request that you forward it to everyone you know, it's not real.

2. If there are several "FWD" comments in the body of a message, showing it's already been forwarded many times, it's not real.

3. If a message claims you'll get something for nothing, it probably isn't real.

4. If a message includes several e-mail addresses in addition to yours in the "TO:" line, you can be pretty sure it's a hoax or legend or chain e-mail.

5. If a message claims such-and-such a thing happened to a friend of a friend (FOAF, in the words of the Urban Legends folks), their aunt or uncle, or someone else, but never them—yep—it's not real.

Even if a message contains technical references, or refers to institutions, or includes addresses and phone numbers, be wary of believing it. If you want to verify that the message is real, go to the Web site of the company, person, or organization that claims to be involved and see if anything is mentioned on their site. Nine times out of 10, there will be a disclaimer, such as the ones noted in this chapter about the Internet e-mail tax.

Scams, Safe Shopping, and Online Banking

Online Scams

The same as scams off-line, where an offer is just too good to be true but some people still fall for it.

Online Shopping

Shopping from the comfort of your home or office via the Internet.

Online Banking

Doing all of your banking online, including paying bills.

There are scam artists and there are scam *artistes*. And it didn't take them very long to discover the Internet. The FBI's Internet Fraud Complaint Center (IFCC, see Figure 5.1) and Internet Fraud Watch (IFW, see Figure 5.2) issued a list of what they consider to be the Top 10 online scams:

1. Online auctions
2. General merchandise sales
3. Securities fraud—stocks, bonds, etc.

4. Credit card fraud
5. Identity theft
6. Business opportunities/work-at-home schemes
7. Advance fee loans
8. Computer equipment/software sales
9. Adult services (pornography)
10. Other (including Nigerian money offers, credit card offers, and discounted travel/vacation offers)

Figure 5.1   IFCC.

Figure 5.2   IFW.

Credit Card Fraud

When it comes to credit card fraud, some scammers are very clever.

Annette was checking her bank statement in September 2000 and found a debit for Skiftelecom in Stavropol, Russia, in the amount of $15.08. Since she and her husband used their bank debit card online for purchases, she asked her husband if he ordered something from Russia. He hadn't. And she hadn't.

"When I reported this unauthorized charge to our bank, I was told that most consumers don't check their bank statements or credit card bills and that's how companies or people such as this Skiftelecom can get away with charging small amounts," Annette says. "If they do it to hundreds or thousands of people, they can make a tidy profit and never get caught."

Annette had the credit cards canceled and replaced with new account numbers. Then she did some checking online and found she wasn't the only one who'd been charged by Skiftelecom. A news site in the United Kingdom first reported it in their August 8, 2000, issue:

> HASTINGS INTERNET SHOPPERS BEWARE!
>
> Do you shop on the Internet? Do you accept your bank or credit card statements without a closer look? If you are one of those people who are busy or trusting and do not check your bank or credit card statements and you also shop on the Internet, now might be the time to change your habits.
>
> Two members of our website team, who are Internet shoppers, have had statements this month which include the same entry for a service of which they have no knowledge.
>
> The amount payable was 722.19 Russian Roubles to a company named as Skiftelecom, Stavropol. The sum in Sterling is £17.84 and was withdrawn on 18th July 2000.
>
> They have both discussed the matter with their credit card company/bank and the site team have reported it to the Hastings Police. So, beware!

Annette was furious but not surprised and did some more digging. She found another person who posted a complaint to his credit card Web site, stating that he'd been charged $10.47 on July 21, 2000, by Skiftelecom. Another woman posted on a newsgroup the information about how she found two of her credit cards were charged approximately $26.30 (one card twice) from Skiftelecom in July. She asked around and found four other friends who had the same charges. Then in October, her credit card was charged $10.05 from www.inetplat.com. Other newsgroup posters chimed in with complaints they had not only been charged by Skiftelecom, but also www.inetplat, both out of Russia.

Annette was glad she reported the charge from Skiftelecom when she had or she might have lost more money. As more people complained, they all seemed to have one common thread—they either had their Web site hosted by a Canadian company called Softcomca or purchased something from a Web site hosted by Softcomca.

When contacted, a spokesman stated, "We are confident that the breach was not at Softcomca. We have received a bank statement from a customer who signed up at July 21, where she was charged on July 18 by Skiftelecom. Also, on some newsgroups, there are several complaints from people who have no relation to Softcomca, yet they were charged by Skiftelecom, too."

This response infuriated those who had lost money, and soon the Web host company was losing customers. To this day, there are warnings about this situation on newsgroups and forums, especially because Softcomca denied the Skiftelecom hack was from their site.

It all came to a head in December 2000, when the media began reporting that hundreds, perhaps thousands, of people reported small charges from four Russian "Internet firms": Skiftelecom, Inetplat, Intelcom, and Global Telecom. When I tried to interview these companies, none replied to my e-mail.

Thoughts were, at the time, that these companies were part of a larger credit card scheme Russian hackers had concocted and pulled off by hacking into a database at CreditCards.com, stealing three million credit card numbers. However, they turned out not to be the ones troubling Annette and others.

As suddenly as the charges appeared, they stopped. But Annette learned her lesson. "Now we use only one credit card for all of our online transactions and it's not our bank debit card," she says. "We haven't had any problems since."

Online Shopping

When it comes to online shopping, we hear about the horror stories more often than we hear about the good experiences. The truth is that online shopping is as safe as off-line shopping, if not safer.

"I've used my credit card and never had a security leak or unauthorized charges from any online store," says Lorian, who lives in Oregon. "I often use coolsavings.com and valupage.com coupons, which gets me free shipping at many online merchants, or $10 off a $25 purchase or some other premium item with purchase."

Yes, there are plenty of happy online shoppers like Lorian, and you can be one, too. Frank Fiore, an e-commerce expert and consultant, has written several books about online shopping and commerce.

"The most common mistake online shoppers make is not using a credit card," says Fiore. "When you use a credit card, you're protected by your bank against scams and merchants who either send you the wrong product or will not take a product back for whatever reason. All you have to do is call your bank and dispute the charge. If you send a check or money order, you have little or no recourse. This is especially important in person-to-person auctions like eBay."

Sites That Offer Tips/Advice/ Comparison Shopping

Scams, Frauds, Hoaxes, etc., on the Internet from A to Z
http://advocacy-net.com/scammks.htm

Scambusters
www.scambusters.com
This is one of the most comprehensive Web sites devoted to online scams, including shopping and banking. They offer a monthly newsletter with the latest information that can be e-mailed to you.

Scamwatch
www.scamwatch.com

Internet Scams Ezine
http://inetscams.hypermart.net

WebAssured.com
www.webassured.com

Planet Feedback
www.planetfeedback.com

Ecomplaints.com
www.ecomplaints.com

Epinions.com
www.epinions.com

BizRate.com
www.bizrate.com

Rating Wonders
www.ratingwonders.com

ConsumerSearch
www.consumersearch.com

Productopia
www.productopia.com

PriceWatch (comparison shopping)
www.pricewatch.com

Copernic Shopper (comparison shopping & reviews)
www.copernic.com/products/shopper/index.html

For auctions, it's recommended that you use a service that allows payment for your winning bid with a major credit card. PayPal and Billpoint are examples of these types of services. They enable you to pay for online purchases securely. If anything happens, such as non-shipment or the wrong item, you can get PayPal or Billpoint to intervene on your behalf. Many online merchants use these services as a way for you to pay for items in their store if they don't accept credit cards.

Also, take a careful look at the location of online merchants.

"Does the merchant have their own domain name—such as www.virtualvin.com—or are they using free Web space such as Geocities or AngelFire? If they have their own domain, it does lend some credibility to the merchant," says Fiore. "You could make a comparison to a merchant with a large storefront downtown vs. a guy with a fold-up cart on the side of the road. If you have a problem with your product, who are you more likely to find again to help get it resolved?"

Once you feel comfortable with the merchant's Web site, look at the site itself. Does it look professionally designed or slapped together? A site that looks professional usually means the merchant spent money to have it designed, showing a commitment to the product(s) he sells online. If you wouldn't go into a store that is small, dingy, and questionable, you shouldn't do business with a Web site that looks like it was put together by an amateur or fly-by-night operation, no matter how good the prices seem to be. If the business doesn't have its physical address and telephone number posted somewhere on the site, that's a warning sign.

"Does the site mention secure shopping?" Fiore says. "Many sites will dedicate an entire page to shopper security to help you feel at ease."

Make Your Online Shopping Experience a Safe One

MasterCard International and the National Consumer's League offer these great tips for making your online shopping experience a good one:

Privacy Protection. Reputable Web site operators clearly state privacy policies in an easily accessible place. Understand what information is collected and how it is used. Look for sites whose policies or privacy programs enable you to choose whether, and in what circumstances, your personal information will be used or shared with others.

Information about the offer. Good companies provide plenty of information and make it easy to find. Make sure you know what you're buying, how much it costs, the terms of any guarantees or warranties, the return or cancellation policies, and how to contact the company if you have questions. This is crucial when shopping online, since you can't actually see or use the product or service before you buy it.

Information about the seller. Look for information about whether the seller belongs to a trade group or participates in a program, such as BBBOnLine, that helps resolve complaints.

Delivery date. Know when the product(s) will be delivered or the service(s) performed.

Security. Good Web sites provide information about how they protect your financial information when it's transmitted and stored.

Guard your personal information. Don't provide information that you're uncomfortable giving. Never give anyone the password you use to log onto your computer or ISP. Don't offer financial account information unless you're paying for a purchase with that account.

Check the seller's reputation. Learn as much as you can about companies or individuals before doing business with them. Check with the Better Business Bureau (BBB) and your state and local agencies to find out about complaints. See if the Web site has a "feedback forum" where people can put information about their transactions. Ask friends about their favorite online merchants. Bear in mind, though, that just because a seller has no complaints or a good reputation, there's no guarantee that things will go smoothly for you.

Consider taxes and shipping costs. There may be taxes or duties on your purchase, especially if the transaction is international. Factor in shipping and handling charges to determine the total costs. You may also have to pay for shipping if you want to return the item.

Ask about insurance. Will the seller pay to insure the shipment, or is it your expense? How much does it cost? Is other insurance available to protect you if you don't get what you paid for or if you're dissatisfied? Some auction sites provide insurance to buyers. Be sure you know how insurance programs work and how much they cover.

Keep records. Print out all the information on your transaction, including the product description, delivery information, privacy policy, warranties, and any confirmation notices that the seller sends you via e-mail.

How can you tell if a site has secure shopping? There are several ways to determine this. Some sites that offer secure shopping show a graphic or logo with "SSL" on the main page, often with a link describing Secure Sockets Layer (SSL), which is a form of encryption that scrambles your credit card number and other information, allowing for safe transmission of the transaction (see Figures 5.3 and 5.4).

Figure 5.3 Unlocked.

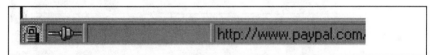

Figure 5.4 Locked.

Once you've selected the items you want and have a virtual shopping cart or an order form, clicking on "Pay now" or something similar should take you to a secure page. This page will either have "https" as the beginning of its URL, such as https://www.virtualvin. com or a "lock" or "key" graphic that appears in the lower left or right hand corner of your Web browser. If the lock or key is closed or whole—essentially locked—then the site is secure. When you leave that page or the site, you'll notice the lock is open or unlocked or the key is broken. Depending on which version of the browser you use, you may get a pop-up window letting you know you're entering a "secure area." This is the same as the lock or key graphic—your payment information will remain secure so that no one can steal it.

Later versions of Microsoft and Netscape browsers have preferences you can set so that you can be alerted when you're entering an encrypted (or secure) site, leaving one, viewing a page with a mix of encrypted/unencrypted information, or sending unencrypted information to a site. (See Figures 5.5 and 5.6.) Remember, though, that checking these preferences will result in quite a few pop-up alerts while surfing the Internet.

If there's something you just have to have and the online merchant who sells it doesn't accept credit cards or seems a bit dubious, consider using Paypal (www.paypal.com), or Billpoint (www.billpoint.com), or an escrow service such as Guzoo Escrow (www.guzooescrow.com). Escrow services hold your money until you've confirmed you received the product or service. Then they release the payment to the seller. There is a small fee, but in many cases the peace of mind will be worth the expense.

If the merchant refuses to allow this, then you'd better look elsewhere or wait until the item you want becomes more widely available. Reluctance on the part of a merchant to provide a secure transaction is a sure sign something's fishy. Don't cave in if they demand a money order or bank draft—or cash, heaven forbid.

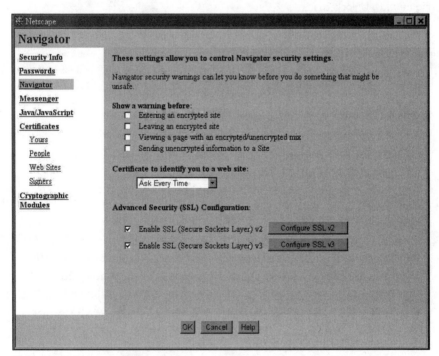

Figure 5.5   Netscape secure.

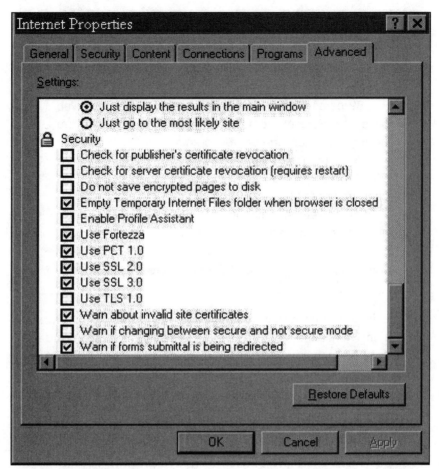

Figure 5.6   MSIE secure.

"One of the best online shopping experiences I had was when I heard of a music group called Gaia Consort but couldn't get their CDs anywhere locally or through a major online merchant," says music fan Cynthia. "The group didn't have any kind of online sales set up on their Web site yet, but we contacted them via e-mail about purchasing their CD. We used PayPal to pay for it with a credit card and got the CD shipped to us overnight—just in time for a party!"

Online Scam and Fraud Statistics

• More than 72 percent of online fraud victims are male.

• 82 percent of online fraud cases originate from Web sites; 12 percent from e-mail offers, 4 percent from newsgroups/message boards/forums.

• 57 percent of victims are ages 31–50; 20 percent are 20–30; 15 percent are 51–60; 6 percent are over 60; 2 percent are under 20.

• The average amount a victim loses is $427, an increase of 27.5 percent in one year.

Compiled by Internet Fraud Watch for the year 2000; released May 22, 2001.

Credit card companies have jumped onto the bandwagon, offering everything from online fraud protection if you use their credit card for all your online shopping, to tips and information on their Web sites to make you a savvy online shopper. Here are some sites to visit:

MasterCard International ShopSmart
www.mastercardintl.com/newtechnology/set

American Express Private Payments
www26.americanexpress.com/privatepayments/info_page.jsp

Discover Financial Services Shopping Guide
www2.discovercard.com/shopguide/sec03_safe.shtml

Visa International Internet Shopping Guide
www.usa.visa.com/personal/secure_with_visa/secure_commerce_program.html

It may seem that finding an online merchant you can trust is a simple task, but Richard M. Smith, a Boston-based independent security consultant, urges careful investigation.

"If you go to a search engine, such as Yahoo! or Google, to look for something you want to buy, don't assume a merchant listed in the search results is legitimate," Smith says. "After you find an online merchant, do some basic research if it's not a well-known name. The best place to start is in newsgroups or forums. Ask if anyone in the newsgroup or forum has dealt with that merchant. You can bet that if they had a bad experience, you'll hear about it."

There are also Web sites where people can post their bad and good experiences with online merchants. With names like Epinions.com and BizRate.com, you can be sure you'll find out what you need to know before you purchase something from a particular merchant (see the Resources section at the end of the book).

Smith also warns against Web sites that force you to register before you can look at what they sell.

"Give fake information," Smith says. "Or leave it blank if you can. If you can't get through that way, then don't register and don't patronize that site. They don't need all your personal information—such as name, address, and phone number—just so you can take a look around."

Top 10 Countries Reporting Internet Fraud

1. United States
2. Canada
3. Australia
4. United Kingdom
5. Singapore
6. Japan
7. Germany
8. Aruba
9. Uganda
10. Hong Kong

In the United States, California tops the list for complaints filed by victims, followed in order by Texas, Florida, New York, Washington state, Pennsylvania, Illinois, Ohio, Virginia, and Michigan.

Compiled by the Internet Fraud Complaint Center for the year 2000; released May 22, 2001.

Top 10 Countries of Alleged Perpetrators

1. United States (90 percent)
2. Nigeria (2 percent)
3. Canada (2 percent)
4. Ukraine
5. Romania
6. United Kingdom
7. Indonesia
8. Hong Kong
9. Netherlands
10. Australia

In the United States, California again tops the list for alleged perpetrators, followed in order by Florida, New York, Texas, Pennsylvania, New Jersey, Illinois, Michigan, Ohio, and Nevada.

Compiled by the Internet Fraud Complaint Center for the year 2000; released May 22, 2001.

How the Government Helps

The FBI has its hands full with the ever-growing number of online-related cases, from harassment and stalking to hackers and fraud. For example, between October 1, 2000, and April 6, 2001, the FBI referred about 800 Internet fraud investigations to several federal law enforcement agencies and more than 1,200 local law enforcement officials. Another 40 cases were referred to international authorities. In addition, since the IFCC opened, 10,370 complaints have been referred to nearly 40,000 law enforcement agencies. With the number of online users increasing daily, the amount of complaints is certain to double, if not triple, in coming years.

"The agency has a hard time gauging the actual incidence of Internet fraud because only a fraction of those affected by fraud schemes online know where to report the problem," says Tracey Silberling, who is with the FBI's Criminal Division. "There is probably a huge percentage of fraud that goes unreported. The IFCC takes all those reports and sends them out to the appropriate agency."

The U.S. Postal Inspection Service (USPIS) has also gotten into the act. If an item was paid for through the postal mail (via check, money order, or bank draft), or if an item received through the postal mail was not what was ordered, the victim can file a complaint with the USPIS, which will look into it and try to get the customer's money back.

One example is the Woodside Literary Agency, mentioned in Chapter 1. Since many writers sent this so-called agency reading, editing, and contract fees via postal mail, the USPIS stepped in. They arrested the two people running Woodside in January 2000 and charged them with mail fraud and perjury, punishable by up to five years in jail and/or fines.

The USPIS is serious when it comes to fraud that occurs while using postal mail. They are so Net-savvy that they offer a number of consumer tools on their site (www.usps.gov/websites/depart/ inspect) so that you can find the address of your nearest U.S. Postal Inspector, see the list of laws enforced, and read news about the latest cons and swindles. The Software Information Industry Association (SIIA) gave the USPIS a recognition award at its annual conference in 2001.

"SIIA has, over the past four years, developed an aggressive Internet Anti-Piracy Campaign to help stop the spread of infringing software online," wrote Mike Flynn, manager of the Internet Anti-Piracy division of the SIIA, in a letter to the USPIS. "To that effect, we have worked in the past with various U.S. enforcement agencies. This past year [2000], SIIA turned to the USPIS for help in a few cases that we were handling on behalf of our members since many, if not all, of the alleged pirates were using the U.S. Postal system to send illegal product. The response that SIIA has received from various USPIS offices has been extremely positive. As you know, often-times good deeds go unrewarded. We'd like to change that."

On March 11, 2001, U.S. Postal Deputy Chief Inspector Michael Ahern accepted the award on behalf of the USPIS in San Diego, California, from SIIA President Ken Wasch, for its success in protecting intellectual property rights and consumer rights from online scams.

Through rain or sleet or snow, and now we can add "online."

FDIC Tips for Banking Safely Online

www.fdic.gov/bank/individual/online/safe.html

- Confirm that an online bank (if you're not using your own) is legitimate and that your deposits are FDIC-insured.
- For insurance purposes, be aware that a bank may use different names for its online banking; understand your rights as a consumer.
- Learn where to go for more assistance from banking regulators.
- Remember that nonfinancial Web sites that are linked to your bank's site are not FDIC-insured.

ALSO:

- Find out what fees are involved to switch to online banking; sometimes it's actually less expensive than keeping your regular checking account.
- Determine if there are any fees should you decide to cancel the service. Is there a contract?

Online Banking

Many banks provide online banking services, often getting customers interested in signing up by offering the first three months free or waiving the standard setup fee. So far, most consumers have balked at moving their checking and savings to the Net. After all, using a credit card for an online purchase may be well and good, but this is *their* money!

If you are ready to take the plunge, or at least study the options, software accounting programs such as MS Money and Quicken offer tips on how to get an online banking account set up so that you can take care of all your finances online, including your taxes, stocks, bonds, and more.

Here are some sites to visit:

Banking and Investing Online Resources Group
www.bank-accounts-online.com

Free Online Banking in America
www.free-online-banking-internet-checking.com

Electronic Banker
www.electronicbanker.com/btn/m_btn2.shtml

Quicken Online Banking
www.quicken.com/banking_and_credit

MS Money Online Banking Page
www.msmoney.com/mm/banking/onlinebk/onlinebk_intro.htm

"Online banking hasn't really caught on yet," says Frank Fiore. "Banks will have to offer more useful services than the ones they currently offer. After all, you can't get cash from your PC!"

Auction Caution

Online Auction Fraud

When a seller offers something that is not what they claim, such as forged autographs or memorabilia; pirated software, videos, or music; and any prize that is not as initially described.

Author's Note: The following example is included for the purposes of illustration only, in order to point out the potential dangers of online auction fraud, and is in no way intended to suggest that shopping on eBay is unsafe in comparison to any other auction site. The principal function of an online auction site is to connect third-party buyers and sellers, and, despite the most diligent efforts of eBay and other auction sites to protect the interests of their visitors, abuses by auction participants are inevitable.

It seemed like it was too good to be true. On eBay there was an 8x10 color photograph of Harrison Ford and Sean Connery from the movie *Indiana Jones and the Last Crusade* signed by both of them (see Figure 6.1). Prospective bidder Anne read the following description:

All of our photos are authentic and come with 100% Money back guarantee. We Have been in business since 1988 and we have never had any problems with any Customer. We give you our word. Negative comments usually come from Competition. Look at our feed back it speaks for itself. Please notify us if you Receive any non-solicited e-mail regarding this item. Please forward complete email To me so that we can forward them to ebay! This is an absolutely gorgeous 8x10 photograph signed in Blue and Black ink by Ford and Connery. We provide money backed satisfaction guarantee and certificates of authenticity. We have other Memorabilia at www.xtruexcollectorx.com. or at Ebay sellers at XXMEM Thank you for visiting and have A great day. ** SORRY ABOUT BAD SCANS !**

Figure 6.1   Indiana Jones.

There was a link to the company's Web site and it seemed legit, so Anne placed a bid on the photo. Three days later, on July 23, 1999, she won it for $41 plus shipping. The seller responded quickly with a shipping address and Anne promptly sent off a check for $45.50.

"Three weeks went by and no photo," Anne said, "so I e-mailed xxmem letting them know I was wondering where the photo was. I got no reply."

She sent two more e-mails a week later and still no reply. She went to the eBay site and got the user ID information on xxmem, which included their address and phone number. When she called, an answering machine picked up. Anne left a message, but received no return phone call.

The next day she got an e-mail from them:

```
We looked up the reciept under your last
name, could it be under a different name?
```

It hadn't been and Anne let them know that in a quick reply, repeating her full name and mailing address for them.

The next day brought this reply:

```
Just got back from the post office and it
was   insured,   it   will   take   30   days   to
process but we will be sending one out to
you on Monday, when it get home I am going
to   email   a   scan   of   the   insured   reciept
showing it was mailed on 7-28-99.
```

By this time, Anne had done some checking on xxmem on eBay and was beginning to doubt the validity of the signatures on the photo. She discovered that xxmem had offered the same photo with the same exact signatures at least 18 times within the past 30 days. Each auction had a winner, which meant there were at least that many other photos of Harrison Ford and Sean Connery out there. She knew it was hard to get autographs from Ford and Connery, and harder still to get them to sign copies of the same photograph that many times. Anne asked xxmem if the replacement photo would be like the one she'd won. The answer was yes.

Anne sent them this e-mail on August 23, 1999:

```
One last question: Can you guarantee me
that this photo has authentic autographs
and does not have autopen signatures? My
```

concern is that after doing a search on ebay under your seller ID, I find that there were/are at least 18 of the same exact photo since 7/19/99, with both Ford and Connery's signatures on it. I don't know how many prior to that date you've sold. How did you get them to sign this many photos? I sincerely think I would rather get my money back at this point. Please send a money order in the amount of $45.50 to me immediately. Forget the photo. If I receive one, I am returning it. I want my money back.

The reply came quickly, and was curt:

After everything we are doing you want your money back sure will have it in the mail today.

But they never answered the question about the authenticity of the autographs or how they'd gotten them. Anne did some more research on eBay and checked out xxmem's feedback.[1] She found out she wasn't the only one having problems with this company, as per these examples of complaints:

Complaint: Never sent item, won't give me refund, won't answer about authenticity of auto's.

Complaint: The item has never been sent. I am very disappointed with the service.

Complaint: NEVER SENT PICTURE .... BEWARE! DO NOT DO BUSINESS WITH Xxmem!!

Complaint: It has taken me over a month + 2 checks to get him to send the WRONG picture!!!!

Complaint: BEWARE; I ONLY RECEIVED ONE OF TWO ITEMS PURCHASED

Complaint: Check cleared 7-22. No photo, just excuses by e-mail. Did not return phone call (finally received a refund on 8/23/99 after repeated emails and calls)

Complaint: well over a month never received item. Will never buy from again!!!!!!!

Complaint: Where's my Griffey Jr. picture? It's been a month. Not even an e-mail.

Anne gathered up these e-mail addresses and sent this message:

We're all in the same club, unfortunately—those who had problems with the seller known as xxmem on eBay. Most of us didn't get the photo we won and/or a refund and some of us got the wrong photo or not the whole order. My case is that I kept emailing them, asking when they'd sent the photo I won out and they didn't answer me until I called and left a message on their answering machine. Then I got the runaround--first I was asked if I'd used a different name, they couldn't find it under my last name, then they mysteriously found the insured receipt they supposedly sent with my photo (under my name), then said they'd send me a new photo. When I discovered they'd gotten four negative feedbacks within the past seven days, I demanded my money back. First I got an okay, then an e-mail claiming I had to wait until they got a refund from the post office first. I told them no. I not only demanded my money back, but told them I would complain to eBay, the southern California BBB, the California State Attorney General, and my lawyer. I think the IRS would be interested to find out that all auction sales on eBay have payment made out to a person and not the company name. I haven't heard back from them, but I want to ask all of you if you will agree to do a combined complaint to the organizations I mentioned. I'll be happy to do the legwork. All I'd need is your okay and have you let me know exactly what happened between you and xxmem.

I've also done some research on their past sales. They seem to have an awful lot of the same photos up for bid signed by some pretty elusive celebrities. I can't imagine Harrison Ford and Sean Connery signing the same photograph from Indiana Jones and the Last Crusade over 20 times. And that was just a listing of auctions from the past 30 days.

I'm sure if eBay did some research, they'd find that xxmem sells the same photos over and over again, leading me to believe this seller may be auctioning forged signatures of celebrities. I don't think most winners are smart enough to see what kind of photos xxmem has sold in the past or are selling now--I think they'd be very surprised to find that their photo may be a fake.

Replies came quickly from most of the people who complained about xxmem. Pat in Texas wrote:

I never got the photo of Stevie Nicks that I won. They (xxmem) had one excuse after another. The last excuse was that one of them had gone on vacation at the time the check was received and that a new person had not posted the check with the item number. They then asked for a copy of the canceled check. I faxed it to them on August 20 and have not received a reply. I asked for a refund in lieu of photo. I was a little leery about the authenticity of the autograph anyway.

And this from Lynette of Massachusetts:

I won two photos from xxmem; one arrived and not the other. They said they would send it right out. They told me that three times. Because I waited the 30 days from the end of the auction, I was unable to file a Fraud report on eBay. They no longer answer my e-mails, ever since I left the negative feedback.

Jeff from North Carolina was also angry:

> I won an autographed Pretty Woman photo
> [see Figure 6.2] and the autographs look fake
> (they don't look the same as others I have
> seen). I have contacted xxmem and they agreed
> to refund my money, but I'm wary about send-
> ing him the photo without any proof.

And another from David of Michigan:

> I was the high bidder on a autographed
> photo of Ken Griffey and Alex Rodriguez. It

Figure 6.2 Pretty Woman.

was a very nice photo, and the signatures looked very good. I've been collecting for some time, and from what I could tell, the Griffey signature was right on! I was excited to get such a great pic for only $42. After I won, xxmem sent me the info on where to send the money order. When the pic hadn't come after a week, I sent them an e-mail asking what was going on. They replied that it had been sent the day before. I waited another week, but never got the pic. I sent one more e-mail, saying that I either wanted my pic, or a full refund. I never got a reply, a picture, or a refund, so I left negative feedback!

Complaints stretched as far away as England, including this one from Christian:

I was the highest bidder for a Pamela Anderson photo for $27 + $10 postage. So I sent $37 on the 14th of July. I then sent an e-mail about 3 weeks later asking if it had been sent out. They replied that they had not received the payment. Another week went by and I sent another e-mail to see if payment had arrived and they said no and asked if I sent it under another name, to which I replied no. Since then I sent five e-mails but have not received any replies.

Anne was intrigued that Christian had also been asked if he sent his payment under another name. Now she was positive something was wrong. She gave xxmem one last chance and e-mailed them on August 30, 1999, that she had not received the refund.

The reply the next day was:

It was mailed to on 8-24-99, just like the photo was mailed to you along time ago. Something is wrong with your post office.

Anne knew there was nothing wrong with her post office. But she did receive the second photo. Jeff sent her his *Pretty Woman* photo "signed" by Julia Roberts and Richard Gere. She called a local autograph dealer who was a member of the UACC3 and asked if he'd look at the photos to authenticate them for her. He agreed.

His e-mail to her was what she thought it would be:

> Anne, it is my opinion that both auto-graphs you sent me are forgeries. Meaning they were intentionally hand-signed by someone other than the pictured celebrity. Sean Connery, Harrison Ford, Julia Roberts, and Richard Gere are perhaps the four toughest Hollywood autographs to obtain--at least the top 10 most difficult. To have jointly signed pieces on these individuals is remarkable.
>
> I would pay up to $150 for legitimate pieces like the ones you sent me. Keep in mind, that I pay wholesale prices so you can imagine what the retail value is. Another thing to keep in mind--authenticat-ing is a risky and difficult job. So, I will state that, in my opinion, the autographs you inquired about are not hand-signed by the pictured celebrity.
>
> You should never buy anything on eBay unless you have a business relationship with the seller--one that you trust. There is so, so much bad material on eBay that, in my opinion, it isn't worth bidding--unless you know the seller. Because of lia-bility issues, this will be my only indication that I felt the pieces you mailed me were not hand-signed.
>
> It is amazing, but some of the most dis-reputable dealers in the industry will sue if they hear someone saying their stuff isn't real--even though they know that it isn't. So, I really try to stay out of the third party authentication game.

Anne got the others to agree to a combined complaint and began filling out forms for all of them. These were sent to the Southern California Better Business Bureau (xxmem was located there), the

California State Attorney General, the USPS Mail Fraud Bureau, the National Fraud Information Center, and eBay's Fraud division.

It didn't take long for xxmem to reply to everyone. And they all received the same e-mail:

> It is hard for us to believe you could do something like this. We went out of our way to get this matter solved and to make you satisfied. We always insure our packages, we have proof showing we sent the photo's out when we said we did. We have almost 2,000 positive feedback's from customers that are satisfied with our business. We even sent you a new photo, and you did not give us the benefit of the doubt. We are not out here to scam anyone, we are trying to earn a honest living.

But—miraculously—refunds began to appear in the mail.

Pat was one of the first to receive his, on August 23, 1999, in the amount of $50. Anne received hers on September 7, 1999, in the amount of $45.50. Lynette finally received her photo of Harrison Ford and Sean Connery on September 21, 1999, and decided to keep it instead of getting a refund. Christian received his refund of $37 on September 24, 1999. David received his refund of $46.50 on September 24, 1999. Jeff was the last to receive his, on October 2, 1999, in the amount of $146.02.

It may seem incredible that nothing can be done to stop sellers from putting up forged autographed items on the auction Web sites, but as more pressure is put on online auction sites to take responsibility, things are bound to change.

When I asked eBay about this, I received this reply from the company's *eBay Life* columnist Uncle Griff:

> Fake autographs and infringing items are two separate kettles of fish. We cannot verify or authenticate an autograph, thus we remind all bidders it's 'caveat emptor' (buyer beware) that should be their watch cry. eBay doesn't handle the merchandise so any sort of authentication from us is impossible. The bidder has to rely on the integrity of the seller and know what they

are buying. That being said, anyone who ends
up with an item that is not what it was
claimed to be has some recourse with our
Insurance program and, if that fails, our
Fraud Reporting form. Items that infringe
upon a person's copyright or property
rights are removed from the site as they are
reported by either the property owner or a
conscientious member. Since eBay is the
biggest player in the person-to-person
trading market, most of the big trademark or
copyright holders watch us like hawks and
immediately report any violations of their
intellectual property rights.

It's interesting to note that by the time most bidders who have had
problems do get in touch with either the insurance program or fraud
reporting on eBay, the 30-day limit eBay imposes (from the end of
the auction) has passed. This means bidders have to swallow their
pride and lose their money, or they can file complaints, as Anne and
the others did. The latter takes time and, often, money.

I contacted several suspected sellers at online auction sites about
the origin of their "authentic" autographed memorabilia. No seller
revealed where they got their autographs from—and no seller claimed
they had procured the photos and other signed objects directly from
the celebrities.

Within a week after contacting these dealers, a major FBI raid
occurred. Operation Bullpen, a two-year-old undercover FBI investigation, cracked down on counterfeit autographs, most of which had
been sold at online auctions in what authorities said was a $1 billion-
a-year industry. As part of the probe, agents and informants posed as
collectors and traders to infiltrate the industry. As a result, more than
50 dealers were raided in California, Nevada, New Jersey, and
Pennsylvania, including some of the ones I had contacted.

"Reverse" Auction Fraud

In 1997, Connie opened the Gray Horse Emporium, an antiques
store in Paris, Virginia, with a friend. Soon, the two began buying and
selling antiques on eBay. Then her friend left the business and Connie
felt she couldn't run the shop by herself because she had no time for

her family and for training her horse. She began selling antiques and collectibles exclusively online, mostly through eBay.

A friend asked if she'd help him auction off watches from his father's estate. Many were expensive, and he didn't want to try to sell them through classified ads in the newspaper. Connie agreed and put the watches up for auction. One Rolex was quickly bid on and had reached $10,000 when she received an e-mail.

It was a request that she end the auction at the reserve price of $13,000 if the bidder paid that day via credit card. She called her friend, advising him to keep the auction going, as she thought the Rolex could fetch much more money. He decided to end the auction instead of waiting, so she e-mailed the bidder back, agreeing to the transaction. Within an hour, she received an e-mail from Tradenable[2] stating that the credit card payment had gone through.

Connie called her friend with the mailing information so that he could send the Rolex out that day. When she got off the phone, she noticed she'd received another e-mail from Tradenable—the credit card was a stolen one and they urged her not to send the Rolex. She called her friend back immediately but he'd already dropped the Rolex off at the post office. When she called the post office, she was lucky—they still had the package.

While her friend picked up the Rolex, Connie called the local police. They asked her what she wanted to do about it. She had the Rolex, so she hadn't lost anything. She told the police officer that she didn't want this guy to get away with the fraud. The officer said he was happy to hear this and they hatched a plan.

Connie e-mailed the fraudulent bidder and let him know that the post office would not insure the watch and she'd have to send it via UPS. She needed a street address for this, not the P.O. Box he'd given her. He quickly e-mailed back a street address. Connie called the police officer with the address and was told to package something similar in size and weight of the Rolex and send it off.

Connie found a broken soap dish, carefully packaged it up and sent it via UPS to the address indicated. The next day, the police staked out the street address, finding it was an abandoned home. They hoped the fraudulent bidder would show up. They called UPS to find out what time the delivery would be. The police were told by UPS that the fraudulent bidder called them and said he'd come to their office to pick up the package. By the time police arrived, the package had been picked up, but they got a good description of the man. Less than a block away, the opened package and broken soap dish were found in a dumpster.

Within a week, the fraudulent bidder was arrested—but not for the credit card fraud; it was for a traffic violation.

Connie says she learned her lesson: Never send an item out to a buyer the same day the credit card transaction has been approved, and never end an auction early. She has adhered to these two principles and has had no further problems.

Safe Bidding Online

Bidders can be auction-savvy if they follow this advice:

1. Check the feedback/comments on the seller. Even if there are only a few negative comments, you might want to contact those people via e-mail to find out why they were dissatisfied with the transaction.

2. See what else the seller is currently selling. If the auction site you're on has the capability, check any past auctions by that seller. If you see more than one of the same item you want to bid on, be wary. If you see a large number of the item you're interested in (such as 10 Joe DiMaggio signed photos, when you know he's been dead for some time, and they're all the same pose and same signature), DO NOT bid on them!

3. Look at other auction items of the same type and see if their descriptions match word for word. Many fraudulent sellers use several IDs or usernames to get as many of the same products out as possible.

4. If you're having doubts, get the seller's user information/e-mail address/mailing address and compare it to similar items up for sale. If more than one seller matches, you'd be wise not to bid on that item.

5. If the seller has only a few feedback comments and you really want an item they have up for auction, see if they take credit cards, PayPal, BidPay, Billpoint, or some other form of online payment. If they don't, and only accept money orders to be sent to a P.O. Box, be wary. Many fraudulent sellers will put "ghost" items up for auction, then disappear once the money is sent. If you use a credit card, make sure it's one that will allow you to dispute a charge in case the seller does turn out to be fraudulent.

6. If you really want an autographed piece of memorabilia, deal with someone legitimate who can absolutely guarantee the item was hand-signed by the celebrity.

More on autographs: Two autograph organizations, Universal Autograph Collectors Club (UACC) and Professional Autograph Dealers Association (PADA), have strict guidelines for their members, which must be adhered to or the members will be dropped and/or penalized. If an auction seller is a member of either of these organizations, then you can be reasonably sure the item you bid on is legitimate.

Founded in 1965, UACC began as a small group of Long Island, New York, autograph collectors and has grown to be the largest federally recognized nonprofit collectors organization of its kind. Reach them at:

UACC
P.O. Box 6181
Washington, D.C. 20044-6181
www.uacc.org
Paul Carr, president: paulkcarrsr@msn.com

Membership in PADA is limited to dealers who have demonstrated expertise and integrity in buying and selling autographs. Reach them at:

PADA
P.O. Box 1729-W
Murray Hill Station
New York, NY 10156
888-338-4338
www.padaweb.org
padamail@padaweb.org

Sellers of fake or forged items really believe a sucker is born every minute. Don't prove them right. Remember what should become your mantra for everything you do online: *If it looks too good to be true, it probably is.*

Endnotes

1. Feedback: Found mostly in online auctions, the seller and winning bidder can leave feedback or comments for each other when an auction sale is completed. Feedback allows you to see if the seller or bidder has had positive, neutral, or negative feedback before you bid on an item.
2. Tradenable (formerly called iEscrow): An online escrow service that protects a buyer and seller from fraud.

Where the Heartache Is: Adoption Fraud

Susan is single, in her 40s, and wants a baby. After much thought, she decided to adopt, but that was easier said than done.

"In late fall of 1998, I was frustrated with my hopes of adopting a child," Susan recalls. "Typical adoption agencies wanted children to go to two parents, not one, and wanted them younger, not middle-aged. I did find a couple of possibilities, but then the birthmom decided to keep the baby. Not her fault, just my luck."

Susan, who lives in southern Maine, occasionally visited an online adoption chat room to find some comfort with other frustrated prospective adoptive parents. They'd discuss the trials and tribulations of domestic and international adoption, mention where they were in the scheme of things, commiserate about failed adoptions, and give each other pats on the shoulder.

"That's where I met Sonya [Furlow]," Susan says. "She seemed to be on just about every adoption-related mailing list I joined, offering her comments about adoption as a facilitator—a person licensed to arrange adoptions—in Philadelphia, Pennsylvania."

Since these mailing lists seemed to have helped other adoptive parents, Susan read Sonya's messages with interest. She was well aware of adoption scams and grilled Sonya with questions and comments.

"Sonya told me she had a Web site, Tender Hearts Family Services Adoption Counseling, so I looked it up, felt it was professional-looking, then called and asked her to send me a packet of information about her services," Susan recounts. "I asked her over the phone if she would work with singles and she told me she would, although I'd be her first."

Even though Sonya's agency was located quite a distance from her, Susan was hopeful.

Adoption Resources

National Council for Adoption (NCFA)
www.ncfa-usa.org

Adopting.com Internet Adoption Resources
www.adopting.com

Adopt: Assistance Information Support
www.adopting.org

The Adoption Guide
www.theadoptionguide.com

Adoption.about
adoption.about.com

Waiting Families: Family/Child Matching
www.waitingfamilies.com

Adoption Resource Directory
www.adopt-usa.org

Adoption Assistance
www.adoption-assist.com

Adoptshop
www.adoptshop.com

National Association of Ethical Adoption Professionals
www.NAEAP.com

Trusting Sonya

Sonya asked Susan questions about her family, what Susan was looking for in a child, essentially interviewing Susan. Susan confessed that all she wanted was a healthy baby—race and sex weren't issues. This conversation took place at the end of 1998.

The New Year rang in and Susan was worried she'd never adopt. Then one night, the phone rang. It was Sonya.

"Susan, I just may have a situation for you that came up a couple of days ago," said Sonya enthusiastically. "I have a birthmom who would be willing to have a single woman adopt her baby."

Susan couldn't believe her luck—maybe she'd finally get her baby! Sonya told her all about the birth mother, Gabrielle, weaving a sad, but believable tale: Gabrielle was a single mother, 27, with an associate's degree and working on her bachelor's. She was of Italian descent with one daughter who was five years old; Gabrielle worked part-time in daycare, and wanted to become a teacher. Gabrielle's boyfriend, Carlos, was a secret affair—he was married with four boys. Gabrielle and Carlos didn't believe in abortion and felt adoption was their only option. The baby was due May 12, 1999.

"I told her it sounded like a good situation," recalls Susan. "Sonya asked me to fill out the paperwork and sign the contract."

Before she did that, Susan checked around and talked to a lawyer in Philadelphia who had completed an adoption with Sonya with no problems. And when she checked with the Better Business Bureau, she got a thumbs-up. Satisfied that Sonya Furlow was for real, Susan sent her a check for $3,500 on February 18, 1999.

"I did not think that everything about Sonya checked out," says Judith M. Berry, Esq., Susan's lawyer and member of the American Academy of Adoption Attorneys. "In fact, I was extremely concerned as soon as I heard about her practices, such as asking for money to be wired to her immediately without receipt of medical records or background information and medical confirmation of pregnancy. Her practices were well outside the scope of traditional and reasonable adoption practice."

The next few months were like a roller coaster for Susan. Sonya started off with frequent reports about Gabrielle's pregnancy and the baby growing inside of her. After that, e-mail messages and phone calls became sporadic. There would be days when Susan wouldn't hear back from Sonya, who claimed she was an extremely busy woman. One time she said she'd been at the hospital with one of the other birth mothers she was working with. Susan believed her.

"Sonya told me she'd send a sonogram to me by Easter, then she changed her mind and called me back saying it was going to be Good Friday instead," Susan says. "That was when I began to feel uncomfortable about the situation."

It turned out Susan wasn't the only adoptive parent waiting for a baby from Sonya Furlow. Forty-three other families had put down deposits ranging from $1,000 to $15,000. And every one of them had found Sonya on the Internet at her Web site.

In early May, Susan heard from a couple who said they had flown to Philadelphia from Missouri to pick up the baby girl Sonya had promised them. They stayed for two weeks, waiting, and finally returned home empty-handed.

"I told them in the adoption chat room that it better not happen to me!" Susan recalls.

The roller coaster ride continued. Gabrielle had false labor a couple of times. Susan never received the sonogram. With a heavy heart, but still hopeful, Susan flew to Philadelphia on May 20th. She carried a baby car seat and bag filled with baby clothes, toys, and other childcare items. Somehow, she felt that if she were there when the birth mother was scheduled to deliver the baby, things would work out.

Sonya was more than surprised when Susan called her from the airport. But she reassured Susan that everything was fine. Susan sat in her hotel room, waiting.

"What went on for the next week was something I never believed would have been in the cards," Susan says. "After many frustrating phone calls never returned, faxes not answered until days later, I got a call from Judith Berry [Susan's attorney]. She asked if I was sitting down. I was. Then she told me the FBI was investigating Sonya."

"I was not surprised when the FBI called me," Berry says. "They wanted to interview clients who had contact with Sonya and found that I represented some of them. What started it all was another couple who reported Sonya to the FBI."

"I was stunned, I was in shock," Susan says, sighing at the memory. "I didn't want it to be true."

Susan flew home the Tuesday after Memorial Day weekend in 1999. She talked with the FBI on June 24, 1999. There was no Gabrielle. There was no Carlos. There was no baby.

"I found the FBI to be very compassionate, professional, and thorough," Berry says. "Sue helped tremendously to make their case."

"In my mind, that baby was real," Susan says. "It was the death of a child who never existed."

Around the country, from Maine to California, 44 families sat down with FBI agents and recounted their stories of trying to adopt through Sonya Furlow. The stories were similar: the birth mothers almost always seemed to be single, young, and the baby the result of a forbidden affair. Some families said Sonya told them the birth mothers had changed their minds. Some couples said they were told the baby was lost due to miscarriage or some other malady. And they all believed Sonya when she told them she'd find them another baby and to send more money. Sonya scammed the 44 families out of more than $200,000.

"Adoption scams have been happening for as long as there have been people seeking to adopt," says Julie Valentine of Adopting.com. "The Internet is simply a new way for people to connect. I don't think it's increased the number of adoption scams. It's simply widened the geographical possibilities for these scams."

Top 10 Online Adoption Tips

1. Go through an official agency or attorney. According to Adopting.org, "Do your homework. Don't rely on your gut instinct—make sure."
2. Don't give in to requests for immediate money. "A birth mother crisis is the common excuse," attorney Judith Berry warns. "Being homeless, out of food, etc. The bottom line is this: don't send money until you have more information, and consult an attorney. Several states prohibit any funds being given to a birth mother—payments can void an adoption and be considered a criminal act."
3. Be leery of e-mail messages or chat rooms. "Don't go into a chat room and write, 'I'm looking for a birth mother,'" says Courtney Frey of Adopting.org. "This is like standing on the street corner with a wad of cash in your hand, waiting for scam artists to approach you. If you get an e-mail with photos of a pregnant birth mother, along with a request for your phone

number or for money to 'help out until the baby is born,' don't fall for it. Most birth mothers use agencies. Very few have the emotional capacity to go online and look for potential parents themselves."

4. Remove any time limits you set. "Allow a minimum of one year to complete an adoption once you have started the paperwork," says Julie Valentine of Adopting.com. "If you're promised a baby faster than that, run the other way!"

5. Ask for information. "You have a legal right to confirmation of the pregnancy, medical records, social, psychological, psychiatric, and genetic information regarding the biological parents," says attorney Judith Berry.

6. Contact others online. "Network with others in the online adoption community," says Courtney Frey of Adopting.org. "Tell them about the person who contacted you about adoption. Share your stories. The online community is quite close and if you use each other to keep an eye out, the more likely you'll be safe."

7. Educate yourself before you adopt and while you're waiting. "There are many books and Web sites on adoption that every adoptive parent should read," says Julie Valentine of Adopting.com. "An adopted child is not the same as a biological child. They have issues and needs that are unique, and adoptive parents should be well-educated and prepared to help meet those needs."

8. Don't be rushed into a decision. "People who say, 'I have a baby now and if you don't send money today, she may not be here tomorrow' are a big red flag," Valentine says.

9. Keep your Web site/messages private. "Use toll-free numbers on your Web sites and in your e-mail messages or in chat rooms," says Courtney Frey of Adopting.org. "Or use your attorney or agency's telephone number as a contact. This protects you from scam artists finding out where you live and from contacting you."

10. It's an old adage, but it's true: If it sounds too good to be true, it probably is.

The Internet Twins

In January 2001, two adoptive families fought over twins they both claimed as their own. One family in California had paid an online adoption agency $6,000 for the twins. When the babies were born in Missouri, the birth mother took them back, then resold the twins to a couple from England for $14,000. The couple flew back to England with the babies in tow. The "Internet twins" were taken by British social services at a north Wales hotel where the British couple had taken refuge. A court fight ensued among the couple in England, the couple in California, and the birth mother.

On April 9, 2001, a judge ruled that the now nine-month-old twin girls would be sent back to Missouri and placed in foster care pending future rulings. Their birth mother claimed she wanted to share custody with her estranged husband and regretted giving them up for adoption.

"Selling babies like that is not as uncommon as you'd think," says Sandra Lennington of Adopting.org. "We had a woman get in touch with us who was pregnant. She and her husband already had a teenager and she wanted to sell the baby for $50,000. We informed her it was illegal to sell a baby and we would prosecute. We never heard from her again."

"Adoptive parents are emotionally and financially at risk," Judith Berry says. "They are vulnerable and want to believe the situation is a dream come true, even when demands are placed on them regarding money. When I questioned Sonya, she stated that maybe she did not want to work with someone who was questioning her practices. Red flags were waving. I warned my clients, but they wanted to believe she was going to give them the baby they so badly wanted."

Sonya Furlow was indicted in April 2000 on charges of 20 counts of mail fraud—for receiving payments through the U.S. Postal Service and private courier services. In June 2000, she pleaded guilty to three of the counts and publicly accepted responsibility for what she did. When the judge sentenced her to nearly four years in prison, he called her conduct "particularly and unusually cruel." He ordered her to repay the $215,000 she scammed from the 44 families, but since she's broke, it's doubtful any of them will see restitution.

"I mourn the loss of a child that never was," Susan says. She still hopes to adopt, but will rely on the expertise of her attorney from now on. She hopes to see new laws enacted that specifically target Internet adoption fraud.

"You need to realize that the Internet is a tool for people to connect," says Julie Valentine of Adopting.com. "It's a wonderfully useful tool that has greatly increased the span and scope of information about adopting. It has also dramatically increased the number of children who have been matched with families, especially older and special needs children. But the anonymity afforded by the Internet is a potential veil for scam artists, so make sure you thoroughly check out anyone and everyone."

8

Cases of Stolen Identity

Identity Theft

When someone steals your identity online, impersonates you, and wreaks havoc in your name; many times the thief charges money to credit cards you never received, takes out loans, orders items, etc.

The words "identity theft" conjure up an image of someone who has had his name and reputation hijacked by an imposter—a thief who has used the victim's social security number, personal data, and credit records for personal gain, and perhaps even committed crimes while impersonating the victim. This is an accurate representation of the problem. It can be devastating, and it takes years for most victims to recover from the experience.

But how does it happen *online?* Much in the same way it does off-line, except that it's easier to steal a person's identity online if the thief is Net-savvy and doesn't mind spending a few bucks. Sometimes it happens with a bit of a twist.

Natalie knows. Her identity was stolen online. She found out when she began receiving postal mail—three letters from different banks that thanked her for her business and enclosed her new credit card. Magazines she'd never ordered began to arrive—with bills asking for payment.

Then she discovered that someone applied for an online loan (it was denied), opened two online accounts with different ISPs, and applied for two more credit cards all in her name. This person joined online clubs based on her interests and waited for her to post to those clubs. Then the person made public, slanderous posts to the whole list in response—pretending to be her.

Who was this person?

Her ex-husband, bent on revenge.

"He broke into two of my e-mail accounts and sent himself harassing e-mails so that they looked like they came from me," Natalie says. "He then had Yahoo! close my accounts based on the fact that 'I' had harassed him."

But he wasn't done yet. He used her e-mail addresses to send messages to her friends, impersonating her, in order to get them to reveal information about her new life. He then sent himself e-mails from her address, this time trying to make it look like she was still crazy about him and wanted to get back together with him. One day, when he broke into one of her e-mail accounts, he found a copy of an e-mail in her Outbox in which she complained briefly about work, edited it to make it seem even worse, then printed it out, and overnighted it to one of her co-workers.

Natalie found herself on damage control alert in every aspect of her life—online and off-line. She filed a complaint with the Arizona State Attorneys Office, her state of residence.

"After I turned over all of my evidence, the office was one step away from a Grand Jury warrant. Unfortunately, they needed something from the ISP proving that my ex-husband was in fact logged in under his account with them during the specified times at which the fraudulent applications were placed," Natalie says. "In other words, they needed the login records from the ISP, which are stored for just such reasons. The ISP had several computers devoted to batches of customer accounts for record-keeping purposes."

But the particular computer that held the batch containing her ex-husband's login records had crashed. All the information was lost. Therefore, it could not be absolutely proven and the Grand Jury would not issue a warrant. Undeterred, Natalie pressed on and got seven e-mail accounts of his shut down based on the ISPs' terms of service and her ability to prove inappropriate use.

When her ex-husband discovered that he was being investigated, he stopped impersonating and harassing her online.

"The most obnoxious thing about this is that although the credit bureaus recognized that the applications were fraudulent and not initiated by me, the inquiries will still stay on my credit report for seven years, making it very hard for me to actually get credit, or get a mortgage," Natalie says. "They say that I am welcome to add a 100-word statement to my credit report that explains the situation but I don't think I should have to."

But she did anyway, knowing it was the only way to keep her good credit rating. I wish I could tell you Natalie's story has a happy ending, but it doesn't. Her ex-husband began stalking and harassing her off-line, even moving less than 90 minutes away from her. Although she has a protective order against him, she fears for her life.

How to Protect Yourself from Identity Theft

Thor Lundberg, founder of Cybersnitch (www.cybersnitch.net) recommends the following:

1. Don't give out financial information, such as your checking account and credit card numbers, especially your social security number (SSN), to a Web site or anyone online unless you initiate the communication and know the person or organization.

2. Never give personal information to a stranger, even if they claim to represent a legitimate organization or credit agency.

3. Notify an organization/company/business of any suspicious e-mail arriving in their name, such as those asking for your information to "verify a statement" or "award a prize."

4. Protect your passwords and Personal Identification Numbers (PIN) for your ATM card, credit cards, and online accounts.

5. Be creative in selecting passwords and PINs for any ATM card, credit card, or online account. Avoid using birth dates, part of your SSN, or driver's license number, address, or children's or spouse's names. Try using passwords that are at least eight characters in length and a mix of letters and numerals and one special symbol, like a punctuation mark.

6. Be sure that any Web site requesting personal information for verifying a transaction, such as making a purchase online, is using Internet-based security (SSL encryption).

According to the Federal Trade Commission (FTC), the number of identity thefts in the U.S. rose dramatically in 2001, the latest year for statistics, but relatively few are happening online.[1]

"Identity theft is expanding and increasing every day," says Jodie Bernstein, director of the FTC's Bureau of Consumer Protection, during the first meeting of the President's Information Technology Advisory Committee in February 2001.

Bernstein claimed the FTC received 2,000 calls per week in June 2001, but less than 1 percent of all reported cases to date can be linked to the Internet.

"We don't see as many Internet solicitations, but we are watching that," says Joanna Crane, program manager for the FTC's identity theft program. "There is evidence, however, that Internet-related thefts, particularly e-mail schemes, are increasing."

Andrea Morin, director of strategic planning at Technology Resources in Boston, agrees with the FTC that there is a misconception that online identity theft happens all the time.

"The role the Internet often plays is one of aider and abettor, if you will," Morin says. "Criminals often purchase fake ID—that in itself is generally considered a separate crime—via Web sites, or other items that could contribute to identity theft such as diplomas, birth certificates, driver's licenses, visas, passports, etc."

Identity thieves are helped by sites that sell personal identifying information on just about anyone. Also, there are sites that advertise books on how to create a false identity.

"The Internet is also a great place for criminals to use the credit of the victim," Morin says. "You can make a transaction online, and unlike an in-person transaction, there are no witnesses and no videotape. You don't even need to show the credit card or sign a receipt."

There have been two primary sources of identity theft via the Internet, according to Morin.

"The first, and most egregious source, is the SEC's[2] Edgar database. Edgar is an identity thief's dream. It contains various publicly available reports that must be filed by people owning more than five percent of stock in a company. These reports list their name, work or home address, social security number, and ownership position," Morin says. Other reports available on Edgar provide a detailed inventory of a person's financial holdings.

The U.S. Securities and Exchange Commission (SEC) stopped requiring that people provide their social security numbers, even though there is a space for this information on the online form. However, many people still fill it in, not knowing it will be displayed online, and others didn't remove their SSN from the Web site because they didn't know it was there—no one notified them. So unless people go looking for their SSN on the Web site, they're oblivious to the fact that it is there.

"The second most used source 'was' the online version of the *Congressional Record*," Morin says. "Its policy was to announce the promotion of every military officer, colonel, or above, and included the military ID number of that person, which was essentially his or her social security number."

The *Congressional Record* has done a partial redaction of the social security numbers in its online version, deleting some of the digits in the ID number; however, the original print editions still have the full SSN information.

Steps to Follow if Your Credit Card Is Stolen

1. Report the crime to the police immediately. Get a copy of your police report or case number. Credit card companies, your bank, and the insurance company may ask you to reference the report to verify the crime.
2. Immediately contact your credit card issuers. Get replacement cards with new account numbers and ask that the old account be processed as "account closed at consumer's request" for credit record purposes. You should follow up this telephone conversation with a letter to the credit card company summarizing your request.
3. Call the fraud units of the three credit reporting bureaus in the United States. Report the theft of your credit cards and/or numbers. Ask that your accounts be flagged. Also, add a victim's statement to your report that requests that they contact you to verify

future credit applications. The three credit bureaus
are:

Equifax Credit Information Services—
Consumer Fraud Division
P.O. Box 105496
Atlanta, Georgia 30348-5496
Tel: (800) 997-2493
www.equifax.com

Experian
P.O. Box 2104
Allen, Texas 75013-2104
Tel: (888) EXPERIAN (397-3742)
www.experian.com

Trans Union Fraud Victim Assistance Department
P.O. Box 390
Springfield, PA 19064-0390
Tel: (800) 680-7289
www.transunion.com

4. Keep a log of all conversations with authorities and
financial entities.

Provided by the U.S. Secret Service

One newsworthy online identity theft case involved a busboy in
Brooklyn who went through *Forbes* magazine's "400 Richest People in
America" issue and victimized more than 200 people who were listed in it.

Abraham Abdullah convinced credit companies to give him detailed
credit reports about the people he wanted to impersonate. He then used
the information to gain access to their credit cards and bank accounts—
all online. This went on for almost six months. Abdullah impersonated
well-known people including Martha Stewart, George Lucas, Oprah
Winfrey, Ross Perot, Ted Turner, Michael Bloomberg, David Geffen,
Steven Spielberg, and Michael Eisner.

How did he do it? First, he got a box at a local mailbox rental company in the name of Microsoft co-founder Paul Allen, conducting the
rental transaction via fax from start to finish, never appearing in person.

Next, Abdullah used online voicemail/fax accounts to receive messages and faxes. He began receiving credit cards in his victims' names, and then ordered items online. When they were delivered to the postal box he'd rented, he had a courier pick up and deliver the packages on deliberately confusing routes to elude any authorities who might suspect something. He never physically did any of this himself.

It was only when he was arrested that the police began to suspect the scope of his criminal activities. They noticed the well-used copy of *Forbes* magazine on the front seat of the car he was driving. A closer inspection revealed detailed notes next to the biographies of the people he had impersonated, including their home addresses, telephone and cell phone numbers, mothers' maiden names, and more.

What led to the arrest of Abdullah was an investigation that had begun a couple of months before, when Merrill Lynch received an e-mail requesting a transfer of $10 million from an account belonging to Thomas Siebel, founder of Siebel Systems, to a new account in Australia. Siebel was contacted and said he never requested the transfer. Merrill Lynch then contacted the New York Police Department (NYPD), who tracked down the e-mail request to two e-mail addresses. Those two e-mail addresses were found in other accounts at Merrill Lynch, with similar requests, though not in the $10 million-range.

The NYPD began contacting other brokerage houses and high-roller banks and discovered the same two e-mail addresses popping up all over. They found out about the couriers being used to deliver packages. This led them to keep track of one UPS delivery that arrived on February 23, 2001, containing $25,000 worth of equipment that could manufacture and magnetize credit cards. When the courier arrived to pick up the package, two NYPD officers nabbed him. One officer took over as the driver while the other hid in the back seat under a trash bag. When they were redirected to a different address, they went and waited. Soon after, Abdullah showed up in a 2000 Volvo.

His crime spree had come to an end.

Identity Theft Resources

U.S. Government's Official Site About Identity Theft
www.consumer.gov/idtheft

Cybersnitch
www.cybersnitch.net

U.S. Secret Service
www.treas.gov/usss/index.html

Identity Theft Resource Center
www.idtheftcenter.org

Endnotes

1. FTC Figures & Trends Identity Theft Report, November 1999–June 2001.
2. SEC: U.S. Securities and Exchange Commission.

Your Personal Life
Exposed

Web Wreckers

People who put up harassing Web pages about another person or persons.

Cyberstalkers

People who track another person or persons' online activities.
Cyberstalking sometimes leads to physical stalking.

Famous people face more dangers online than do average private citizens. Besides threatening e-mails, a celebrity has to contend with the fact that their address, the type of car they drive, and the places they frequent in town are posted by fans on various Web sites and newsgroups. But movie stars and other celebrities have the money and resources to protect themselves. Regular folks have to fend for themselves.

Askance Romance

Brenda was surfing the Web one night and typed a query into a search engine, looking for information in New Jersey, where she lived. When she saw a link to a Web site that bore her ex-boyfriend's name in the URL,[1] she clicked on it, curious to see what he was up to.

At first glance, the site was tame, but when she clicked on a link for Romance, she discovered that, along with other ex-girlfriends, he'd posted her name, where she lived, photos of her, and intimate descriptions of their relationship for anyone to read.

Devastated, Brenda sought advice from a friend, who suggested she contact him via e-mail and ask him to remove her information. She did and he wrote back that although he was disappointed, because she had been a part of his life, he would do what she asked and remove the link.

Brenda breathed a sigh of relief. Two days later, she checked his site. When she clicked on Romance, she got a pop-up window asking for a password. Panicked, and not knowing if her information was still on his site, she again e-mailed him, trying to remain calm.

"I asked him why he didn't remove the link like I'd asked and like he'd agreed to," Brenda says. "He just ended up writing me back, and not in a very nice way, that he was not going to remove the page and that he was expressing himself and I would just have to deal with it."

She didn't. Brenda contacted the ISP he was using, explaining that he was doing more than just expressing himself, and she was concerned about who may be reading her information on his site and what they might do with that information.

The site was pulled. When Brenda found that the site was back online a few weeks later, all the Romance links and information were gone from the site.

Sites about Online Stalking That Should Scare You

The Stalkers Home Page
www.glr.com/stalk.html

Opening paragraph from the Stalkers' Web page: "What could be more absurd than a home page for stalkers? We thought so, but we're finding more and more personal information widely available to any prying eyes...Of course, we don't encourage anyone to engage in stalking or other impolite behavior...but look at the resources!"

Although this site tries to be more pro-stalking than anti-stalking, it does offer some links to interesting and helpful sites victims can use to their benefit, as well as links to sites that some may find questionable and unsettling.

For the Love of Julie
www.creepysites.com/julie/julie

What began as a public relations stunt soon became a serious problem. People began calling the Los Angeles Police Department in 2000 when they stumbled onto this site of a stalker who is obsessed with Julie. Be forewarned if you go to the site: it contains disturbing videos, tape recordings, photos, a journal, and more.

It turns out that Julie is a hired actress, and the creator of the site is a filmmaker hoping to get attention. He got the attention when the media and police came calling, wondering why he'd put up a site like this one with no disclaimer (now there is a clear disclaimer that states the site is fictional).

Sorry, Wrong Number

Cindy, who lives in Los Angeles, began finding messages on her answering machine from men she didn't know. These men stated they'd gotten her number from a Web site, one she'd never heard of. She never called them back and thought it was just an odd coincidence or a wrong number. Then, while home sick one day, she answered the telephone and found herself in a conference call with two men claiming they were online with her right at that moment. She told them she was not online; they in turn told her what Web site she was supposedly on. There were photographs of her and a description that said she wanted to be a "white sex slave to an all-black gangbang, men and women."

Cindy was lucky because when she contacted the owners of the Web site, she found out who was impersonating her and was able to get her local police to press charges against the man. It turned out to be an ex-boyfriend.

Lawmakers Understand

"I first became aware of this issue [cyberstalking] after reading a magazine article appearing in an NCSL [National Conference of State Legislatures] publication," says Florida State Senator Steven A. Geller, District 29. "I saw that this [cyberstalking] legislation had been passed in other states, and based on my service on the Florida Information Technology Development Task Force and the extensive amount of Internet legislation I've been working on, I felt this was important legislation to be passed."

At press time, Florida had not passed the cyberstalking legislation that was introduced in 2001 and reintroduced for the 2002 session. It will be reintroduced in 2003. Many Florida legislators said they believed current stalking and harassment laws covered cyberstalking.

John Laurence Reid, Legal Counsel/Legislative Assistant, Florida State Senate, District 29, disagrees. "I've been speaking with numerous women from Florida who are being stalked over the Internet. Because of jurisdictional problems, the current stalking statutes have been ineffective for them, and they desperately need this legislation. This law is good for these women, and it is good for the people of Florida," says Reid.

Cyberstalking Facts

- SafetyEd.org (www.safetyed.org) claims it receives more than 50 requests for help each month.
- WHOA (www.haltabuse.org) claims it receives 100 requests for help each week.
- CyberAngels (www.cyberangels.org) claims it receives more than 200 requests for help each week.

This represents more than 80,000 cyberstalking cases per year, and the number is growing.

The Amy Boyer Story

Amy Boyer of Nashua, New Hampshire, was also a victim. Her story has a tragic ending.

Figure 9.1   Amy's smile.

A vivacious 20-year-old, Amy lived at home with her mother, Helen; stepfather, Tim; and 10-year-old sister, Jenna. She had a boyfriend, her own car, and a job at a local dentist's office. Life was good. When Amy and her mother went online on October 12, 1999, they surfed several sites for a few hours. What they didn't think to do was search for Amy's name.

"Maybe if we had, she'd still be alive today," Helen says.

Liam Youens seemed like an unassuming young man. He was 21, tall, thin, and wore glasses. But Liam harbored a dark secret—his obsession with Amy. Although he didn't tell anyone around him about his crush, Liam spilled his thoughts onto two Web sites, one located at Geocities and the other at Tripod. Both Web sites offered the same disturbing information and had been online for some time, one of them for over two years, yet no one was alerted to them.

The main page opened with two black-and-white photos of Amy (see Figure 9.1) and scarcely any text. One link, labeled "age 17" went to a page where Liam commented on how he felt Amy's smile was forced in the top photo and how he airbrushed the other photo so that it was more in keeping with how he wanted her to look.

A click on ENTER took visitors to a page that began: "Greetings Infidels, I am Liam Youens," and showed a photo of him holding an automatic weapon (see Figure 9.2). "Who am I?" the text continued. "Well if i had 20 people buried in my backyard my neighbors would have described me as 'Quiet, basically kept to himself'."

Thus begins the tragic online journal of how Liam began stalking Amy in real life. What may have started as a way to blow off steam for his unrequited "love" for Amy soon became a series of rants and raves and ultimately a death watch: When would be the day he would decide to kill her?

Figure 9.2   Infidels.

He claimed he fell in love with Amy in the 10th grade during alge-
bra class. She never knew it. His thoughts on the Web site about this
were: "Oh great, now I'm really depressed, hmmm…looks like it's
suicide for me. Car accident? Wrists? A few days later I think, 'hey,
why don't I kill her, too? =).'"

He wrote about how he tried to be in the same classes as Amy in
his senior year of high school (she was a junior), how he would stare
at her in the hallways and at lunch, positive she knew he loved her,
although her parents claim Amy knew Liam only in passing.

As he accumulated weapons and ammunition, Liam became braver
in his pursuit of Amy. He added a Web page that showed off all the
weapons he'd purchased (see Figure 9.3), with descriptions of where
he purchased them. He kept thinking everyone knew he was stalking
Amy, even the Nashua police, and noted this on the Web sites, but it
was just another delusion. Or could it have been a cry for help?

Liam wrote on his Web pages about killing Amy's boyfriend
and others from the same youth group they belonged to, even a

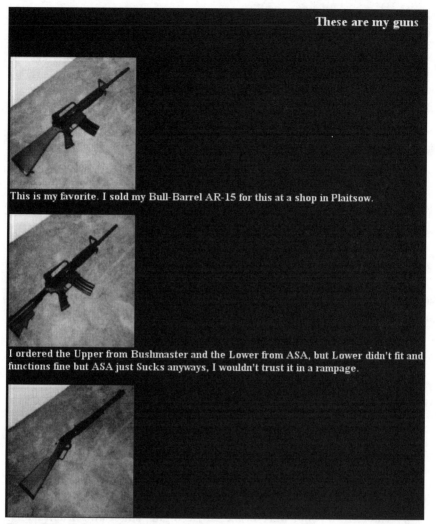

These are my guns

This is my favorite. I sold my Bull-Barrel AR-15 for this at a shop in Plaitsow.

I ordered the Upper from Bushmaster and the Lower from ASA, but Lower didn't fit and functions fine but ASA just Sucks anyways, I wouldn't trust it in a rampage.

Figure 9.3   Guns.

"Columbine-style" shooting at Nashua High School (see Figure 9.4), but Amy remained his primary focus.

By the time Liam had worked up his courage to set the date, all it took was less than $100, visits to Web sites where anyone could purchase information, and he had what he needed: the address where Amy worked.

He wrote, "It's accually obsene what you can find out about a person on the internet."

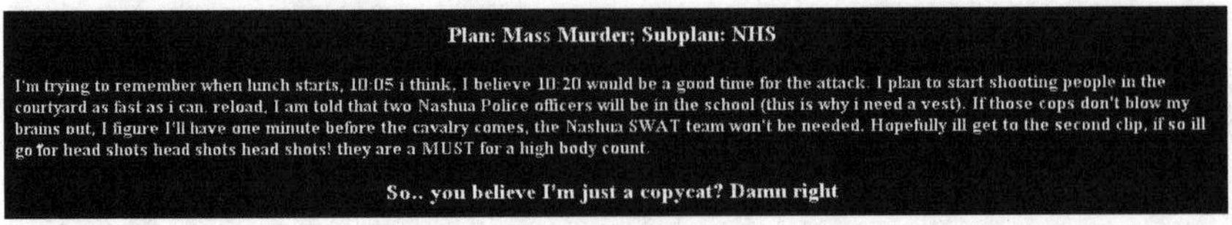

Plan: Mass Murder; Subplan: NHS

I'm trying to remember when lunch starts, 10:05 i think, I believe 10:20 would be a good time for the attack. I plan to start shooting people in the courtyard as fast as i can. reload, I am told that two Nashua Police officers will be in the school (this is why i need a vest). If those cops don't blow my brains out, I figure I'll have one minute before the cavalry comes, the Nashua SWAT team won't be needed. Hopefully ill get to the second clip, if so ill go for head shots head shots head shots! they are a MUST for a high body count.

So.. you believe I'm just a copycat? Damn right

Figure 9.4 Plan.

On October 15, 1999, at 4:29 P.M., Liam showed up outside the dentist's office where Amy worked part-time. He waited for her to come out and get into her car, and then he drove up alongside her car and shot her several times in the face with his 9mm Glock. He reloaded the gun, put the barrel in his mouth, and killed himself.

Amy's parents were more than grief-stricken—they couldn't take out their anger at the killer because he was dead, too. And as parents, they couldn't get angry with Liam's parents. They found themselves directing their anger at Tripod and Geocities, where the Web pages resided, and at DocuSearch, the company that provided Amy's work address.

"It would be one thing if he'd written this in a private handwritten diary," Amy's stepfather, Tim, says. "But he wrote this on the Internet. Now don't you think he expected someone to read this?"

A representative who worked for Tripod at the time removed the site the same night Amy died, after a Nashua police detective called him. He said Tripod would have notified authorities if anyone had seen the site. Later, the Tripod representative claimed that the number of visitors to the site were in the single digits, suggesting Liam had been the only visitor to his site. But had he been?

Cyberstalking Estimates

The Los Angeles District Attorney's Office estimates that e-mail or other electronic communication was a factor in approximately 20 percent of the 600 cases handled by its Stalking and Threat Assessment Unit.

> The chief of the Sex Crimes Unit in Manhattan District Attorney's Office also estimates that roughly 20 percent of their cases involve cyberstalking.
>
> The Computer Investigations and Technology Unit of the New York City Police Department estimates that almost 40 percent of their cases involve cyberstalking.
>
> From the U.S. Department of Justice Report on Cyberstalking, May 2001.

If Amy Boyer's stepfather has his way, Web page hosts such as Tripod and Geocities (now owned by Yahoo!) will be required to police themselves.

"They should be monitoring sites where the word 'kill' is used ..." Amy's stepfather says. "They should have someone sitting in front of a computer all day, doing nothing but hunting for the people who're hunting for us."

A Tripod representative, who wished to remain anonymous, claims the company does its best to monitor pornography and online threats, which are a violation of the terms of service (TOS) agreement that each Tripod member must follow. But the technology to weed out threatening pages hasn't been perfected. In March 2001, a filtering program used by Tripod ended up deleting legitimate Web pages along with ones that did violate the TOS. If a human reviewed each of the sites (as Tim suggested) instead of a computer program, this might not have happened.

In March 2000, Tim stood before a Senate subcommittee in Washington, DC, and testified, "We must show Amy that we care about what happened to her and that we are going to act to see it doesn't happen to anyone else."

Within days of his testimony, New Hampshire Senator Judd Gregg announced he was co-sponsoring legislation that would outlaw the sale of Social Security numbers online. With the Social Security Administration and the White House on board, the Amy Boyer Bill was introduced. Although passed by the House and Senate, organizations such as the American Civil Liberties Union (ACLU) vigorously opposed it. The bill passed in December 2000,[2] but Tim and his wife asked that they take Amy's name off the bill, as the approved bill was not what they'd initially supported. The bill applies to violations effective on or after December 21, 2002, two years after its enactment.

Amy's parents filed a wrongful-death suit against Docusearch.com in April 2000, claiming negligence and invasion of privacy. They haven't done anything about Tripod and Geocities, mainly because of the Communications Decency Act, which doesn't hold ISPs or Web hosts such as Tripod and Geocities responsible for their customers' actions.

"These companies have a 'get out of monitoring free' card," Amy's parents claim on their Web site, www.amyboyer.org. "This law ... eliminates the Web site servers from having any responsibility for anything printed on the space they provide on the Web."

If the Web hosts had monitored their sites correctly, as they claim they do in their TOS, Amy might still be alive today. Yet, these same Web hosts are fearful of the First Amendment, the right to free speech, and the opposition from members to monitoring member pages. They should have the same concern when it comes to threats of violence. Let's hope somebody has the conscience to do the right thing and report it before someone else is hurt or dies.

Cyberstalking Statistics from WHOA

• Over 57 percent of victims harassed/stalked online are Caucasian.

• Over 80 percent are women.

• 47 percent are 18–40 years of age.

• Over half of the offenders are strangers to the victims.

• 63 percent of offenders are male.

• Most cases begin with e-mail threats, followed by message boards, chat, and IMs (Instant Messages).

• Texas has the most cyberstalking cases, followed by New York, California, Florida, and Illinois.

• Over half of all reported cases were resolved by WHOA by contacting the offender's ISP.

These statistics are based on a sampling of 609 cases WHOA handled in 2000 and 2001 from victims who completely filled out the questionnaire on WHOA's site; providing location/gender/age information is not required to receive help from WHOA (www.haltabuse.org/resources/stats).

Unwanted Fantasy

Gary Dellapenta was angry that a woman at his local church had spurned him in 1996. He followed her at first, keeping his distance, but his anger grew so much that he decided he wanted to get back at her in a more serious way. He went online during the summer of 1998 and began signing up for sex-related chat rooms and placing personal ads, all in Randi Barber's name. He opened up free e-mail accounts using sexually attractive usernames such as "playfulkitty4u" and "kinkygal30."

Randi didn't own a computer, had never been online, and went about her daily life until the first man came knocking at her door wanting to fulfill her home-invasion rape fantasies.

She told him she had no idea what he was talking about. The man left, then called later that night asking if she'd changed her mind. She demanded to know why he thought she was interested in something as sick as that and discovered that someone was impersonating her online.

Six men in all came to Randi's home, and by the time the last one arrived, she had stopped answering the door and the phone.

Dellapenta wasn't through yet. He replied to anyone who e-mailed Randi, claiming she was playing hard to get and gave explicit instructions on how to break into her apartment, even how to bypass her home security system.

Randi didn't know what to do at first. She filed a complaint with her local police department, but they told her they couldn't help her. She turned to her father for help. He went online, and with help from some of the men who had called Randi or stopped by her home, he finally learned Dellapenta's identity.

Randi and her father then went to the police. The FBI and Los Angeles County Sheriff's Department worked together and in November 1998, Dellapenta was arrested on charges of cyberstalking—the first case to test the new cyberstalking law passed in California earlier that year.

Police who worked on the case said that the computer-related evidence they collected was almost better than telephone recordings. They ended up finding proof that the personal ads placed in Randi's name originated from Sprynet, the ISP Dellapenta used, as evidenced by transcripts of chat logs and other information gathered from his computer.

Dellapenta ended up getting six years in prison for stalking and soliciting others to commit rape. The court stated that probation was not an option because of the "enormous difficulty in controlling what a person does at his computer on the Internet."

The Psychology of Cyberstalking

Cyberstalking is the most prevalent type of online harassment. When a harasser is not stopped in the beginning stages of harassment, such as via e-mail, chat rooms, forums, or newsgroups, the perpetrators begin to feel powerful. The harassing escalates so that the harasser follows the victim everywhere online, becoming a cyberstalker. Cyberstalkers can find a victim's new e-mail address, put the victim on their AOL Instant Messenger Buddy List so that they are alerted when the victim is online and then bombard them with e-mail, and subscribe the victim to mailing lists, free offers, and pornographic Web sites.

It's the anonymity of the Internet that provides the cyberstalker with their feelings of invincibility. Using a free e-mail account or changing the "From" line in e-mails to show a bogus e-mail address all feed into this feeling of power.

If not stopped, the cyberstalker can become obsessed with the victim, with the stalking escalating off-line (in real life), which is a new hell for the victim to endure.

This is why it's so important to contact an online safety organization, the offender's ISP, and/or the police if someone is harassing you online. Don't end up like Amy Boyer.

Endnotes

1. URL (Uniform Resource Locator): A Web site address, such as http://www.disney.com.
2. P.L. 106-553; 42 U.S.C. Section 1320B-23.

Ugly Beasts
Lurking Online

Troll

Someone who visits a chat room, newsgroup, message board,[1] or other online forum and writes messages meant to get the other people online upset.

Flame

A public response to a message or posting on a newsgroup, mailing list,[2] or chat room, which goes beyond polite disagreement, belittling the author's point of view and frequently insulting him personally. If the author responds just as nastily to the flame, a "flame war" often ensues. On moderated lists, flaming can frequently be stopped before it gets out of control.

Spoofer

Someone who impersonates another person online. A spoofer will sometimes open several e-mail accounts in the victim's name, then use those accounts to post messages on Web sites, send offensive e-mail messages to others (typically employers, family, and friends of the victim), pose as the victim in chat rooms, newsgroups, and mailing lists, sign guestbooks,[3] and commit various online transgressions in the name of the victim; a form of identity theft.

Don't Feed the Troll

Trolls are more than ugly beasts hiding under a bridge in a fairy tale. Online trolls are people who love to cause trouble. Trolls will visit a chat room, newsgroup, or message board and post a message intended to get other folks upset. Then trolls sit back and enjoy the havoc and infighting they have created (sometimes adding to the mayhem by taunting the group). Once they have been sufficiently entertained, trolls typically leave for another newsgroup, chat room, or message board, and start all over again.

The newsgroup alt.sports.hockey.nhl.ny-rangers is an example of an online forum that was "trolled," which began when someone calling himself Gene posted a one-word message to the newsgroup: "Suck!"

"Gene" was no stranger to the newsgroup. He would pop in every once in a while to start trouble. Over the course of more than 50 replies to his Suck! post, Gene answered with taunts. As the messages progressed, so did the length and content of Gene's posts, with messages becoming especially vile at times. Instead of ignoring Gene, others on the newsgroup kept it up and began fighting with each other, which is exactly what a troll wants.

It turned out Gene only went to the newsgroup to cause trouble. Out of several newsgroups he visited, this sports newsgroup responded to his posts in such a way that he kept coming back ... and back, and back.

So, what can you do in this type of situation?

If you notice that a new person has appeared in a newsgroup, message board, chat room, or other forum and he is making all sorts of rude comments, you can be fairly sure this is a troll. Ignore the troll. He feeds on replies and attention. No matter what the troll writes, avoid any sort of reply. In fact, put them on "ignore" in a chat room, filter them out of the newsgroup, or stop visiting that message board for a while. Don't give in to what the troll wants, which is attention and the chance to start a huge fight.

If you insist on defending yourself or others, you could be asking for more trouble than it's really worth. Your best defense is to simply complain to the troll's ISP and let them take care of the troll.

Flames are an appropriate name for another situation that often gets out of control. Often, it starts out innocently, with someone making a sincere comment. Then someone will write a nasty reply. The flamee usually defends herself with something just as nasty, and a flame war breaks out between the two. Many times others will join the war, which cools off only when the flamer or flamee stops sending messages.

Flaming Beatles

A good example of flaming is what happened on the rec.music.beatles newsgroup. A group of Beatles fans had been sharing thoughts, stories, and silly messages with each other for quite some time. One day, a new person named Garik showed up in the group and began lambasting one of the participants for being a Beatles freak. The person responded by telling Garik to "buzz off," but he wouldn't leave. Garik began to target other members of the rec.music.beatles newsgroup, even going so far as to forge messages in other members' names, such as this one, "from" Ted:

> I like child molestors. As long as they confess to their crime, and then do what the courts order them to do as part of their sentence, I have no problem with them. I would like to molest children myself. I read all about Gary Burnore's child molestation, his confession, his sentence, what a sick fucking piece of shit he is, and I have to say, I got quite turned on. I masturbated all day thinking about Gary molesting that girl, and the thought of her being upset, and perhaps permanently scarred by it made me cum harder than I ever did before.

Then he listed Ted's full name, home address, and phone number.

Regulars on the group complained to Garik's ISP, who canceled his account. But instead of letting it go, Garik got a new e-mail account and started flaming the newsgroup again; the regulars flamed right back. Garik ended up losing several more e-mail accounts due to complaints from the regulars, but he kept coming back. It got to a point where many of the regulars began receiving e-mails and threats from Garik, and they ended up looking for legal help.

Another incident involved Dean Stark, a regular on the scruz. general newsgroup. He had some disagreements with a few people in the group and flamed them for disagreeing with him. They fought back in full force. One member in particular, who went by the user-name anus_astonished, was particularly brutal, and is thought to be the creator of more than 200 newsgroups about Dean, among them alt.fan.dean-stark, alt.recovery.dean-stark, alt.fan.dean-stark.diapers (many of them are still there). Soon Dean's name was all over the newsgroups, with discussions asking just who Dean Stark was. But Dean did the right thing. He stopped responding to messages about him, stopped posting messages, changed his e-mail address/user-name, and is more careful now when posting online.

The best solution, besides what Dean did, is e-mail the person who flamed you, swallow your pride, let them know you apologize if you offended them and "shake hands." This often works. If it doesn't, and the other person continues to flame you on the newsgroup, chat room, etc., *don't* respond but *do* report them to their ISP. Your nonresponse will prove to the ISP that you didn't encourage the flaming.

Spoofing

Spoofing can happen without your knowledge, and it should be considered a serious problem. Someone can open an ISP account in your name. Or a person can open an account in her own name or a fictitious name, go online, and pretend to be you.

Sound impossible?

Susan, who lived in Maryland, didn't even own a computer. She discovered she was being spoofed (impersonated) online when she began to receive phone calls about items she supposedly put up for sale on a local newspaper's Web site. Susan hadn't.

Carol, who lived in Michigan, found out someone was going into chat rooms pretending to be her, then berating the other chatters and getting into arguments with them. Carol would receive e-mail messages asking why she was being so awful or threatening to complain about her to her ISP. She'd have to explain that she'd never been in that chat room.

Gerald, a Maryland college student, received phone calls from gay men saying they'd answered his ad on a gay Web site. He hadn't put the ad there.

But someone did.

Why did this happen to these people? Most of the time it turned out to be a spurned lover, friends who had argued, or a jealous classmate. Sometimes it was a total stranger who took a dislike to the victim's e-mail address or chat room user ID,[4] didn't like what the victim "said" in a chat room or wrote in an e-mail or newsgroup, or some-times took offense to something written in a guestbook. There was no real single factor that set off these spoofers.

The scariest thing is that spoofing happens more often than it should. Why? Because it's far too easy to forge another person's name on messages, e-mails, and in chat rooms.

You need only to provide a valid credit card, money order, or sometimes just a cash deposit to an ISP and you can open an account. ISPs rarely check to make sure the name of the person opening the account is the same as on the credit card or check. Even less often do ISPs check to see if that person was kicked off of their service or another ISP for harassing someone or abusing the service.

Once someone has an account, she can do all sorts of damage to another person. Even if the account is in the spoofer's real name, the spoofer can easily change the "FROM" line in e-mails or newsgroup postings so that they look like they came from someone else. Or, a spoofer can get a free e-mail account (such as from Yahoo!, Hotmail, or Juno) and use that to forge the victim's name everywhere. Or they can use an anonymous remailer—a service (usually free) that allows someone to send an e-mail or newsgroup post with all of the associ-ated identifying information stripped away so the recipient can't determine the origination.

But that's just the beginning.

If someone knows your current e-mail address or chat room user ID, they can go to Web sites and leave nasty messages in guestbooks using your name and e-mail address, put your information on contro-versial or sex-related Web sites "offering your services," order pizzas to be delivered to your house (this happened to Jackie—the pizza par-lor called her to confirm that she'd actually ordered 10 pizzas with the works when she hadn't), subscribe you to online newsletters and mailing lists, impersonate you in chat rooms—the list goes on because there are so many things spoofers can do to you on the Web, all for free.

Then there are the newsgroups. Pick a newsgroup, any newsgroup. Someone can post a message on a newsgroup that claims the people there are a bunch of idiots—or worse—and make the message look like it came from you. You'd surely get nasty e-mail messages about "your" behavior on that newsgroup or any others "you" visited. Then you have to deal with telling these people that you didn't put that mes-sage on their newsgroup and try to figure out what happened and why.

So, what can you do to avoid being spoofed?

If you don't own a computer, but are listed in the telephone book and someone has taken a dislike to you, there may not be much you can do to prevent being impersonated online. Your name, phone number, and address information can wind up on newsgroups and Web pages, in chat rooms, and on message boards. An unpublished phone number can help you avoid problems, and you may decide it's worth spending a little extra each month to have one.

If you own a computer and have an Internet connection, the likelihood of your being spoofed increases. The flip side is that you can discover fairly easily if someone is spoofing you, and take steps to resolve the problem. If you have reason to believe you are being spoofed, I recommend the following.

On Newsgroups

First, go to a newsgroup search engine, such as Google Groups as shown in Figure 10.1 (www.groups.google.com). Look for Google's "Advanced Search" link, click, and input your first and last name in the "with the exact phrase" text box, then click the Google Search button.

If you like, you can refine the search by selecting certain dates, newsgroups, and other criteria. You can also type any e-mail address or chat room user ID you use in the text box and click on the Google Search button.

If the results list (see Figure 10.2) includes messages that may have been written by you (remember, there may be messages by someone

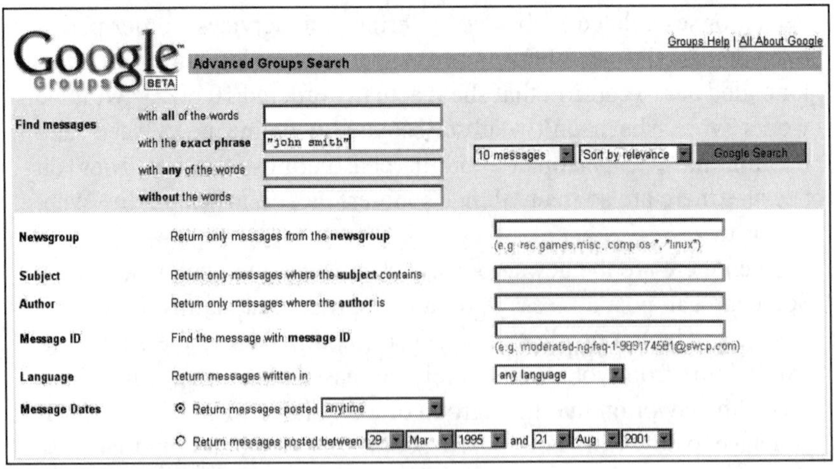

Figure 10.1   Google.

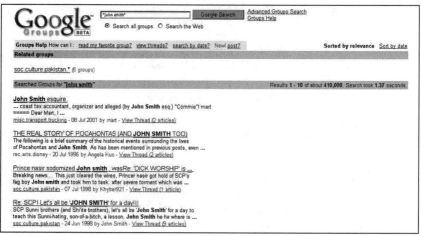

Figure 10.2   Google results.

with the same name as yours), click on the associated link to view the message.

Here, as an example, is a message forged in my name:

```
From: "J.A.Hitchcock"   <latakia@ix.net-
com.com>
        Newsgroups: rec.climbing
Subject:     CLIMBERS ARE SICK PEOPLE
Date: Tue, 24 Dec 1996 04:53:47 -0800
I'm an international author who knows
what she's talking about. Read my books.
Climbing is a disease and pointless.
```

If a given message is clearly associated with you and your e-mail address, and you're sure you didn't write and post it, click on "View Original Article" in Google Groups to learn which ISP the message was posted from (or, alternatively, get a newsreader program, such as Free Agent at www.forteinc.com/agent, which offers the option to show full headers).

In this example, the headers expanded quite a bit:

```
Path:
ix.netcom.com!ix.netcom.com!worldnet.att
.net!feed1.news.erols.com!news.idt.net!nnt
p.farm.idt.net!news
```

```
From: "J.A.Hitchcock"   <latakia@ix.net-
com.com>
        Newsgroups: rec.climbing
 Subject:    CLIMBERS ARE SICK PEOPLE
 Date: Tue, 24 Dec 1996 04:53:47 -0800
        Organization: INTERNATIONAL AUTHOR
        Lines: 2
        Message-ID: <32BFD25B.3D9E@ix.net-
com.com>  NNTP-Posting-Host:  169.132.8.11
(ppp-9.ts-12.nyc.idt.net)
        Mime-Version: 1.0
        Content-Type:          text/plain;
charset=us-ascii
        Content-Transfer-Encoding: 7bit
        X-Mailer: Mozilla 2.01 (Win16; I)
 I'm an international author who knows
what she's talking about. Read my books.
Climbing is a disease and pointless.
```

The full headers[5] will help you determine where the message originated; this is crucial for the next steps. In the above example, the NNTP-Posting-Host line shows the message originated from 169.132.8.11 (ppp-9.ts-12.nyc.idt.net; you can identify the ISP from the last part, idt.net).

Now you have some options.

If you are a newsgroups user, open your newsreader or the program you use to view newsgroups. Find a newsgroup called news.admin. net-abuse.sightings and post a new message with the subject line exactly as it appeared when originally posted, with [usenet] in front of it. In the text area, type in something like "I've been spoofed on Usenet and did not post the following. Please cancel this message [or "these messages" if there is more than one]," then paste a copy of the newsgroup message in its original Usenet format, with the full headers. Here's an example of how you'd post the above to news.admin. net-abuse.sightings:

```
From: J.A. Hitchcock (latakia@ix.netcom.
com)
        Newsgroups:  news.admin.net-abuse.
sightings
```

Subject: [Usenet] Climbers Are Sick
People
Date: Tue, 24 Dec 1996 09:15:47 -0800
Hello, I'm being spoofed on Usenet and
have found many messages forged in my name.
I've reported these to news.admin.net-
abuse.sightings but would appreciate any
help you can give me. One of the messages
is as follows; you'll see by the headers
that it did not originate from my netcom
account, but from idt.net.
Thank you,
The real J.A. Hitchcock

Path:
ix.netcom.com!ix.netcom.com!worldnet.att
.net!feed1.news.erols.com!news.idt.net!nnt
p.farm.idt.net!news
From: "J.A.Hitchcock"   <latakia@ix.net
com.com>
        Newsgroups: rec.climbing
   Subject: CLIMBERS ARE SICK PEOPLE
   Date: Tue, 24 Dec 1996 04:53:47 -0800
        Organization: INTERNATIONAL AUTHOR
        Lines: 2
        Message-ID: <32BFD25B.3D9E@ix.net-
com.com> NNTP-Posting-Host: 169.132.8.11
(ppp-9.ts-12.nyc.idt.net)
        Mime-Version: 1.0
        Content-Type: text/plain;
charset=us-ascii
        Content-Transfer-Encoding: 7bit
        X-Mailer: Mozilla 2.01 (Win16; I)
   I'm an international author who knows
what she's talking about. Read my books.
Climbing is a disease and pointless.

If you are not a newsgroup user, register on the Google Groups
site, then find the newsgroup news.admin.net-abuse.sightings and follow the instructions given above for posting to it.

After you've posted to news.admin.net-abuse.sightings, go to the
newsgroup news.admin.net-abuse.misc and post a new message

with the subject line: "I'm Being Spoofed - Please Cancel." In the text area, explain that someone is spoofing you on one or more newsgroups and that you have posted those messages on news.admin.net-abuse.sightings but request any help that can be offered. You may be surprised by how willing other Internet users are to help victims of spoofing.

On Web Pages

Go to a major Web search engine or service, such as Yahoo! (www.yahoo.com), type your name in quotes, and click on the Search button, as shown in Figure 10.3. You should also try searching on any e-mail addresses and chat room user ID you use.

If there are Web page matches, follow the links to see if they are legitimate: You may be surprised at how often your name or user ID might be out there, as indicated in Figure 10.4.

If the Web pages you turn up were obviously designed to harass or embarrass you (as was the case with Gerald, who had his name and phone number placed on gay Web sites), then send an e-mail to the site's Webmaster or support person (an e-mail link can be found somewhere on almost any site). Explain that you did not authorize use of your name or information on the site and would like it removed immediately. Most of the time, this will work. If it doesn't, read Chapter 19 to find out how to trace the origination of the Web site to the person or company who owns that site.

One of the benefits of using Yahoo! is that after the initial search you are given an option that allows you to run the same search through other search engines (see Figure 10.5).

Just click on one of the other search engines, such as Google or Ask Jeeves or whatever search engines are available through Yahoo! (they change from time to time), to see if there are any matches to

Figure 10.3 Yahoo! search.

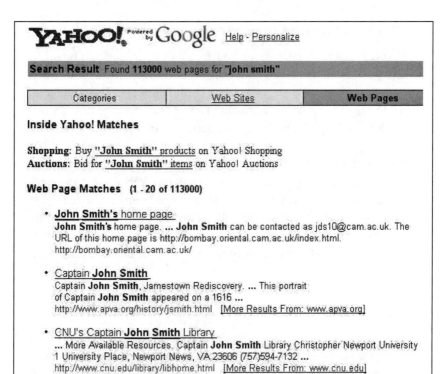

Figure 10.4   Yahoo! results.

your name. If there are not, then click on the BACK button of your Web browser and click on a different search engine until you've checked them all. Another option is to use a metasearch engine. Metasearch engines, like Metacrawler (www.metacrawler.com) and DogPile (www.dogpile.com), search a number of major search engine databases at once.

Other Search Engines
AltaVista - Google - Ask Jeeves - More...

Promotional Links
Free Cell Headset - Find Low Airfares! - Free CDs See Details - Find Old Friends! - Cut Debt By 60%

Yellow Pages - People Search - City Maps - Get Local - Today's Web Events & Chats - **More Yahoos**

Figure 10.5   Yahoo! other search.

In Chat Rooms and on Message Boards

If you find that a chat room you frequent or a message board to which you often post suddenly shows messages from you when you're not online, change your user ID immediately. This change is easy to perform in a majority of chat rooms and message board sites. Then alert the Webmaster or support person of the chat room/Web site via e-mail that you are no longer posting under your old user ID. Explain to them that someone is impersonating you with certain user IDs and list the one(s) you know about. Ask the Webmaster to remove these user IDs from the chat room or message board immediately. If that doesn't work, a telephone call almost always seems to do the trick. Although e-mail is the wave of the future, a human voice over the telephone tends to have more impact than an electronically sent message.

Be Alert and Informed

If you don't own a computer and someone is impersonating you online, you probably won't know about it unless a friend or acquaintance mentions something or, even worse, when you start getting phone calls or home deliveries you did not initiate.

Remember Jackie, who supposedly ordered pizzas online? She was able to cancel the order when the pizza parlor called to confirm the order. Then she went a step further. She asked that they send her a copy of the online order placed in her name so that she could find out from where it originated. Jackie asked for help from someone she knew who was Internet-knowledgeable and they were able to track down the order to a particular ISP, which was contacted and informed of the impersonation. Once she provided a notarized statement that she did not open the account used to order those pizzas, the ISP canceled it.

How about Susan, who received phone calls about items "she" offered for sale on a local newspaper's Web site? She was also able to get the information she needed, this time from the Web site owner—the newspaper. She contacted the Maryland State Police Computer Crimes Unit, who took the case from there. They ultimately tracked down the spoofer to a local library system—the spoofer was an employee at one of the libraries. It turns out he was a neighbor of the victim and was getting back at her because she wouldn't carpool with him.

YAHOO! Powered by Google   Help - Personalize

Search Result Found **113000** web pages for **"john smith"**

| Categories | Web Sites | Web Pages |

Inside Yahoo! Matches

Shopping: Buy **"John Smith"** products on Yahoo! Shopping
Auctions: Bid for **"John Smith"** items on Yahoo! Auctions

Web Page Matches   (1 - 20 of 113000)

- **John Smith's** home page
  John Smith's home page. ... **John Smith** can be contacted as jds10@cam.ac.uk. The URL of this home page is http://bombay.oriental.cam.ac.uk/index.html. http://bombay.oriental.cam.ac.uk/

- Captain **John Smith**
  Captain **John Smith**, Jamestown Rediscovery. ... This portrait of Captain **John Smith** appeared on a 1616 ... http://www.apva.org/history/jsmith.html [More Results From: www.apva.org]

- CNU's Captain **John Smith** Library
  ... More Available Resources. Captain **John Smith** Library Christopher Newport University 1 University Place, Newport News, VA 23606 (757)594-7132 ... http://www.cnu.edu/library/libhome.html [More Results From: www.cnu.edu]

Figure 10.4   Yahoo! results.

your name. If there are not, then click on the BACK button of your Web browser and click on a different search engine until you've checked them all. Another option is to use a metasearch engine. Metasearch engines, like Metacrawler (www.metacrawler.com) and DogPile (www.dogpile.com), search a number of major search engine databases at once.

Other Search Engines
AltaVista - Google - Ask Jeeves - More...
Promotional Links
Free Cell Headset - Find Low Airfares! - Free CDs See Details - Find Old Friends! - Cut Debt By 60%

Yellow Pages - People Search - City Maps - Get Local - Today's Web Events & Chats - **More Yahoos**

Figure 10.5   Yahoo! other search.

In Chat Rooms and on Message Boards

If you find that a chat room you frequent or a message board to which you often post suddenly shows messages from you when you're not online, change your user ID immediately. This change is easy to perform in a majority of chat rooms and message board sites. Then alert the Webmaster or support person of the chat room/Web site via e-mail that you are no longer posting under your old user ID. Explain to them that someone is impersonating you with certain user IDs and list the one(s) you know about. Ask the Webmaster to remove these user IDs from the chat room or message board immediately. If that doesn't work, a telephone call almost always seems to do the trick. Although e-mail is the wave of the future, a human voice over the telephone tends to have more impact than an electronically sent message.

Be Alert and Informed

If you don't own a computer and someone is impersonating you online, you probably won't know about it unless a friend or acquaintance mentions something or, even worse, when you start getting phone calls or home deliveries you did not initiate.

Remember Jackie, who supposedly ordered pizzas online? She was able to cancel the order when the pizza parlor called to confirm the order. Then she went a step further. She asked that they send her a copy of the online order placed in her name so that she could find out from where it originated. Jackie asked for help from someone she knew who was Internet-knowledgeable and they were able to track down the order to a particular ISP, which was contacted and informed of the impersonation. Once she provided a notarized statement that she did not open the account used to order those pizzas, the ISP canceled it.

How about Susan, who received phone calls about items "she" offered for sale on a local newspaper's Web site? She was also able to get the information she needed, this time from the Web site owner—the newspaper. She contacted the Maryland State Police Computer Crimes Unit, who took the case from there. They ultimately tracked down the spoofer to a local library system—the spoofer was an employee at one of the libraries. It turns out he was a neighbor of the victim and was getting back at her because she wouldn't carpool with him.

If you begin receiving phone calls or—heaven forbid—you find someone knocking on your door claiming to be taking you up on your online offer, don't hang up on them or slam the door in their face. If you ask for the source of their information, they may be able to pinpoint the Web site, newsgroup, or chat room where they "met" you online. From there, you can contact the Web site or chat room administrator, or go to Google Groups to find out what newsgroup posted the message and from where the message originated. This will allow you to contact the appropriate ISP about resolving the problem.

Some spoofers won't take no for an answer and will open up several e-mail accounts in a victim's name, jumping from one account to the other as the accounts are canceled, or changing a chat room user ID as often as they can. This is when you need to be diligent and continue to report them to the proper ISP, Webmaster, or support folks to get those accounts canceled. If your state has an online harassment or related law, take advantage of it and file a complaint with your local, county, or state police (see www.haltabuse.org/resources/laws for more information).

If the advice I've given in this chapter does not do the trick, and your state doesn't have an applicable law, then it's time to consider hiring a lawyer and filing a civil suit. While most of us would rather avoid this step, spoofing is a serious offense and, unfortunately, there are times when legal action is the only solution.

Endnotes

1. Message Board: Similar to a newsgroup, but located on a Web site; usually they are unmoderated, which opens the door for trolls and spoofers.
2. Mailing List: Similar to a newsgroup, but all messages (new ones and replies) are sent to your e-mailbox. If the mailing list is especially active, this could be as many as 100 messages or more in your e-mailbox daily.
3. Guestbook: Much like a guestbook at weddings, this is on a person's Web page/site so that a visitor can add a comment about the Web page/site in the guestbook.
4. User ID: Also known as a "nickname," this is your "name" when you go into a chat room.
5. Full Headers: Technical information in the header of e-mail and newsgroup messages; the information is hidden when you receive/send mail.

A Little Harmful Chat

┌─ **Chat** ─────────────────────────────────────
Real-time or live conversation online. This happens in an online room
where anywhere from a few people to a hundred or more congregate;
or the conversation can take place one-on-one in what is called a
Private Room. People chat about anything and everything, whether or
not it has to do with the name of the chat room. Names of chat rooms
range from "The TV Room" to "Adults 30+" to "Los Angeles Teens."

Marci's Story

Marci, a Massachusetts resident, decided to visit a chat room on a
local Web site. A legal secretary, she created the username "legalsec"
and began chatting with others in the room. A message popped up
from someone named MetalOne:

"I don't like your name, legalsec."

Taken aback, her first reaction was surprise, then anger.

"So what?" she replied.

Responding in kind to rude remarks is a natural reaction, but it's
the wrong one if you want to avoid trouble in chat rooms, newsgroups, and the like. In Marci's case, it led to big problems.
MetalOne began to make it his mission to find out more about her:
her real name, where she lived, and her telephone number. That was
in the fall of 1998.

In November, he posted her real name, address, and cell phone
number in the chat room. Marci reacted angrily, telling MetalOne he

133

had no right to publicize her personal information. He taunted her. She defended herself.

It soon became a tangled web of people from her local area fighting one another. Marci heard from someone else in the chat room that MetalOne's real name was Donnie and he lived at home with his mother, not far from Marci. Without thinking twice, and for revenge, she mentioned in the chat room Donnie's real name and where he lived.

Donnie changed his username to MachismoMan and in March 1999, he posted this in the chat room:

```
Marci, you are a slut, a blowhole - I like
to bother you because it gets me going,
bitch. I'm going to get you.
```

Marci was afraid now. She changed her cell phone number, and then moved to a different apartment in the next town. She made sure her new phone number was unlisted and got Caller ID. She called the police. They told her there wasn't much they could do because it was all happening online.

In April, Donnie aka MachismoMan wrote in the chat room:

```
Hey Marci, I am going to kick your teeth
down your f-ing throat, you c-t.
```

Even with this obvious threat of physical harm, the police still wouldn't help her. Marci stopped going to the chat room for a few weeks, but when she returned in early June, Donnie was waiting for her.

```
There's a girl watching for you, Marci.
She's going to beat the crap out of you,
you bitch.
```

Marci knew the police wouldn't help, so she created a new username, PrimedUp, and made believe she was someone else. Soon Donnie confided to PrimedUp:

```
Marci is gonna get it, she's going to die.
```

The police finally listened to Marci and began an investigation when she provided them with a copy of this chat room conversation. But it wasn't fast enough for Marci.

Donnie found her new, unpublished phone number and began calling her in July. She let the answering machine pick up. He IM'd[1] her, demanding she answer her phone and that she had "two weeks."

"Two weeks to what?" she recalls. "To die? Before he'd come over to my house? Burn it down? What? I was terrified."

He IM'd her again, telling her to watch herself everywhere she went. By then, a court date had been set for August. Marci was counting the days, praying nothing would happen to her before then. She had an alarm system installed and went to the pound to adopt a large dog for protection.

The last week of July, Marci answered the phone. It was Donnie.

"I'm your worst nightmare, bitch. I am going to kill you, you c—t."

As the court date came closer, Donnie's harassment increased. He not only IM'd and called her at home, but seemed to magically appear in the chat room every time she logged in.

He wrote in the chat room, "You're all done, Marci. You'll end up in a wooden box and I'll piss on your grave when you're four feet under."

Others in the chat room finally told him to stop threatening Marci. He defiantly wrote back, "NO, she's mine!"

In court, a woman accompanying Donnie admitted he asked her to beat up Marci. Donnie admitted nothing. The case was dismissed.

Angry, Marci went to the District Attorney's office with proof of the threats, both online and off-line. In March 2000, the DA filed new charges against Donnie for telephone threats and annoying calls. In court in early May, Donnie finally admitted to what he'd done and was found guilty.

On Memorial Day weekend, Marci looked out her living room window and saw Donnie getting out of his car. She said he looked drunk and had duct tape in one hand and rope in the other. She immediately tripped her alarm, grabbed her dog's collar, and called the police. They were there within minutes and arrested Donnie.

Since then, Marci has moved once again, changed her online account to a different Internet service provider, put her new phone number in another person's name, and doesn't go to chat rooms anymore. She finally won her case in the summer of 2001. Donnie was ordered to pay her more than $20,000 in restitution, but received no jail time.

The Urge to Chat

"At any given moment there are literally hundreds of thousands of people chatting around the world," says Paul Hook, founder of TheGuardianAngel.com, an online safety organization. "Of those, 33 percent have been in a chat room at least once. When you consider that in the U.S. alone there are over 100 million people on the Internet, that translates to a staggering 33 million people. Break that down even further and suppose that only one percent become regulars in chat rooms and that's still a staggering 2.2 million people!"

Why do people love chat so much? It gives folks the chance to mingle with people they never have to meet face to face (unless they want to). People can talk about everything and anything, whether it's how their day went, what last night's TV show was like, complaints about their boss, or just goofiness. Because chat is immediate and live, people tend to say things they wouldn't normally say to a stranger standing next to them in an elevator or on the street corner. Online chatters tend to show their feelings to the world, and most forget that the world is reading everything they write. Many times what people write can get them in trouble, even though they feel they can remain anonymous when using chat rooms on Web sites such as Yahoo!

A Matter of Free Speech?

The line between exercising the right to free speech and the harassment of another individual can easily blur. Here's a perfect example: Let's say someone is in a chat room and complains bitterly about their employer. This person is letting off steam and may feel better, but they do forget that there are many people in the room reading the chat.

Now, if one of those lurkers[2] happens to be an assistant to the president of that person's employer and reports that someone is bashing the company online, the chatter could be sued. Often the company involved is small to midsized, and they'll subpoena the records from the chat room provider to find out who belongs to that anonymous username before filing a suit. The company doesn't expect to actually file and win the suit, but it hopes to make the person complaining keep quiet—and it usually works.

Even though the U.S. Supreme Court ruled that Internet speech should be accorded the same protection as speech in any other medium, many chat room providers are only too happy to turn over those anonymous identities to anyone who provides a subpoena, often without notifying the owner of the username.

There have been several cases where privacy advocates have supported these anonymous chatters, claiming the subpoenas are illegal, and they've won. So, where do you draw the line between harassment and free speech? The law clearly states that the plaintiff must prove the defendant not only made a false statement but did so maliciously. To do this, the defendant needs to be deposed, but if they're anonymous, that's hard to do. However, if an anonymous chatter is clearly harassing someone else, making threatening statements, posting personal information about the person, following them from chat room to chat room, and e-mailing them, then that should be more than enough to allow chat providers to disclose the anonymous chatter's identity when a subpoena is provided.

When Chatting Becomes Harassment

If you don't believe harassment in chat rooms is a problem, conduct your own experiment. Go online to a chat Web site, such as Yahoo! or AOL. Create a female-sounding username, such as MissKitty, then go into any chat room and wait. I guarantee that within minutes someone in that chat room will be asking you questions about where you live, how old you are, if you're single—and sometimes even nastier things. You'll probably be hit with PMs (private messages), which usually pop up in a small, separate window so that chatters can talk one-on-one, and you can bet their chat will not be about the weather.

While you're waiting for the first come-on, take a look at the usernames of the other chatters in the room. Some will be pretty shocking. Many are obviously female or male, and depending on the chat site you're on, if you check their profiles, you'll find that people list far too much personal information in their profiles.

Why would anyone put sensitive personal information online for the whole world to see? It's quite simple: people online forget the world can see the information.

Chat Room Tips from Paul Hook of TheGuardianAngel.com

- Don't give out personal information such as your address, telephone number, work address/telephone number.
- Never agree to get together with someone you "meet" online without first checking them out to the best of

> your ability; if you do decide to meet, make sure it's in a public place.
> - Do not send anyone your picture unless you are sure to whom you are sending it.
> - Do not respond to any messages that in any way make you uncomfortable; your first reaction may be to defend yourself, but it could make the situation worse.
> - Don't fill out your chat profile; this is the first place people look for personal information!

If you were at a party chatting with various people and someone came up to you and made rude comments, you'd probably move on to another conversation. If this person continued bothering you, following you from conversation to conversation, and the host (much like a chat room moderator) didn't ask him to leave, it's likely you would leave the party and avoid the place in the future, right?

If that's what you'd do in the real world, wouldn't you act in a similar fashion online? But Internet users return again and again to chat rooms where they have previously encountered problems.

Chat room moderators can help keep out the riffraff, but not all chat rooms are moderated, and some moderators do not deal effectively with problem visitors.

Consider what happened to Annie in Illinois.

"I used to go to a chat room on AOL all the time," Annie says. "Then this group began harassing all the women in the room. We notified AOL on a continual basis for an entire month. Some of the chat room moderators saw what was going on but did nothing. The response was mostly the general form letters from AOL. None of these people were kicked off."

Annie and the others fought back, defending themselves, and telling the harassers to leave them alone. Suddenly, they all received viruses via e-mail, then found their AOL accounts had been hacked and their passwords stolen.

When Annie called AOL and finally talked with a representative there, he chided her for giving out her password. But she hadn't.

Annie and the others began receiving harassing messages via e-mail, IM, and mailing lists, all on or through AOL. They continued to complain to AOL, but nothing was done. Finally, tired of fighting back, they stopped going to the chat room or changed their usernames.

Some canceled AOL and got new accounts with other ISPs, and then blocked the harassers' usernames in their chat preferences so that the harassers couldn't get through.

"It's not fair that I had to leave a chat room I really enjoyed going to," Annie says. "These people should have been taken care of when they began harassing us."

Annie was lucky. Her chat harassers were content with online abuse. Sometimes the harassment goes off-line.

"A man allegedly from Florida started chatting with one of our students," Steve Thompson, Sexual Assault Coordinator at Central Michigan University, recalls. "After about a month, he showed up at her apartment, talked a bit, and raped her. She came to me for help and we worked with local police to resolve the case."

Central Michigan is just one of the many universities and colleges taking online harassment and stalking-related cases seriously, and educating not only students but faculty, too.

"I began seeing these types of cases in 1996," Thompson says. "Not many, but I've seen them. We do try to address this issue at orientation, but I have a feeling not all students having these problems come to us for help. It's hard to get the word out there that we are here to help."

Common Chat Terms (Also Used in E-Mail, Newsgroups)

Here are some common terms you'll come across in chat rooms. For a complete list, go to the Tech Dictionary at www.techdictionary.com/chat.html

ADN – Any day now
AAMOF – As a matter of fact
AFAIK – As far as I know
AFK – Away from keyboard
AISI – As I see it
B4N – Bye for now
BAK – Back at keyboard
BBFN – Bye bye for now
BRB – Be right back
BTW – By the way

CSG – Chuckle, snicker, grin
CUL8R – See you later
DIY – Do it yourself
F2F – Face to face (or in person)
FOAF – Friend of a friend
FWIW – For what it's worth
FYI – For your information
GMTA – Great minds think alike
HTH – Hope that helps!
IAC – In any case
IIRC – If I remember correctly
IMHO – In my honest opinion
IRL – In real life
KIT – Keep in touch
LOL – Laughing out loud
MYOB – Mind your own business
NBD – No big deal
OBTW – Oh, by the way
PDS – Please don't shout (when someone types in cap
    ital letters, that's considered "shouting")
ROTFL – Rolling on the floor laughing
RTBM – Read the bloody manual
SO – Significant other
THX – Thanks
TTFN – Ta ta for now
WB – Welcome back
YMMV – Your mileage may vary

Angela

Most people are too embarrassed to come forward when they've been harassed in a chat room, mostly due to the stigma chat rooms have—that they're frequented by lonely people looking for romance, which isn't always the case.

Angela is in her early 20s, pretty, outgoing, and lives in suburban Virginia. She likes to hang out in chat rooms and has made many online friends through chat. One night, Andrew began chatting with her. He was from Rhode Island, friendly, funny, and said he wanted to be online buddies. As their chats continued, he asked her to trust him, and they exchanged photos. A few weeks later, he let her know he thought the relationship had progressed to another level— boyfriend-girlfriend. Angela was uncomfortable with this and told him she wanted to stay online buddies.

He did not.

Angela e-mailed Andrew and asked him to leave her alone. He wouldn't. She complained to Hotmail, where his e-mail was coming from, and they quickly canceled the account. Then she got an e-mail from Andrew, who had gotten another Hotmail account:

> oh wow angela how funny you got me locked out of my hotmail account wow baby you're dangerous at least now i have one less account to worry about so thank you for that you hillybilly inbred c—k licker and if you are as f—ing stupid as i think you are you will have this account closed too. so once again big deal i lose one or hundred hotmail accounts i will just get a new one haha so funny you can't stop me i know how to get your e-mail no matter how many times you change it i could make your life hell if i wanted to

A few days later, when Angela didn't respond, he sent her another e-mail, more chilling than the first:

> hey ang get this one closed too while you're at it oh by the way it's amazing what you can find online—credit reports, income tax reports, personal info, ss #, and tons of other stuff to so go and have this hotmail account closed you dumb ass s—t!

Angela went to her local police for help.

"They said that most likely they couldn't really do anything," she recalls with a sigh. "And that I should just stay off the computer. They said it was a misdemeanor and Virginia probably wouldn't bring him from Rhode Island for that."

Frustrated, she contacted WHOA[3] for help. WHOA was able to cancel Andrew's free e-mail accounts and advised Angela to change her e-mail account and username again. But Andrew wasn't content with that. He began prowling the chat rooms, first pretending to be her, then asking where she was. Although Angela happened to be in the chat room the same time he was, he didn't know her new chat name, and she always left the room before he could figure out she was there.

Andrew was banned from several chat rooms but he began getting more usernames and managed to continue to prowl the chat rooms looking for Angela.

He found her new e-mail address and sent her one final message:

"It's all a matter of time. I'll be paying you a visit very soon. You're going to die."

WHOA had a contact at the Providence, Rhode Island Police Department, Captain Jack Ryan, to whom WHOA provided all the information from Angela, including Andrew's address and telephone number. When Captain Ryan called Angela, she wasn't too optimistic.

"My first feeling about this was, 'Why am I even trying? He's going to be like the other cops and not help,' but boy was I wrong," Angela says. "In the first five minutes of talking with him, I can't describe how wonderful I felt."

Captain Ryan called Andrew's home and his father answered, claiming Andrew was asleep. Captain Ryan said he'd call back and when he did, suddenly Andrew wasn't there. Captain Ryan told the father what his son had been doing and Andrew came on the phone and admitted to harassing Angela. He then offered to come to the police station.

Later that afternoon, Andrew sat with Captain Ryan at the Providence Police Department and admitted to everything. Andrew turned out to be 24 years old, unemployed, had no driver's license, lived with his father, and never got past the 8th grade. He spent his life online.

"When Captain Ryan told me Andrew said he would stop, the relief that came over me was amazing, too much emotion in fact for me to handle," Angela says. "I can never repay Captain Ryan or WHOA for what they did, but I hope they know they are amazing people who will always hold a very special place in my heart."

Endnotes

1. IM: Instant message, similar to chat except the conversation is one-on-one instead of in a room with many other people; popular IM programs include AIM (AOL Instant Messenger), ICQ, and Yahoo! Messenger.

2. Lurker/Lurking: Someone who goes to a newsgroup or chat room and reads what's going on but does not participate in the discussion.

3. WHOA (Working to Halt Online Abuse): An online safety organization that helps adult victims of online harassment and cyberstalking.

Other Ways
They Can Get You

Yes, there's more. Just about any part of the Web can be used for harassment, fraud, or scams. From greeting cards to personal ads to PC Webcams, you need to know what to look out for and how to handle it if it happens to you.

Personal Ads

Personal ads can be great for people who want to meet someone online, but these ads can also be used against someone for revenge. This is what happens: a personal ad is placed in someone else's name. It ranges from the obscure to downright nasty, often including personal information about the person, which could be dangerous if the wrong person answers the ad.

"This woman—the ex-wife of a friend of my brother—decided to harass me by making up screen names using my name in the Yahoo! personals," Anita says. "Why she did this, I still don't know. She then solicited men to 'fantasy rape' me by giving out my name, phone number, and address. I had over 400 men approach me. It was pure terror."

In this case, Yahoo! was cooperative, canceled the account in question, and held all the information regarding it for subpoena, but her local police claimed they couldn't do anything, even though Anita was put in harm's way.

"What if one of those men who contacted me did try to rape me?" Anita says. "I ended up confronting her, telling her that Yahoo! had all the evidence and if she didn't stop, I'd sue her. She stopped."

Marie started receiving phone calls asking about a personal ad she'd placed in Yahoo!

"I had no idea what they were talking about," Marie recalls. "I checked Yahoo! Personals and sure enough, there was an ad placed about me. It listed my name, that I was looking for a 'bisexual female,' and it also listed my cell phone number and home phone number."

Marie received phone calls about this ad for days, stressing her out and humiliating her. She ended up changing both her home phone and cell phone numbers and made sure neither was publicly listed. She had to contact Yahoo! several times before they finally pulled the ad. And she never found out who placed it.

What happened to Sue was a little different.

Sue began receiving e-mail from people who claimed they'd heard about her through someone else. One e-mail read:

> We received your name from someone via yahoo personals listing and were told that we should contact you. We have no idea if this contact was being straight with us but we were told that you are exactly what we are looking for. We don't want to go into more detail yet until we hear back from you and find out if this is for real. You can look up our ad/profile on yahoo (bbvel-vet69). If this person was not being sincere we apologize for any inconvenience. Hope you will set us straight either way.

Another:

> Hey there. Glad to hear your very horny. Did you see my ad on Excite or did I reply to one of yours? I'm rather horny as usual myself. (-: Maybe you could help me out with that..mmmmmm

And yet another:

> I was given your e-mail by seegulred@ yahoo.com. I am a married man 6'4" 230 lbs, blonde hair, green eyes, and I live in Roanoke. I'm in need of an exciting sexual relationship. He said that you are very sexual and that is something I am looking for. I am 27 years old. So do you think you

would be interested in getting with me
sometime? Please e-mail me back and tell me
what you look like.

Sue was upset and answered the e-mails, asking for more information and explaining she definitely was not interested and had no idea who this seegulred was. Only one person replied, in the form of an e-mail message that read:

If you want a nurse that will do anything, contact sueoromo@yahoo.com she will
do anything, and likes it all. Her profile
is earthpiggy.

Sue was flabbergasted. Someone had opened an account at Yahoo! called "earthpiggy" to impersonate her, then sent other Yahoo! members e-mail messages encouraging them to get in touch with her. Sue contacted Yahoo! to remove the earthpiggy account and the seegulred account, which was used to e-mail people with her information. Within a day, they did so. Sue never found out who did this to her, but she hasn't had any problems since.

Yahoo! does seem to attract a lot of people who are out for revenge or who want to harass someone. It's probably because of the variety of services it offers—e-mail, chat, personals, clubs, groups, and more—and the ease of opening up an account. But, it is gratifying that Yahoo! is very quick to act when something like Sue's situation occurs, which helps Yahoo! keep its reputation as one of the most popular sites on the Web.

Dealing with Fraudulent Personal Ads

There's no way to know if someone has placed a personal ad in your name until you begin receiving phone calls or e-mail. But, once you do, follow these steps:

1. Try to remain calm and ask the person who has contacted you where they saw the ad.
2. If possible, get a URL, then go to the Web page and print out several copies of the ad to keep as evidence.

3. Contact the Web host of the page/site where the ad was placed and ask that the ad be removed.

4. If the Web host refuses to remove the ad, contact your local police to ask them to intervene and make a phone call on your behalf to get the ad removed (this is where the printout of the ad comes in handy). This usually does the trick.

5. Contact an online organization such as WHOA or SafetyEd for help.

6. You may also want to seriously consider changing your e-mail address to prevent future problems. If you do this, keep your new e-mail address private and give it only to people you know and trust. Open a free e-mail account on a Web site such as Hotmail or Yahoo!. Use that for everything else you do online.

E-Newsletters

It's easy to sign yourself up for free accounts on the Internet, but it's also easy to sign up other people for services they didn't request, such as e-mail newsletters, subscriptions to magazines, and more.

"Someone was signing me up for all sorts of wedding and child-birth e-subscriptions and having free items or brochures from these sites sent to my home or work place," Doug says. "I thought it was someone I work with who had a crush on me and was upset that I had announced my engagement to my longtime girlfriend."

Doug spoke with the woman and asked her to stop subscribing him, but she denied doing it and the number of subscriptions increased, online and off-line. He began receiving trial issues of magazines related to weddings, babies, and romance. He finally approached his supervisor and explained what was going on and that he had no proof but was pretty sure it was this woman. The company Doug worked for installed security software on the computer network so they could keep track of which Web sites each employee was visiting and when.

Doug again approached the woman and asked her to stop subscribing him. She again denied she was doing anything at all. Within an hour, Doug began receiving more newsletters via e-mail, and more messages from sites offering information about weddings. Later that day, the woman was called into her supervisor's office and confronted with a printed report of her online activity right after she spoke with Doug. All of the Web sites from which he had received e-mail were sites she had visited.

She was warned to stop the harassment or she'd be fired.

Doug stopped receiving free things in his e-mail and mail at home. He's now happily married. The woman eventually left the company and he never heard from her again.

Greeting Cards

You've probably received or sent an online greeting card to someone in your family, a friend, or co-worker. They're usually cute and funny, some with animation, some with music. They're a quick and easy way to stay in touch with people. But it didn't take long for the twisted among us to use online greeting cards against others.

Lisa opened her e-mail one morning and found a message that claimed there was a greeting card waiting for her at Yahoo!Greetings. It was from someone named "chrisjimbob," a name not familiar to her. Thinking it was a joke from a friend, she clicked on the URL link in the e-mail message and found a colorful beach scene. She was due to take her vacation soon, so she assumed the card was from a friend. She clicked the "cover" of the card and it opened to reveal the following text:

    want to go to the beach? or do your tribe
    of halfbreeds have you tied to your house.
    Just think if you had started sleeping with
    black men earlier you could have a half-
    breed yourself.

Lisa noticed more greeting card announcements in her e-mail box from Yahoo!, Blue Mountain Arts, and other greeting card sites. She hesitantly opened them. All had the same or similar message. She began thinking about who could have done this and remembered a message board she'd been on the prior week.

"There were some disagreements on the board, and we exchanged some angry posts," Lisa says. "I received e-mails from some of the people but put them in my trash and never read them. Then I began getting more e-cards, but most were sent to me 'from me' or from bogus e-mail addresses, so that I couldn't figure out exactly who was sending them."

Lisa contacted the greeting card companies, and they made sure that she didn't receive any more greeting cards. She changed her e-mail address but soon the greeting cards began arriving again.

"I felt like I was being held hostage by these people," Lisa says. "It was horrible. For a long time, no one I knew could contact me because I had to keep changing my e-mail address. I finally gave up. I stopped visiting that message board and the harassment stopped."

Dealing with Junk You Never Requested

Are you suddenly being inundated with subscriptions to e-mail newsletters, greeting cards, and more? Follow these steps to stop them:

1. Go to the Web site that the subscription or other nuisance originated from and contact their abuse department via e-mail (many are simply the word "abuse" then the domain, such as abuse@yahoo.com) and ask to be removed from their list(s), explaining that you did not subscribe to them.

2. If you received an abusive greeting card, make sure you print out a copy of the page the card is on for evidence, then contact the abuse department at the greeting card Web site, providing them with the URL where the card is currently located and letting them know you printed out copies of the card in case you need to go to the police.

3. If the site does not remove your name from their list or remove the greeting card(s) and you continue to receive more, a phone call to the company involved usually works. Ask to speak to the manager in their abuse department, explain what's been going on and ask them to intervene.

4. If this doesn't work, then you can go to your local police for help, contact an online safety organization, or cancel your e-mail address and get a new one. Many ISPs are willing to help people who are receiving abusive or harassing e-mail, so a phone call and brief explanation may save you a few dollars.

Guestbooks

Most personal pages and many professional sites have a nifty feature called a guestbook. People who visit the page or site can sign the guestbook and leave comments. At least, that was the guestbook's original design.

A professional racecar driver's Web site suddenly began to get odd messages in its guestbook.

"Several times a person tried to post descriptive messages about the driver's wife and weird sexual fantasies about her," says Candi, the Webmaster. "He described what she was wearing at the race track, so we knew this person has gotten close to her and we were very concerned."

Although Candi deleted the messages from the guestbook, she kept copies of them as evidence. Soon, the person was posting more messages to the guestbook and to a message board on the site, but they were disturbingly odd:

> Madeline Thomas [not her real name] will wear her red FLEECE SWEATSHIRT and have her hands tied behind her back. Then she will have 100 cream pies smashed into her face and be covered in chocolate syrup. Then she will have a cake smashed into her pretty little face. Then she will put on her black FLEECE SWEATSHIRT and have 10 cream pies smashed into her face and covered in mustard. Then she will put on a gorilla costume and be thrown into a huge mud puddle. Then she will get covered in mayonnaise and oil. This will totally humiliate pretty little Madeline and then we will see how she walks around the pits in her nice little RED AND BLACK FLEECE SWEATSHIRTS!!!

"We were able to determine which ISP this person posted from," Candi says, "and found out it was a small and fairly new ISP, only about 20 minutes from the race track where Madeline's husband is based."

Since this was the first case of harassment for the ISP, they weren't sure how to handle it or how to figure out who was posting the messages. Meanwhile, the messages in the guestbook and on the message board continued, escalating at a rate where Candi almost couldn't keep up to delete them.

The local ISP was doing nothing and Candi was getting worried. Then a new message appeared in the guestbook:

> Can someone get a hold of Madeline and tell her that at Port Royal this Saturday she WILL get a pie in her pretty little face. There will be three people there with cream pies and whoever sees her first and gets the best shot at her will smear that pie in her face and hair. Then this will be the end of these messages.

"We'd been scratching our heads trying to figure out what these messages meant as *every* post mentions a pie," Candi says. "We had been trying to decode them and finally came to the conclusion that it must be some weird sexual fetish. We'd heard about a group of people who pied celebrities like Bill Gates, but it never occurred to us that the pie could actually be a weapon. That's when we began to get really worried."

Madeline and her husband finally went to their local police and filed a complaint. The local police contacted the state police, who began narrowing down the search to six users at the local ISP. They finally narrowed that down to one person and left a message on the man's answering machine.

"That's when the posting escalated even more," Candi says. "And this time he began sending e-mails to my address in addition to the posts in the guestbook and on the message board."

> Madeline will wear her red fleece sweatshirt and I'll tie her hands behind her back. Then I'll wrap plastic around her whole body so she is helpless and put her black fleece sweatshirt on her. Then I'll hit Madeline in the face with 30 cream pies. Then I'll dump chocolate, ketchup, mustard, syrup, and salad dressing all over Madeline. What would your dream date be like with the very pretty Madeline?

The state police arrested the man responsible for the "pie posts" less than a week after the above message was posted to the guestbook. He was the 18-year-old son of a truck driver at a speedway where Madeline's husband raced. He admitted to everything and was charged with harassment—he received 90 days in prison and a $300 fine. His parents made him send a letter of apology to Madeline, which was a nice end to the whole mess.

"The police said they didn't think the kid was deranged," Candi sighs. "He was apparently shy and overweight and just hung his head and cried when they asked him about the posts."

Good Guestbooks

An online guestbook can be a good and useful feature. Whether you get a guestbook program through a Web site that offers them, or design your own from scratch, make sure it:

- sends you an e-mail each time your guestbook is signed,
- shows the IP address of everyone who signs your guestbook (this will allow you to contact a visitor's ISP in the event of abuse), and
- allows you to edit and delete guestbook messages.

Many guestbooks also allow you to set preferences so that a person can only sign your guestbook one time, or to block certain e-mail addresses/usernames from signing the guestbook.

Some recommended ones (they're also free) are:

1-2-3 Web Tools
www.freeguestbooks.com

Guestbook.de
http://two.guestbook.de

Dreambook
www.dreambook.com

Guestworld
www.guestworld.com

Creation Center
www.creationcenter.com

The Other Side of Online Auctions

What happens when a high bidder reneges on an auction and takes revenge on the seller? This happened to Eve, who regularly auctions items at eBay. Some of these items are very ugly.

"The Butt Ugly is a contest we hold every month for fun," Eve says, laughing. "A group of us have been doing this for what seems like forever. Each of us finds the ugliest item we can and puts it up for bid. We do it differently from normal eBay auctions—the winner is determined by which Butt Ugly item gets the most bids, then that person can either keep the item or give it to the high bidder if they want it. We pay all the eBay fees involved, so there is no deception."

Sometimes real bidders who aren't part of the group place bids, not knowing a thing about the Butt Ugly contest (BU contest, as it's called), but they gladly join in on the fun when told at auction's end if they are the winning bidder. A few really want the item and are more than happy to pay for it.

"I had one that was a really ugly porcelain chicken. I put it up with the description, 'BU Chicken thingie that wouldn't die,'" Eve says. "This is the one that started the problem."

A bidder who had won an earlier auction of Eve's and was told of the BU contest did not take the news lightly. In fact, he was outraged and claimed she and the other sellers were shill bidding, which means bidding on each other's auctions to artificially raise the bid. "Crusadeworker" wrote to the BU Chicken bidders:

> The auction you bid on is part of a shill
> ring perpetrated by a group of users on
> ebay. The bidders in the auction except
> yourself are all friends of the ring.
> Unless you really want this item I suggest
> you retract your bid. Are you aware that
> the BU in the description stands for Butt
> Ugly. Just thought you wanted to know.

Crusadeworker then began checking Eve's auctions and e-mailed every one of the bidders for any auction she was running, whether it was a BU auction or not.

One bidder was so alarmed, she contacted Eve:

> Hello. I received this message concerning the BU item you have up for auction. While I am not concerned about the ugliness of the item (which is rather obvious), I am concerned about the legitimacy of the auction. Does the item exist and is it really for sale? If you do not reply to my message, I am afraid I will follow the advice of retracting my bid. Thanks!

eBay suspended Crusadeworker's user ID, but he kept coming back and creating new IDs. Although eBay continued to suspend the new user IDs, there wasn't much else they could do. Eventually, Crusadeworker either got tired of creating new IDs or wasn't getting enough attention, because he stopped e-mailing bidders on BU auctions, which continue to this day.

Another way to cause problems in online auctions is through the feedback or comments section. When a bidder wins an auction and completes the transaction with the seller, he is supposed to leave feedback. If the bidder doesn't pay for the item won, the seller leaves negative feedback to warn others of possible problems with that bidder. This didn't sit well with one bidder.

"This guy was a high-bidder on six of my auctions," Patti says. "I followed the standard contact timeframe specified by eBay but never heard from him. When I posted negative feedback, he seemed to have exploded."

The bidder posted a retaliatory negative feedback against Patti in each of the six auctions he'd won, which she had expected him to do. But the ferocity stunned her.

"I was really baffled as to why he didn't just tell me he'd changed his mind, as I am a reasonable person and hate to resort to posting negative feedback," Patti says. "In my final note to him, I advised him I would have to post negatives in keeping with eBay's recommendation, but would still consider not doing so if he would just reply to my e-mail with an explanation."

He not only left negative feedback but began signing her up for online services, one of which was weather specific to her ZIP code.

Patti managed to cancel these as they came in, but she knew he was-n't going to give up easily. And he didn't:

> Of course, the loss of the $12 that you have initiated all of your little war over, will seriously damage your ability to pay for the counseling you so obviously need, won't it...? If you had one bit of sense, you would have relisted the items and gone along merrily. Did that never occur to you? Or were you so busy focusing on pestering us and slandering us to everyone you encounter, that the thought never crossed your mind? Well, I really don't have the time for any more nonsense from you...Go and take some Prozac and lie in a dark room for a while...it might begin to help. Get it right up ye, you nasty cow!

This was just one of the many e-mails he sent Patti. He began bidding on her auctions under other user IDs, then leaving more negative feedback when he won. She complained to eBay and they canceled the user IDs of this unhappy bidder, but Patti finally had to change her own eBay user ID and basically start all over again.

"I had to change my Web page on eBay, all my links, contact people who were repeat bidders, and others I did business with," Patti says. "It took a huge amount of my time to do this, but it did end the harassment by this man."

PC Webcams

They're cute, fun, and easy to install and use. PC Webcams are a great way to keep in touch with family and friends around the world—more personal than just e-mail because you can chat and see each other live or send videos back and forth. It didn't take long, however, for the cute and versatile Webcam to be used against someone.

A pre-teen in the Los Angeles area was wandering around his bedroom in his underwear, getting ready for school. His computer was on, but he didn't notice the green light on his Webcam. It was recording.

A hacker had broken into his online connection and was busily recording the kid. Suddenly, the kid heard that familiar, "You've got mail!" and went to check his e-mail. When he saw there was an attached graphic, he didn't think twice and double-clicked on it.

Imagine his surprise when he saw himself, in his underwear, in his bedroom. He looked up at his Webcam, noticed the green light, and unhooked the Webcam. From then on, he only hooked up the Webcam when he wanted to chat with friends or send pictures and videos.

Webcams Can Be Fun— if You Follow These Simple Tips

1. Get a Webcam that has a lens "shutter" so that you can slide it closed when it's not in use.
2. If you want to broadcast a "show," choose a site that has a good privacy policy and does not tolerate harassment or abuse. Some great sites let you put on a show of your own, post photos taken with your Webcam, and more. Some of the more popular sites include:

SpotLife
www.spotlife.com/home.jhtml

CUSeeMe
www.cuseemeworld.com

CamCities
www.camcities.com

CamCentral
www.camcentral.com

MyCams
www.mycams.com

What's Next?

As technology advances and the online world expands, the number of possible ways to harass others increases. That abusive phone call you get could come from someone's computer, not a telephone. A fax sent to you with a nasty message on it could have been sent from someone's computer. Both methods are virtually untraceable avenues, paving the way for law enforcement to try to find new ways to deal with situations like this.

Work is underway to develop a computer that emits odors when you surf the Web or get your e-mail, and CD-ROM and DVD drives that will play CDs or DVDs encoded with scents, so that as you go through a program or game, you can smell the green grass, honeysuckle, bread baking, or whatever.

And you know that when players are made, recorders are not far behind, so someone out for revenge could easily make a scented CD or DVD encoded with the smell of feces, rotting garbage, or something equally disgusting and send it to someone they dislike. Or a harasser could send a scented e-mail that probably won't smell like roses.

Harassers, stalkers, scam artists, and other criminals are finding new ways to ply their trade. Just make sure you don't become their next victim.

Protecting the Children

It's simple. Nothing will happen to your child online because you're a good parent, right?

Wrong.

The truth is any child can become an online victim of child predators, harassment, stalking, pornography, and more.

Ruben Rodriguez, Jr., director of the Exploited Child Unit, National Center for Missing and Exploited Children (NCMEC, see Figure 13.1) makes a bold statement: "Over 95 percent of the complaints and leads we receive via our CyberTipline are related to child pornography. These are followed by online enticement (child luring) and child molestation."

The NCMEC launched its Exploited Child Unit in 1997 specifically to address online issues. It then added CyberTipline to its Web site a year later for the public to report Internet and non-Internet-related child sexual exploitation. It's worked. The CyberTipline has received more than 37,000 leads and complaints since it was created.

Concrete statistics are hard to come by because of various state and federal statutes under which people are prosecuted and because many online-related cases involving children never go to court.

"My records show just over 120 federal convictions for Internet-related child sexual exploitation," says Colin Gabriel Hatcher, founder of SafetyEd International, an online organization that helps child victims of online harassment/stalking. "I don't have the same records for state convictions, but my educated guess is that there are thousands of these cases per year."

SafetyEd handles more than 150 cyberstalking cases and more than 200 online child sexual exploitation cases per year.

www.cybertipline.com
1-800-843-5678

If you know about a child who is in immediate risk or danger, call your local police.
If you have any information on a missing child, call 1-800-THE-LOST.

The CyberTipline handles leads from individuals reporting the sexual exploitation of children.

• possession, manufacture, and distribution of child pornography • online enticement of children for sexual acts • child prostitution • child-sex tourism • child sexual molestation (not in the family)	**CLICK HERE**  **REPORT ONLINE**

NCMEC, in partnership with the Federal Bureau of Investigation, U.S. Customs Service, and the U.S. Postal Inspection Service, serves as the national CyberTipline and as the national Child Pornography Tipline 1-800-843-5678. Please contact us if you have information that will help in our fight against child sexual exploitation. Your information will be forwarded to law enforcement for investigation and review, and, when appropriate, to the ISP. The U.S. Congress has funded these initiatives for reporting child sexual exploitation.

Figure 13.1 NCMEC.

Just for Kids

Tips for making friends online
(from Colin Gabriel Hatcher of SafetyEd International)

1. EVERYONE YOU MEET ONLINE IS A
   STRANGER—EVEN YOUR "FRIENDS." A stranger
   is a stranger until you know them well and have
   your parents' approval. That cannot happen until you
   meet face to face. Online friends are still strangers
   because you have not yet met them in person.
2. DON'T BELIEVE EVERYTHING YOU READ WHEN
   CHATTING ONLINE. Anyone can say anything in live

chat or in e-mail. That 17-year-old sweet-talking boy online may not be 17 and may not even be a boy.

3. DON'T GIVE OUT PERSONAL INFORMATION ONLINE TO STRANGERS. Avoid giving out your family name, home phone numbers, or your address to strangers online.

4. DON'T RUSH. Meeting someone online and then arranging to meet the following week is reckless and dangerous. Give it time. If they are rushing you—be suspicious.

5. ANY SUCCESSFUL FRIENDSHIP MUST BE BASED ON HONESTY. It's easy to exaggerate or deceive with online communications. But successful friendships are based on common interests and honesty. Don't lie about yourself as you begin to make friends online.

6. DON'T EVEN THINK ABOUT MEETING OFF-LINE WITHOUT DISCUSSING IT WITH YOUR PARENTS. If they want to meet you alone—be suspicious. If they don't want you to tell your parents about them—be suspicious! Involve your parents just like with school friends.

7. TELL YOUR PARENTS OR A TRUSTED ADULT IF SOMEONE SAYS ANYTHING TO UPSET YOU ONLINE, OR SHOWS YOU A PICTURE THAT UPSETS YOU, MAKES YOU SCARED, OR DIS-GUSTS YOU. Don't keep it to yourself. It is NOT your fault that it happened.

8. KIDS + RUNNING AWAY = BAD MOVE! Running away from your family to be with someone you met online won't solve your problems. There is a HIGH chance that the person you are running to will be a BAD PERSON and you will get hurt.

9. Finally: DON'T BE PARANOID!

Figure 13.2   SafetyEd.

Agencies and Organizations Are Here to Help

There are a number of important resources you should know about. The U.S. Department of Justice has created the Child Exploitation and Obscenity Section (Criminal Division), and the FBI has created the Innocent Images National Initiative (IINI), a multiagency investigative initiative that addresses online child pornography and the sexual exploitation of children.

Operation Blue Ridge Thunder (Internet Crimes Against Children Task Force) is often spotlighted in the media when the organization busts an online child predator. (See Figure 13.3.)

These are just a few of the many organizations and individuals trying to combat online child exploitation, harassment, and stalking.

"I got involved in early 2000 when I watched a 13-year-old girl I knew experience the trauma of being targeted by a predator," says Paul Hook, founder of TheGuardianAngel.com (see Figure 13.4). "She developed a contact through a chat room who identified himself as being 14 years old, and made arrangements to meet her."

Figure 13.3   Operation Blue Ridge Thunder.

The teenage girl approached Hook for advice. He became alarmed upon hearing that her parents hadn't been informed that this so-called "14-year-old" was making a 700-mile trip to meet her.

"I convinced her to let me pretend to be her in a conversation with this person in the chat room," Hook says. "After 10 minutes of conversation and asking this 'kid' to prove who he was before 'I' met him, he got very frustrated and angry. He then told me his 'mom' (who was supposed to drive him the 700 miles) was now in the hospital and his uncle would be bringing him. At that point, with the agreement of the girl and her parents, we deleted her accounts and created new ones for her, and she quit going to her normal places online."

This resolved her problem—there was no more contact—but the incident left trauma and fear in its wake. It also got Hook fired up initially to start TheGuardianAngel.com, a counseling site for child and adult victims of online abuse. By December 1, 2000, the Web site was up and operational and it didn't take long for people to visit and ask for help. Hook and his staff make sure someone is available 24 hours a day. In addition, there are several Internet Safety Forums on the site, where people can talk about problems they encountered online, child-related or not.

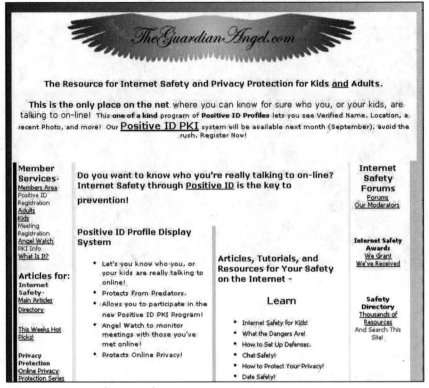

The Resource for Internet Safety and Privacy Protection for Kids _and_ Adults.

This is the only place on the net where you can know for sure who you, or your kids, are talking to on-line! This **one of a kind** program of **Positive ID Profiles** lets you see Verified Name, Location, a recent Photo, and more! Our **Positive ID PKI** system will be available next month (September), avoid the rush, Register Now!

Member Services-		Internet Safety Forums
Members Area Positive ID Registration Adults Kids Meeting Registration Angel Watch PKI Info What Is It?	Do you want to know who you're really talking to on-line? Internet Safety through _Positive ID_ is the key to prevention!	Forums Our Moderators
Articles for: Internet Safety- Main Articles Directory This Weeks Hot Picks! Privacy Protection Online Privacy Protection Series	**Positive ID Profile Display System** • Let's you know who you, or your kids are really talking to online! • Protects From Predators. • Allows you to participate in the new Positive ID PKI Program! • Angel Watch to monitor meetings with those you've met online! • Protects Online Privacy! Articles, Tutorials, and Resources for Your Safety on the Internet – **Learn** • Internet Safety for Kids! • What the Dangers Are! • How to Set Up Defenses. • Chat Safety! • How to Protect Your Privacy! • Date Safety!	**Internet Safety Awards** We Grant We've Received **Safety Directory** Thousands of Resources And Search This Site!

Figure 13.4   Guardian Angel.

"Because our approach to the problems online are awareness and preventative based, when someone comes to us with an existing problem, we provide whatever counsel we can to try to diffuse the situation and take the perpetrator's weapons out of his hands," Hook says. "If this doesn't accomplish the desired result, we refer cases to organizations that are equipped and accustomed to deal with them."

The people at Operation Blue Ridge Thunder find they are overwhelmed at times by the caseload. But they do take each case seriously and try to resolve it quickly.

"We see more child porn/pedophile cases, mainly because of the dollars involved," says Lieutenant Rick Wiita, supervisor of the operation's Special Investigations Division. "We've found there are over 100,000 Web sites related to child exploitation. One particular site was in operation for 90 days. During that period, they received 150,000 hits and 3.2 million images were downloaded. Six people were arrested."

This increase in cases is the reason why so many online safety organizations, including Operation Blue Ridge Thunder and the NCMEC, are involved in passing legislation state by state and federally.

Monitor Your Child

More than half of U.S. parents with home Internet access say parents should monitor their child's Internet use at all times, according to a study from DSL provider Telocity dated May 16, 2001.

The study found that:

- 59 percent of mothers and 51 percent of fathers say children's Web browsing should be constantly monitored;
- more than 90 percent say children's time online should be limited;
- 82 percent say child-filtering and spam-blocking applications are necessary to protect children from unsuitable material;
- almost three-quarters of those polled said it's acceptable to read their children's e-mail without permission.

"Although we're not involved in helping pass legislation, we have had discussions about the Children's Online Privacy Protection Act [COPPA at www.coppa.org] and the Children's Internet Protection Act [CIPA at www.ala.org/cipa]," Hatcher of SafetyEd says. "We are also monitoring closely the Child Pornography Prevention Act (CPPA), a law against computer-generated child pornography, which many claim is unconstitutional."

Changing the law doesn't necessarily mean the laws will work. The American Civil Liberties Union (ACLU) came to the defense of North America Man-Boy Love Association (NAMBLA) when they were sued in a federal civil rights case by the family of a 10-year-old Massachusetts boy who was killed by a man, allegedly after the man viewed the group's Web site.

"NAMBLA has the right to have adequate representation in court, regardless of their philosophy," says Rodriguez of the NCMEC.

"While we don't agree with their positions on children's issues, this is a country founded on rights of the individuals and that above all else must be preserved."

Hatcher agrees but puts it a slightly different way. "The ACLU isn't defending pedophilia. It is defending the First Amendment right of pedophiles to speak out and say who they are. Frankly, I want that to continue so that I know who they are. Silencing pedophiles does not make the problem go away. The best way to deal with it is to shine a light on it."

Hook doesn't pull any punches with his thoughts on the issue. "The fact that the ACLU has aligned with NAMBLA under the banner of the First Amendment defense has, I believe, finally brought to light the true nature of the ACLU's fundamental principles. Anyone with an ability to understand the issues must be able to see through the ruse that this is a freedom of speech issue."

How Bad Is It?

The Crimes against Children Research Center (CCRC) conducted a study in 1999 called "Online Victimization: A Report on the Nation's Youth."[1] Included in the study were 1,051 youths, ages 10–17. The older the child, the more likely they were to go online regularly (meaning at least once a month for the previous six months). Fifty-two percent of the 10-year-olds surveyed were Internet users, while almost 90 percent of 17-year-olds were Internet users. These results are eye-opening:

- 19 percent experienced a sexual solicitation or sexual approach online (2/3 female, 1/3 male)
- 25 percent had unwanted exposure to sexual material
- 6 percent experienced harassment
- 49 percent did not tell anyone about the solicitation
- 24 percent told their parents
- 97 percent of the solicitors were strangers (48 percent of the solicitors were under the age of 18; 24 percent were 18 or older; 28 percent were of unknown age)
- 70 percent of the solicitations happened when the youth was using a home computer
- 71 percent of the solicitations occurred in chat rooms

The CCRC estimates there are 23.81 million youths[2] between 10 and 17 years old who are regular Internet users. If 19 percent have received a solicitation for sex or been approached online, that's a staggering 4.52 million youths.

Why are so many kids at risk online? There are several reasons, according to Hatcher.

"Parents aren't learning about the Internet themselves," Hatcher says. "They don't understand it and don't want to understand it. Some think what they see on talk shows is the whole story. Others use the Internet as a babysitter. Still others make it impossible for their child to tell them if something nasty happens by threatening the child with dire consequences if anything bad happens."

Hatcher feels kids should be told about the good and bad aspects of the Internet.

"Everyone thinks all you need is a computer and the Internet and that's fine," he says. "Schools think it's the parents' responsibility to teach their children to be safe on the Internet. Parents disagree. They think it's the schools who should take responsibility. How can parents teach children about the Internet when many parents still don't know how to use it themselves?"

To that end, Hatcher's group, SafetyEd International, worked with McAfee.com, RippleEffects.com, and the San Jose Sharks to form McAfee.com Kids (see Figure 13.5), a Web site that teaches kids—

Figure 13.5   McAfee Kids.

and their parents—all about Internet safety. Launched in March 2001, the program includes "Guard Your Net," which is co-produced with Dr. Lawrence Kutner, a Harvard University child psychologist. The program includes teaching materials and a student guide and has been distributed to middle schools nationwide.

On the Web site, kids and parents can find guidelines for safe chatting, advice, and lesson plans for teachers, information about cyberstalking and child exploitation, and an extensive summary of child protection laws. A popular part of the site includes "Do's & Don'ts" of Internet safety and privacy, tips for making friends online, and more.

Not only kids in middle and high school become targets of predators online. Parents are allowing their very young children to go online, too, simply because kids take to computers quickly and easily. They all seem to want to go online and see what's out there. And that can be dangerous, especially if they go to the wrong Web sites, or get unwanted e-mail messages, IMs, or questions in chat rooms.

"Many predators send children sexually explicit pictures," says Hatcher. "This is done to encourage the child to see sexual activity as normal and fun. Sometimes, the child can be persuaded and guided to experiment with cybersex, where a sexual fantasy is typed out on the screen between the child and the adult. Then the cybersex can advance to masturbation, as the child and the adult masturbate and share the experience online in words."

"If you put the right tool in the wrong hands, something bad can happen," says Hook of The GuardianAngel.com. "We need to provide children with an informed understanding of the dangers they may encounter through their online activities, through the choices they make, and through how they elect to utilize this wonderful tool. By showing the good things that can result from things like chats and the bad that could occur, you give them the power and knowledge they need to make the right decisions."

It's Not All Bad

The Internet can be a wonderful educational tool. Because it's international, kids can go online and learn about different cultures. Also, they can access documents and information they probably wouldn't find in their school or local library. And this can all be done from the comfort and safety of their own home.

There are hundreds, if not thousands, of educational sites on the Web. For instance, there are the TV-related sites—such as Nickelodeon, Sesame Street, and the Fox Family Channel—that help children learn. On the Web, kids can play interactive games that actually teach them something, or play games that are just plain fun. They can download printable coloring books and even find out how to play new off-line games with their friends.

Here are some activities parents can share on the Web with their kids:

1. *Plan a trip*: Whether families are planning to go to Walt Disney World, drive across the country, or go to the beach for the weekend, parents can sit with their kids and plan the trip together online. See if there's something interesting about where you're going that you wouldn't find out from the brochures or travel agent. (For instance, have you ever heard of the world's largest rubber band ball? No? You'll find out about it online at www.recordball.com.) Figure out what you want to do, where you want to eat, and if the hotel you're staying at has a swimming pool with a water slide.

2. *Plan a pretend trip*: Go on safari in Africa, walk the outback in Australia, or experience haunted castles in Ireland (there are plenty of those!)—all without leaving the house.

3. *Build your family tree*: Get your kids started with your parents' and grandparents' names and see how far back you can trace your family online. You may find you have a long-lost cousin in the next town.

4. *Get an online pen pal*: Help your kids find an online pen pal in a foreign country so they can share what it's like living in the US vs. Japan or Brazil or Iceland or even Nova Scotia.

These are just a few of the many fun and educational things you can do online. Use your imagination!

What's a Cache and How Do You Check It?

A cache is your computer's backup of all the Web sites that have been visited, including graphics and any of the pages accessed. This is a great way to find out where your child has been. The following is how to check the cache, depending upon which Internet browser you use:

Netscape Communicator Versions 4.x and higher

Check the History first, by hitting the Ctrl and H keys, or by going to the pull-down menu on the top toolbar and clicking on Communicator, then Tools, then History. (See Figure 13.6.)

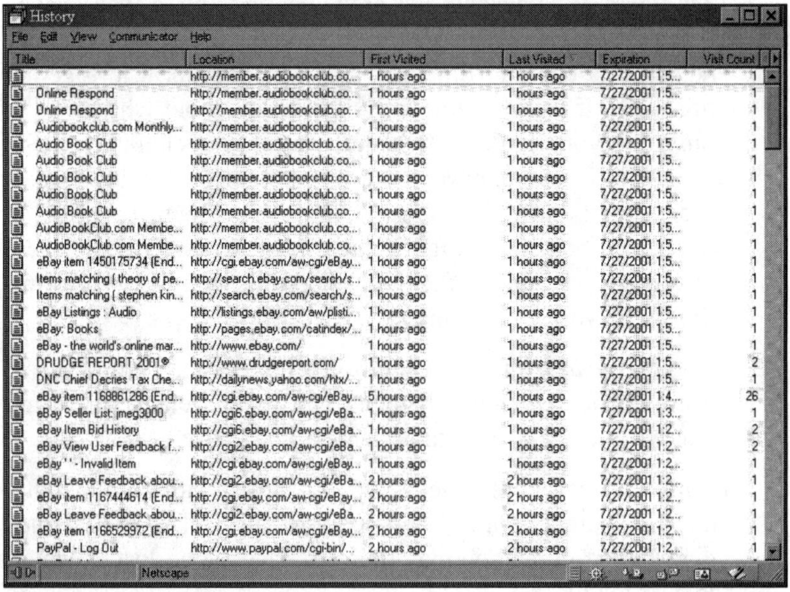

Title	Location	First Visited	Last Visited	Expiration	Visit Count
	http://member.audiobookclub.co...	1 hours ago	1 hours ago	7/27/2001 1:5...	1
Online Respond	http://member.audiobookclub.co...	1 hours ago	1 hours ago	7/27/2001 1:5...	1
Online Respond	http://member.audiobookclub.co...	1 hours ago	1 hours ago	7/27/2001 1:5...	1
Audiobookclub.com Monthly...	http://member.audiobookclub.co...	1 hours ago	1 hours ago	7/27/2001 1:5...	1
Audio Book Club	http://member.audiobookclub.co...	1 hours ago	1 hours ago	7/27/2001 1:5...	1
Audio Book Club	http://member.audiobookclub.co...	1 hours ago	1 hours ago	7/27/2001 1:5...	1
Audio Book Club	http://member.audiobookclub.co...	1 hours ago	1 hours ago	7/27/2001 1:5...	1
Audio Book Club	http://member.audiobookclub.co...	1 hours ago	1 hours ago	7/27/2001 1:5...	1
Audio Book Club	http://member.audiobookclub.co...	1 hours ago	1 hours ago	7/27/2001 1:5...	1
AudioBookClub.com Membe...	http://member.audiobookclub.co...	1 hours ago	1 hours ago	7/27/2001 1:5...	1
AudioBookClub.com Membe...	http://member.audiobookclub.co...	1 hours ago	1 hours ago	7/27/2001 1:5...	1
eBay item 1450175734 (End...	http://cgi.ebay.com/aw-cgi/eBay...	1 hours ago	1 hours ago	7/27/2001 1:5...	1
Items matching (theory of pe...	http://search.ebay.com/search/s...	1 hours ago	1 hours ago	7/27/2001 1:5...	1
Items matching (stephen kin...	http://search.ebay.com/search/s...	1 hours ago	1 hours ago	7/27/2001 1:5...	1
eBay Listings : Audio	http://listings.ebay.com/aw/plisti...	1 hours ago	1 hours ago	7/27/2001 1:5...	1
eBay: Books	http://pages.ebay.com/catindex/...	1 hours ago	1 hours ago	7/27/2001 1:5...	1
eBay - the world's online mar...	http://www.ebay.com/	1 hours ago	1 hours ago	7/27/2001 1:5...	1
DRUDGE REPORT 2001®	http://www.drudgereport.com/	1 hours ago	1 hours ago	7/27/2001 1:5...	2
DNC Chief Decries Tax Che...	http://dailynews.yahoo.com/htx/...	1 hours ago	1 hours ago	7/27/2001 1:5...	1
eBay item 1168861286 (End...	http://cgi.ebay.com/aw-cgi/eBay...	5 hours ago	1 hours ago	7/27/2001 1:4...	26
eBay Seller List: jmeg3000	http://cgi6.ebay.com/aw-cgi/eBa...	1 hours ago	1 hours ago	7/27/2001 1:3...	1
eBay Item Bid History	http://cgi6.ebay.com/aw-cgi/eBa...	1 hours ago	1 hours ago	7/27/2001 1:2...	2
eBay View User Feedback f...	http://cgi2.ebay.com/aw-cgi/eBa...	1 hours ago	1 hours ago	7/27/2001 1:2...	2
eBay ' ' - Invalid Item	http://cgi.ebay.com/aw-cgi/eBay...	1 hours ago	1 hours ago	7/27/2001 1:2...	1
eBay Leave Feedback abou...	http://cgi2.ebay.com/aw-cgi/eBa...	2 hours ago	2 hours ago	7/27/2001 1:2...	1
eBay item 1167444614 (End...	http://cgi.ebay.com/aw-cgi/eBay...	2 hours ago	2 hours ago	7/27/2001 1:2...	1
eBay Leave Feedback abou...	http://cgi2.ebay.com/aw-cgi/eBa...	2 hours ago	2 hours ago	7/27/2001 1:2...	1
eBay item 1166529972 (End...	http://cgi.ebay.com/aw-cgi/eBay...	2 hours ago	2 hours ago	7/27/2001 1:2...	1
PayPal - Log Out	http://www.paypal.com/cgi-bin/...	2 hours ago	2 hours ago	7/27/2001 1:2...	1

Figure 13.6 Netscape history.

The History shows the Web sites visited, the date and time visited, and how many times it has been visited. If you want to go to that site, just double-click the URL. If there's a questionable site listed there, it's a good idea to check the cache. To do this, you need to know where your browser cache is stored on your hard drive. Just go to the top toolbar and click on Edit, then Preferences. A separate window pops up. Now select Advanced, then Cache, as shown in Figure 13.7.

Look for "Disk Cache Folder" and you'll see where it's stored. The default is usually C:\Program Files\Netscape\

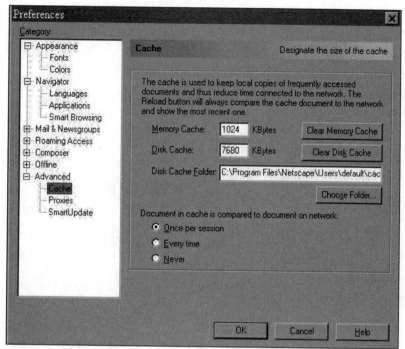

Figure 13.7   Netscape cache.

Users\default\cache. To get there, you need to open up Windows Explorer (your file directory). Click on the Start button, and then look for "Windows Explorer" in one of the subdirectories if it isn't on the main list.

When Windows Explorer is open, click on My Computer, then the plus sign (+) next to C: (your hard drive). This expands the listing to show all the directories on your C: hard drive. Now look for the directory where the cache is stored: Program Files, Netscape, Users, Default, and click on Cache. You should see a lot of files here. If you don't, they have been manually deleted and you need to talk with your child.

Microsoft Internet Explorer (MSIE) Version 5.x and higher

MSIE is different in its setup (see Figure 13.8). To check the history and cache, you need to go to the top toolbar

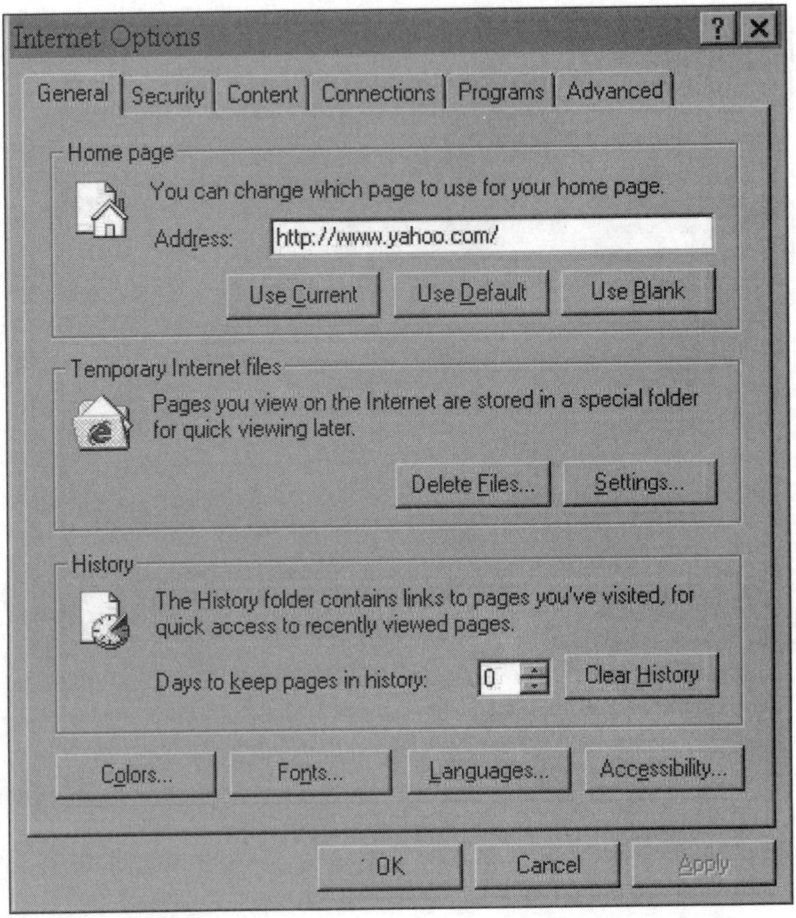

Figure 13.8   MSIE cache.

and click on Tools, then Internet Options. A separate tabbed window pops up.

Go to "Temporary Internet Files" (MSIE's name for the cache file) and click on Settings (see Figure 13.9). This shows you the current location for the cache, which is usually C:\Windows\TemporaryInternetFiles.

If you click on View Files, you'll be able to see names of the sites visited, graphics, etc.; the dates and times visited; and how many times a site was visited. Again, if this is empty, it's time to talk to your child.

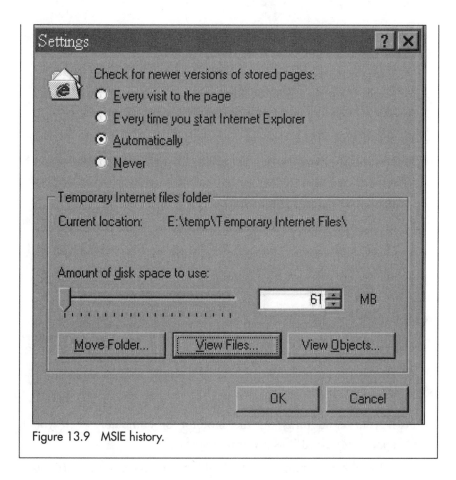

Figure 13.9   MSIE history.

How to Protect Your Child Online

The experts interviewed seem to agree that the following will help:

1. Get actively involved in your child's online life. Know what he is doing online. If your child has created a personal Web site, what information has she posted on it? If there's anything personal or that could easily identify where you live or where your child goes to school, explain why it needs to be changed. The same goes with profiles. Make sure as little as possible is filled in, and select a username/e-mail address for kids that is gender-neutral to make it harder for predators to guess their age and sex.

2. Place the computer in a den, family room, kitchen, or other high-traffic location. Don't allow your child to keep a computer with an Internet connection in his or her bedroom where the

door can be closed while online. If they close the door whenever they go online, regard it as a danger sign.

3. Use a filtering/screening program such as Cyberpatrol, Net Nanny, Guiding Light, or Surfwatch.

4. Set use of the computer to specific times so that your child does not spend an excessive amount of time online.

5. Monitor how frequently your child gets unfamiliar e-mail—and read it.

6. Become more computer literate. The best way to do this is to sit down with your child and ask them to show you how the Internet works. You may be surprised to find how much they enjoy the role of teacher.

7. Sit and work alongside your child while they are online.

8. Warn your children to be cautious with online strangers.

9. Monitor your long-distance phone bill for evidence that your child has been in contact with a stranger.

10. If your child receives strange phone calls or gifts from strangers, find out what's going on.

11. If your child turns off the monitor or computer when you approach, regard it as a warning sign.

12. Know what your children are looking at on the computer. If you find that it's pornography, it's time for a chat. If you check the Web browser cache and find it's already been cleaned out or that it's empty, it's time for a chat. If you check the Recycle Bin to see if the cache info is there and it's not, it's time to disconnect the computer from the Internet and have a serious chat.

If something does happen to your child online, do not panic. Yes, you're upset, but understand that your child may be more upset than you are, and frightened—not only about what happened to him but about the possibility that you'll be angry. Remain calm and find out what happened and when. Then contact an online safety organization such as Operation Blue Ridge Thunder, SafetyEd, TheGuardianAngel, or the NCMEC for advice. If a predator has arranged to meet your child, call your local police.

How the Filtering Software Rates

Consumer Reports magazine tested six filtering software packages[3] on 86 sites known to contain objectionable material such as sexual content and the promotion of crime, bigotry, violence, tobacco, and drugs. It found that CyberSnoop and Net Nanny offered poor protection, while Cyber Patrol, Cybersitter 2000, Internet Guard Dog, and Norton Internet Security offered fair or good protection.

AOL's parental control settings were also tested by the magazine. It found the Young Teen settings were the best protection because they blocked 63 percent of undesirable sites. In one test where *Consumer Reports* pitted six Net filtering programs against a list of 86 Web sites that contained sexually explicit content or violent graphic images or promoted drugs, tobacco, crime, or bigotry, AOL's Young Teen control allowed only one site through completely, while 20 other sites only came through partially (meaning some words and pictures but not the entire site). The other Net filtering programs permitted at least 20 percent of the sites through completely.

Filtering Programs

Mention Net filtering programs and watch organizations such as the ACLU, Center for Democracy and Technology (CDT), and Electronic Frontier Foundation (EFF) come out swinging. For these organizations, it's a freedom of speech and First Amendment issue. But these are your children—should you use a Net filtering program? It's really a choice, and it's yours to make.

Steven Leshikar is the father of three children, all in their early to late teens. When he introduced the Internet to his home in the mid-1990s, information on Internet safety wasn't readily available, and he and his family made up the rules as they went along. Their rules still hold up today: Don't give out personal information; don't open attachments from unknown sources; don't look at porn. They have always kept the computer in a centrally located place and only allowed the younger ones to surf with Mom or Dad.

As the years passed, computer and Internet usage in Leshikar's household increased, and the rules were relaxed. He trusted his children and thought, as most parents do, that they'd be fine online.

"At some point we noticed changes and became concerned," says Leshikar. "Grades were slipping, avoidably. Online friends were being mentioned in conversations. Computer viruses were somewhat common and important data was being lost. Files were being downloaded that caused the computers to stop functioning properly. Auto-dialers were being automatically installed and unusual items were appearing on telephone bills. Items also started arriving in the mail."

At this point, Leshikar decided to try an Internet filter. But he found that these early filters were troublesome and ineffective. Not only did they slow his computers, but important sites for school projects were inaccessible unless he or his wife entered passwords. He also noticed that, for the most part, inappropriate content was still slipping through.

"The real problem with filters was that we were relying on the software to do the parenting," Leshikar says. "Filters didn't provide us with any useful information to instruct or train our children. They did nothing to protect our children from potentially dangerous online relationships. We were still getting viruses and downloads were still causing computer problems. In other words, what our children needed were parents that were involved with their online experience, not uncaring 'Internet sitters.'"

Leshikar didn't know what to do. When he was winding down his Internet advertising company and looking for a new project, he happened to bring up the problem with Net filters to programmers and colleagues. They brainstormed, looked closely at "spy software," and ultimately decided that although the technology was there, the approach was wrong. Parents should trust their children and watch them, not spy on them.

Leshikar knew he was on the right track. He set to work with these goals in mind: a program that was easy to install and use, that was informative and educational, could assist with time management, would allows parents to determine content appropriateness, teach children self-respect and self-control, and empower parents to set intelligent and enforceable guidelines.

"Parental involvement should be required and open communications encouraged," says Leshikar. "We also thought it should be most effective for parents of children between the ages of 8 and 14. We viewed Internet access for entertainment and communication as a privilege."

The Lighthouse program was born, but it was more than just software. Guiding Light Software (www.guidinglightsoftware.com, see Figures 13.10 and 13.11), founded by Leshikar and presided over by Adam Aiken, also provides advice and more on their Web site. They offer educational Internet safety seminars where they define parental involvement as:

1. being informed of children's computer usage

2. understanding what children are doing and viewing

3. communicating concerns openly

4. setting good examples

"We are strongly opposed to parents spying on their children," Leshikar says. "It was our intention that parents discuss Internet safety and notify the child that the software was being installed. The child, knowing the parent is watching, would be generally encouraged

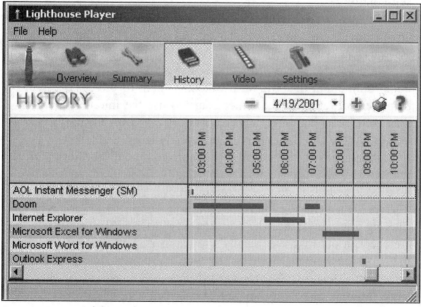

Figure 13.10   Lighthouse history.

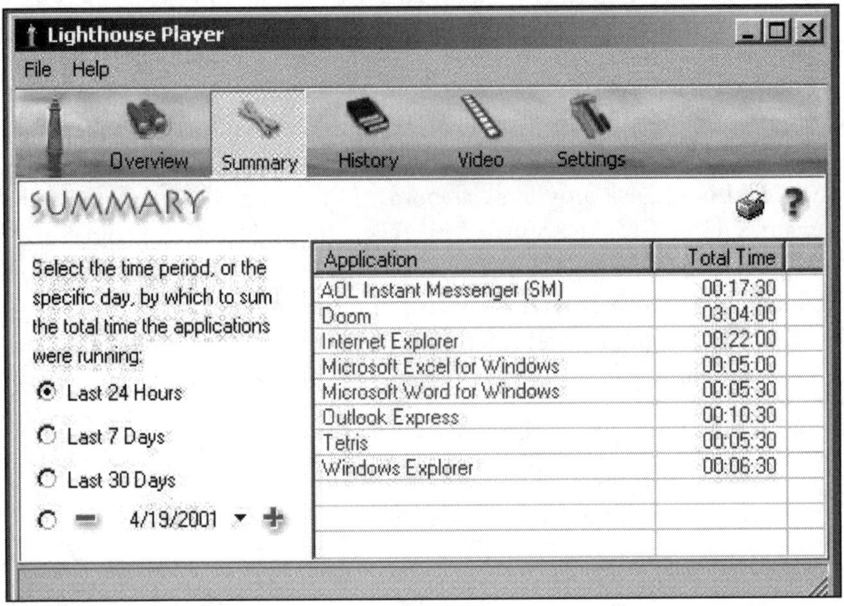

Figure 13.11   Lighthouse summary.

to follow the parent's guidelines for online activity, thus developing self-control."

Leshikar tested Lighthouse out on his own children first, discussing the Internet safety rules again and showing them how the new software worked.

"We pointed out that Mom and Dad would know what they were doing online and that we were watching them to protect them and help them develop the skills necessary to use the Internet safely on their own," Leshikar says. "Once a week, we go over the past week's online activity, discuss concerns, but mostly laugh and talk."

Lighthouse is an alternative to the more common Net filtering programs because sites are not automatically filtered. Parents decide what goes and what stays after talking it over with their children.

CyberPatrol (www.cyberpatrol.com, see Figure 13.12) is a typical filtering program. It includes a preset list of filtered Web sites, which are checked out by the company's researchers. You can override the list and customize filtering to your preferences, a positive CyberPatrol feature. (Be forewarned: there are hundreds of sites to wade through, although they are categorized and subcategorized to try to make it easier.) Another benefit is that access to the Internet can

Figure 13.12   CyberPatrol.

be restricted to certain times of the day or for a certain amount of time. Your child won't be able to stay online past the allotted time.
Other available filtering programs include:

CyberSitter
www.solidoak.com/cysitter.htm

Net Nanny
www.netnanny.com

Internet Guard Dog (McAfee)
www.mcafee.com

Norton Internet Security 2001 Family Filtering
www.symantec.com/sabu/nis/nis_fe

If you don't want to install software, there is an alternative (besides keeping a computer out of your child's hands): Filtered Internet Providers.

A Filtered Provider is like an ISP except it automatically filters out certain Web sites. The good news is that the Filtered Internet Providers are competitive with regular ISPs, and many offer free trials so that you test them for yourself. The bad news is that you can't choose which Web sites you want filtered or accessible. Also, the Filtered Internet Provider may not be available for access as a local telephone number. Some offer portals, which essentially allow you to use their filtering process while using their Web site as your browser. However, if your kids are as smart as most kids are, they can figure out how to back out of this site and surf the "old way."

Filtered Internet Providers include:

Familynet
www.family.net

Family Connect
www.familyconnect.com

Mayberry USA
www.mbusa.net

Safe Access
www.safeaccess.com

Internet4Families
www.net4fam.net

More Filtered Internet Providers can be found at The List (thelist.internet.com). Type "filtered" in the search text box.

While your kids may gripe about your concern, they will appreciate it when you take the time to show them you care about what happens to them—online or off-line. Just be open with them, and encourage them to be open with you so that if something *does* happen you're the first person they go to for help.

Endnotes

1. Funded by the U.S. Congress through a grant to the NCMEC; the study was conducted by David Finkelhor, Ph.D., Kimberly Mitchell, Ph.D.; and Janis Wolak, J.D. of the CCRC at the University of New Hampshire, Durham.
2. Figures based on the 1999 Census.
3. Published in March 2001, available at www.consumerreports.org.

Office Know-How:
Stay Safe in the Workplace

Each day, you arrive at work and don't think twice about safety while using your office computer. But listen to this: whether your company has an intranet or Local Area Network (LAN),[1] you can still become an online target. Trouble can come from someone within the company *or* outside of it.

Melanie's Surprise

Melanie received a puzzling e-mail at work from Escorts.com, thanking her for the information she submitted and telling her they'd be in touch soon.

"I replied and asked them to remove me from their mailing list," Melanie says. "And I left a message for the network administrator at Escorts.com to find out who submitted my information in the first place."

Melanie went to lunch. When she returned, there was an e-mail from someone else with the subject line: "thanksgiving." When she opened the attached file, it was a two-minute video of a man masturbating. Melanie was Net-savvy enough to know how to show the full headers in the message and she tracked the message back to the pornographic Web site from where it originated. She learned that the fiancé of Sharon, one of her co-workers, was the network administrator for the pornographic Web site. She printed everything out and brought it to the president of the company for discussion.

The president told her the company couldn't do anything because it wasn't an employee who had harassed her. Melanie approached the vice president, who was friendly with Sharon. The vice president approached Sharon, and when he explained the situation she said she knew Melanie had received the e-mail, but that it had been a mistake. The message was intended for her. When Sharon was asked about Escorts.com, she said she had no idea what that was about.

The vice president felt this was good enough and advised Melanie to drop it. Melanie argued that even if it had been a mistake, wasn't there something wrong with Sharon receiving pornographic e-mail attachments through the company e-mail system? She was told that if Sharon had been sending pornographic e-mail she would have been terminated.

Even though Melanie received no additional offensive e-mail messages, this incident left her feeling uncomfortable at work. She soon left to take another job.

Was the company legally responsible for what happened? No. A company cannot be held responsible for the actions of an employee's friend, relative, or significant other who is outside of the workplace. Since the e-mail had stopped by the time they were brought to the company's attention, no further action was required. So, the company's conduct in this case was legally defensible, but—given that Melanie had received the messages through her e-mail account at work—could the company have done more to help her?

The answer, in my opinion, is yes. The company could have helped Melanie contact the ISP and Web sites involved, letting them know the situation. They could have said that the messages were sent to a company e-mail address, that this was unacceptable, and that they expected some action to be taken. Sharon could have been reprimanded for knowingly accepting obscene e-mail messages at work. Melanie's superiors might also have offered to move her to a different department or branch office in order to make her work environment as comfortable as possible.

However, this company had no guidelines or policies in place regarding online harassment. If they had, they could have addressed this situation more effectively and possibly avoided losing a good employee.

E-mail Usage Study

A study conducted by Vault.com in 2001 found that of the 1,004 employees interviewed who had received sexually explicit or otherwise improper e-mail messages:

- 9.2 percent forwarded it to friends
- 8.58 percent closed it and left it alone
- 4.7 percent forwarded it to co-workers

One year later, a study of 451 employees by Vault.com showed that the percentages had almost doubled, which explains why many employers now monitor employee e-mails:

- 14 percent said they forward sexually explicit or otherwise improper e-mails to friends and colleagues
- 13 percent said they often received such e-mails at work
- 12 percent said they sometimes received such e-mails at work

Sexual harassment is a form of sex discrimination that violates Title VII of the Civil Rights Act of 1964. This is how the definition appears:

> Unwelcome sexual advances, requests for sexual favors, and other verbal or physical conduct of a sexual nature constitutes sexual harassment when submission to or rejection of this conduct explicitly or implicitly affects an individual's employment, unreasonably interferes with an individual's work performance or creates an intimidating, hostile or offensive work environment.

Sexual harassment of a woman or a man can occur in a variety of circumstances. Note the following important points:

- The victim does not have to be of the opposite sex of the harasser.
- The harasser can be the victim's supervisor, a co-worker, a supervisor in another area, an agent of the employer, or a nonemployee.
- The victim does not have to be the person harassed but could be anyone affected by the offensive conduct.
- Unlawful sexual harassment may occur without economic injury to or discharge of the victim.
- Conduct must be unwelcome for it to be considered harassment.

Advice for employers:

1. Develop and distribute a company Internet policy that offers guidelines for employee conduct and covers online-related abuse and harassment issues.

2. Install firewall protection and anti-virus software on each computer in the company, not just on the LAN/intranet.

3. Consider installing monitoring software on company computers. You need to know if an employee is downloading obscene material, visiting pornographic Web sites, stealing company secrets, sending or receiving harassing e-mails, etc. Make sure your written policy advises employees that their electronic communications and activities may be monitored.

4. Don't use an employee's first and last name as her e-mail address; allow employees to select something gender-neutral or assign a gender-neutral username.

5. Don't list all of the e-mail addresses of employees on the company Web site unless the employee needs to be listed there (as a public relations contact, for instance).

6. If an employee comes to you with a complaint of online harassment/stalking, whether or not the perpetrator is within the company, change the employee's e-mail address immediately, as well as his or her voicemail extension. Do not post the new e-mail/voicemail information anywhere, online or off-line, for as long as there is a threat of continued harassment.

7. Take all employee complaints seriously. Investigate and act on them immediately. Being proactive in these situations will say a lot to your employees.

8. Consider involving local law enforcement. If you attempt to handle a harassment case yourself and the perpetrator physically harms the victim and/or others at the company, you will regret not going to the police in the first place. Hiring a private investigator may also be a viable option.

I Spy

Many companies have turned to filtering, monitoring, and what many employees call "spy software" to keep track of what employees do online—whether it's receiving or sending e-mail, surfing on the Web, Instant Messaging through the company system, or putting games or obscene material on the computer hard drives at their desks.

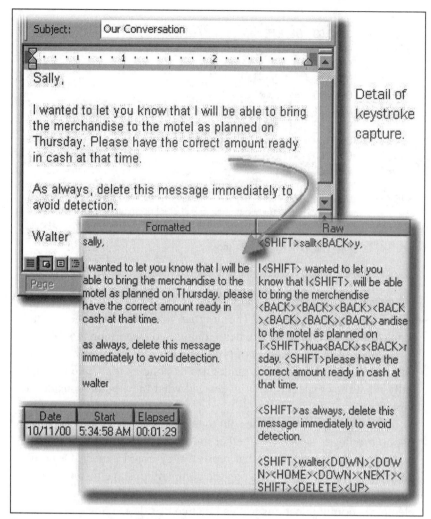

Figure 14.1   WinWhatWhere.

WinWhatWhere (www.winwhatwhere.com, see Figure 14.1) is a spy program. It allows employers to monitor all computer-related activity (not just online-related), selectively exclude particular programs from the log, or monitor only selected programs. It can specify certain days and times to monitor the activity. This means that every time employees run a program or application, it can be logged. If they have a game on their hard drive and they play it, that activity can be logged. Every keystroke they make on the keyboard can be logged—Web sites

3:13:17 AM	00:00:00	DELETE:A:\Web Site Visitors.xls
3:13:17 AM	00:00:00	DELETE:A:\INVEST.BAK
3:13:17 AM	00:00:00	DELETE:A:\AMEX.TXT
3:13:17 AM	00:00:03	3½ Floppy (A:)
3:13:20 AM	00:00:00	My Documents
3:13:20 AM	00:00:21	My Documents
3:13:41 AM	00:00:02	3½ Floppy (A:)
3:13:43 AM	00:00:00	Moving...
3:13:43 AM	00:00:00	3½ Floppy (A:)
3:13:43 AM	00:00:00	CREATE:A:\Government Charges 120 People in Nationwide Securities Fraud Crackdown.url
3:13:43 AM	00:00:02	DELETE:C:\My Documents\Government Charges 120 People in Nationwide Securities Fraud Crackdown.url

Figure 14.2   WinWhatWhere—stealth mode.

they visit, the contents of e-mail messages sent or received, even if the messages have been deleted. The program has a stealth mode so that employees never know they're being monitored (see Figure 14.2).

Because of the availability of programs like WinWhatWhere, more employers are implementing guidelines or policies that state specifically what they expect of employees and what they would consider a violation.

In the past, some companies put together guidelines outlining telephone privileges—such as whether an employee can make personal or long-distance calls and what reprisal they could expect. Or companies laid out the rules for using the company postage meter, photocopier, or computer printer for personal use. It makes sense to add electronic communications to this practice of rule making.

"Every company should have this policy. But make sure it's not hidden so that no one sees it or knows about it," says Eric Rolfe Greenberg, director of management studies, American Management Association (AMA). "So many companies tend to throw new policies or guidelines in the back of an already unwieldy publication and neglect to properly inform employees and new hires about it. When they implement a new policy, such as proper use of online communications in the workplace, every employee needs to be trained in it, not just given the policy printed on paper to read. This would easily take care of potential problems."

Eric Friedberg of Stroz Associates, a computer crimes consulting business, agrees. "Obtain appropriate consents from all employees and consultants that their e-mail accounts, office-issued laptops, PDAs,[2] cell phones, and text messaging devices can be monitored or searched," Friedberg says. "Often, an incident that appears to originate from an unknown person is being perpetrated by a fellow employee. Consents in employment agreements give an extra level of comfort to executives and in-house counsel in conducting internal investigations."

Office Netiquette— More Than Just Manners

Here are some important do's and don'ts for employees:

- Don't give out your password or PIN number and don't write it where others can easily see it.

- Be polite when you are communicating within your company or on the Internet. Remember that you're using your work account and if you do something that could be considered harassment or even rude, you could lose your job.

- Don't put personal information about yourself in a company profile (if your company requires one). List only basic information, such as the initials of your first and middle name, then full last name, your work extension number, and your work e-mail address/username.

- When you write an e-mail message, make it look professional, as though you were typing it to be printed and mailed via regular postal mail. Don't hit the SEND key until you've reread it at least a couple of times to make sure spelling and grammar are correct. Don't use "smileys" or cute acronyms. Always sign your e-mail messages with your full name and title.

- If you're using your work e-mail account to send messages containing your personal opinions, clearly state that this is your opinion and not necessarily that of your employer.

- Don't compose messages in all capital letters, SUCH AS THIS. It's considered shouting and may offend some people.

- Accessing pornographic material while at work—whether on the Internet or from a diskette you bring in or borrow from a co-worker—could get you fired!

- Don't send or forward any chain letters or "Forward this to everyone you know" messages while at work or to your work associates.
- If you do become a victim of online harassment at work, Eric Friedberg of Stroz Associates suggests you report it immediately. "Harassing conduct can escalate quickly into a violent situation," he says. "Employees and companies are far better served in addressing the problem immediately. Under no circumstances should the employee attempt to deal face to face with a person who has been harassing him or her over the Internet."

To Monitor or Not to Monitor

Three-quarters of U.S. businesses electronically monitor employees in some fashion, according to an AMA study in 2000; double the rate of 1995. The survey found that 77.7 percent of the 1,600 companies polled record and review some sort of employee communications and activities while on the job. The results indicated:

- Internet connections were monitored by 63 percent of respondents
- telephone use was tracked by 43 percent of respondents
- computer use (when logged on, or keystroke counts) was monitored by 19 percent of respondents
- video surveillance for security purposes was used by 38 percent of respondents

In addition, the survey found that more than 25 percent of the companies polled fired people for misuse of company technology, and 75 percent have disciplined people.

Perhaps you will remember these headline stories:

Two Salomon Smith Barney executives were fired for accessing pornography and transmitting it between themselves.

The New York Times *fired 20 staffers for sending "inappropriate and offensive" e-mail, citing a need to protect itself against liability for sexual harassment claims.*

Another company offering filtering/watching software is SurfControl. In addition to the software, SurfControl offers many resources on their site (www.surfcontrol.com, see Figure 14.3),

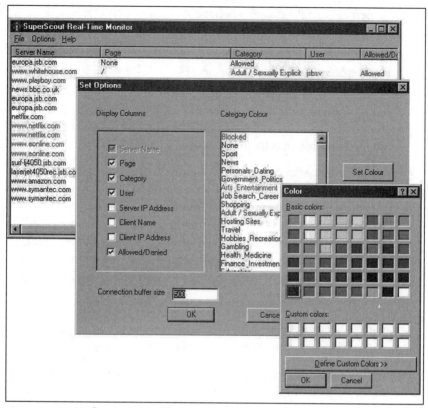

Figure 14.3   SurfControl.

including a sample "acceptable use policy." (See: www.surfcontrol.com/resources/business/acceptable_use_policy/index.html.)

SurfControl conducted a survey in May 2001 that polled both information technology (IT) managers and corporate Internet users on their views about the use of filtering software within their organization. The results indicate that:

- nearly 83 percent of overall respondents believe that employees use the Internet at work for personal use

- more than 75 percent view Internet monitoring and filtering procedures as an absolute necessity

- 42 percent of IT managers surveyed cite Internet monitoring and filtering software as standard operating procedure (SOP) within their organization

- 70 percent of IT managers believe it should be SOP
- 60 percent of overall corporate Internet users agree with IT managers' positions on incorporating filtering into their Internet Acceptable Use Policy
- 54 percent of IT managers state enhanced security as the primary reason for adopting Internet filtering software within their organization, followed by increasing productivity (20 percent) and protecting corporate reputation (20 percent)

The other side of the coin is that this kind of "Big Brother" approach upsets many employees. They feel their voicemail, their e-mail, etc. should remain private and none of the company's business.

"Workplace privacy is a contradiction in terms. It's an oxymoron," says Greenberg. "I know the illusion of privacy is there, but don't forget, you are not using your own stuff. The phone, the keyboard, the connections, the job itself—they don't belong to you. They belong to the company, legally."

When the AMA conducted a study in April and May 2001, in which they polled 435 companies regarding online issues in the workplace, they discovered the following facts from their interviewees:

- 62.5 percent had business interruptions due to a virus/Trojan attack on the company network
- 6.9 percent conducted mandatory software audits (for pirated software)
- 4.6 percent experienced Denial of Service (DoS) attacks
- 3.9 percent had computer networks attacked/sabotaged by former employees
- 2.1 percent had their computer networks sabotaged in other ways

Speaking of employee sabotage, Mark Greenlaw turned on his office computer one day and found that something odd was going on. Programs were opening and closing by themselves, files were being copied, and some files were missing from the hard drive—most importantly a presentation he was set to give the following week. Panicked, he let his supervisor know and soon the company IT tech was in his office. A Trojan horse virus had been planted in his computer. The IT tech took Mark's computer and analyzed the hard drive. After a few days, the computer was returned to him, but this time his computer (and the rest of the computers in the company) was equipped with firewall and anti-virus software.

"They found out that an employee who was upset I'd been promoted over him put the Trojan in my computer," says Mark. "It was set to go off on a certain day at a certain time and when it did, he gained access to my computer and was wreaking havoc with it."

The IT tech was able to trace the Trojan to the employee by watching the activity on Mark's computer, then using "sniffer" software to track it down. The employee was fired.

"Luckily, I had a copy of the presentation on my laptop, so I didn't have to redo it," Mark says. "But we all learned a lesson—even the IT guy who thought he knew everything about computers—make sure all the computers have firewall and anti-virus protection and keep it updated."

Endnotes

1. LAN (Local Area Network): Sometimes known as an intranet, LAN is an internal "Internet" for that company; only employees and those within the company can access it; LANs are not available to the general public; some large corporations have an intranet/LAN accessible by a branch of that corporation, whether they're across the USA or on the other side of the world.
2. PDA: Personal Digital Assistant, such as a Palm Pilot or other handheld "mini-computer" used for keeping track of appointments, to store phone numbers, etc.

Police Duty:
Our Nation's Finest Boot Up

The Internet is filled with dark alleyways. People who would proceed with caution down dark alleys in real life often throw caution to the wind when they are online. So what can you do if you are "accosted" online? There is a good chance your local or state police or even a federal agency will help you—even if they haven't worked on an online-related case before. This chapter will take a look at what law enforcement professionals—from the East Coast to the West Coast—are doing in regard to online crime.

Kennebunk, Maine

Lobsters and lighthouses are what most people think of when they think of Maine. It's the postcard of picturesque views and moose roaming the land. And it doesn't have any online crime.

Wrong.

But at least police Lieutenant David Gordon and former Detective Tom Cannon of the Criminal Investigation Division (CID) at the Kennebunk Police Department are on top of things.

"The first online crime I was involved in and made an arrest for was a child porn case in 1997," says Gordon. "The suspect was also arrested for child sexual assault—a felony—of over 100 counts with two victims. In this case, the children could not testify and the suspect would have gone free, but the online pornography involved made for a good case on its own."

The perpetrator received only one year in jail plus eight years probation, but Gordon was pleased because the perpetrator would be monitored for close to a decade.

Another case did try Gordon's patience, though. It was a stalking case that became an online stalking case.

The suspect was a former boyfriend of the victim. He had been stalking her in person and then he created a Web page. There he related the sexual activities the two had engaged in while they had been a couple. He included her real name and other identifying information.

The victim was mortified and went to Gordon for help. The suspect claimed he had a right to include what he wanted on his Web page. He said it was freedom of speech. Gordon felt otherwise. He was able to get the Web site revised through a court order. It wasn't easy, though, because Maine didn't have a cyberstalking law at the time. Gordon had to do what he could with the existing laws.

At the conclusion of this case, the suspect was found not guilty of stalking. The victim was given a two-year Order of Protection, which included the conditions that the suspect was not to use the Internet to communicate with the victim or post any information online about her.

So it was a partial victory.

"After that case, I strongly feel that victims have no rights while the suspects have many—he stalked her online as well as off-line. We had the proof, but the court felt otherwise. And that makes it hard on victims," says Gordon. "I think advocacy groups like the ACLU should apply common sense when it comes to areas where people are having their lives ruined by a criminal who waves the flag of free speech."

Former Detective Tom Cannon agrees. "I feel that free speech is important, but I never saw anything in the Constitution granting the right to stalk and harass," he says.

The two made a formidable team, with Gordon handling the sex-related and some cyberstalking cases and Cannon handling all other online and off-line crimes, including homicides, deaths, aggravated assault, and robbery. In addition, Cannon helped Gordon, who unfortunately has plenty to keep him busy.

"We're seeing a great increase in computer-related crimes of all types," Gordon says. "We're getting three to eight cases a month and it's our fastest growing problem crimewise. In fact, I predict we'll need a full-time computer crimes investigator on staff within the next few years."

Gordon's concerns about online crime caused him to become involved—along with me—in the writing of the Maine Cyberstalking Bill, which was introduced in March 2001. Gordon represented law enforcement and I represented cyberstalking victims (see my own story in Chapter 1). I also presented myself as an expert who teaches cyber safety, and I testified on behalf of this bill. It passed with a minor change and was signed into law in June 2001 by Maine Governor Angus King.

"Online-related laws need to be passed," says Gordon, "but the hardest thing is getting them enforced. People committing online crimes are not arrested often enough. The courts need to hold these people accountable for their acts."

Another Maine Unit

Taking care of online crimes in the state of Maine is a unit called the Maine Computer Crimes Task Force. While the unit conducts criminal investigations and performs computer forensic exams (the testing of evidence such as hard drives, diskettes, etc.), it also provides public outreach programs and law enforcement training. The task force is composed of detectives from different law enforcement agencies throughout the state—the Maine State Police, the Lewiston and Brunswick Police Departments, and the Maine Department of the Attorney General.

The task force has investigated various Internet crimes, with crimes against children, stalking, and harassment taking up a large portion of their time.

"Our detectives respond to any report of a crime involving computers," says Michael Webber, a computer crimes investigator and forensic examiner on the task force. "We do this by coordinating with the local law enforcement agency where the crime occurred. The investigation is primarily their responsibility, while we provide the necessary technical and online expertise needed for the case."

Webber says that Internet-related laws are proliferating across the country, and the impetus has been that many times the victim lives in one state and the suspect in another. With the passage of these laws in more and more states, the task force's job is eased.

"The officers in Maine are becoming better trained, but we still lack any training for prosecutors," Webber says. "They rely on the detectives as the experts, and this may cause them to shy away from aggressively pursuing the case to its full potential. I'd really like to see that improve."

Webber feels there are still many unreported computer crimes simply because victims aren't completely comfortable turning to police for something that happens to them online.

"Although," Gordon says, "as the days go by, it does seem to be getting better. We're getting the training we need and we want victims to come to us first instead of trying to handle it on their own or ignoring the situation."

Nashua, New Hampshire

When the New Hampshire online harassment bill was signed into law in June 1999, it was a year after Amy Boyer was murdered by Liam Youens (see Chapter 9), who then killed himself. Liam had posted on his Web page details of how he was going to kill her.

Detective Lieutenant Donald Campbell of the Criminal Investigation Division (CID) of the Nashua Police Department was assigned to the Amy Boyer case. He sees the new online harassment law as a hopeful sign.

"We've seen a distinct rise in online-related cases since 1998," Campbell says. "They include harassment, identity fraud, fraudulent auctions, child pornography, and more. We haven't been inundated with them, but there certainly has been an increase in the number."

The Nashua CID has been able to handle most of its cases without referring any to outside agencies. But CID officers have invited federal authorities to join in cases that involved interstate suspects.

"We used New Hampshire's online harassment statute in the prosecution of a man who sent anti-Semitic material by e-mail," Campbell says. "He received a guilty verdict after a trial. So we know the law works."

Massachusetts

The High Technology and Computer Crimes Division was set up by the Massachusetts Attorney General's Office (AGO) in 1997 after officials noticed an increase in online crimes reported by police departments throughout the state.

"I used to get calls from police departments and hear them say 'These aren't crimes anyway,'" says John Grossman, chief of the High Technology and Computer Crimes Division. "I rarely hear that anymore."

The Massachusetts AGO provides support to local law enforcement agencies. Most of the cases involve cyberstalking, primarily via Instant Messaging (IMing), but sometimes by e-mail and chat rooms.

"The difficulty is tracing the source of these threats and then working on an inter-jurisdictional case in what is often only a misdemeanor,"

Grossman says. "Personally, I'd like it to be more difficult for people to be anonymous online, from a law enforcement standpoint. But advocacy groups do make the important point about just how difficult the balance between protecting victims and protecting privacy can be."

Alexandria, Virginia

"Our first and in some ways worst case took place in January 1998," recalls Sergeant Scott Gibson of the Domestic Violence Unit of the Alexandria Police Department. "The case was both cyber and in-person stalking. We contacted WHOA because we had no idea how to trace the e-mails. They were able to tell us where the e-mails were coming from."

The suspect followed the victim and left e-mail messages, handwritten notes at her room, and voice messages, which the victim gave to Alexandria police as proof that he was stalking her.

The suspect also e-mailed messages to her at work with obscene pictures attached and sent them to her fellow employees and to her employer's central fax line. He then posted her name and telephone number online with the message that she liked sex with men over age 60.

"We helped stop the e-mails and got the personal ads removed, but we normally don't handle this type of case," Gibson says. "We don't have any one person in the department to even handle them."

Because Virginia didn't have an online harassment law at the time, the police charged the suspect with the in-person stalking. During the trial, the e-mail and personal ads were introduced as part of the evidence. The suspect was convicted and seemed to have gotten the message. The victim hasn't been bothered since.

"Whenever we get a case now, we work with WHOA," says Gibson. "They've been a tremendous help. Some of us have also attended workshops to help us understand how to work on these types of cases and to get to know the Internet a bit better so that we can not only help the victims, but understand what they're talking about when they come to us in the first place."

Somerset, Kentucky

At the Somerset Police Department Criminal Investigative Division (CID), cases of e-mail harassment are on the rise. Officer Mike Grigsby believes the trend will continue.

"I believe this is the new type of prank call," Grigsby says. "Instead of using a pay phone to order 100 pizzas for someone, a prankster can use online services to harass people via e-mail since they think they can do it anonymously."

"We have no local agencies set up to handle such cases," Grigsby says. "We attempt to help the victim in any way possible, and may refer them to specialized groups when needed, such as the FBI, especially if it involves a death threat."

Online crimes pose problems for the department and Grigsby lists his concerns: "You may have prosecutors that don't understand, victims who are frustrated because they feel like no one can or is helping them, few laws under which to prosecute the person when they're identified, and then the preparation and collection of evidence and how to present it to a jury is very difficult. I can't testify to something if I really don't understand how it works myself, so how can I explain it to a jury of 12 laypersons, many of whom may have never used a computer?"

Grigsby is optimistic that through training and experience, his police department and departments throughout the country will become more knowledgeable about online crimes and how to deal with them.

San Diego, California

District Attorney offices are also getting on the online crime bandwagon. The San Diego County District Attorney (SDCDA) has two units that are involved in the investigation of online crimes: the Stalking Unit and Economic Fraud Division, which handles primarily high-tech crimes (see Figure 15.1).

Figure 15.1 San Diego DA.

In the spring of 2000, SDCDA Investigator Dave Decker wrote a grant request through the California Office of Criminal Justice Planning (OCJP) for a multijurisdictional group to investigate high-tech crimes. As a result, in June 2000 the Computer and Technical Crime High-Tech Response team (C.A.T.C.H.) was formed.

The C.A.T.C.H. team consists of more than a dozen investigators from San Diego-based federal, state, and local law enforcement agencies that work together to investigate high-tech crimes in San Diego County. The team also includes two prosecutors and a support staff.

C.A.T.C.H. takes the case when the following circumstances occur: A computer is the target of a crime—meaning intrusions, denial of service, etc.; a computer was the primary means to commit a crime; and/or a computer is the primary means to investigate a crime. C.A.T.C.H. investigators have varied authority in computer crimes, which means they conduct preliminary and follow-up investigations, assist law enforcement agencies with investigations, write and serve search warrants, conduct forensic examinations of seized computer evidence, make arrests, and prepare criminal cases for trial.

C.A.T.C.H. may handle the more involved high-tech cases, but that doesn't mean the SDCDA itself isn't busy with other online crimes.

"Approximately 10 percent of our stalking cases involve the Internet," says Wayne Maxey, DA Investigator of the SDCDA Stalking Unit. "I believe that for almost every crime that occurs in the real world, we are seeing or will see those crimes committed on the Internet, such as fraud, forgery, gambling, prostitution, child porn, stalking, threats, and more."

Maxey says that e-mail is the number one medium for harassing and stalking online.

"Following at a close second is the posting of victim's information on message boards or forums," Maxey says. "We liken it to the old 'For a good time, call …' message you might see on a bathroom wall."

Maxey knows that it's hard for law enforcement to keep up with this new type of crime, especially when suspects use anonomizers and remailers. He would like to urge small organizations that have a network to take measures to protect it from intrusions. Hackers and crackers, he notes, can break into a system and use it to relay their venom and destruction.

"Computers and the Internet are the new tool of terror for the stalker," Maxey says. "We in the criminal justice system will just have to keep up the good fight."

Stalking
resource center

Figure 15.2   The National Center for Victims of Crime.

National Center for Victims of Crime

The National Center for Victims of Crime (NCVC, see Figure 15.2) is handling more online-related cases every day.

"Most victims initially contact our victim services [VS] department first, and VS advocates provide them with basic information regarding privacy and Internet safety," says Seema Zeya, former director of the NCVC's Stalking Resource Center. "The VS advocates always refer victims to external organizations, such as victim service organizations online or in their local communities, local law enforcement agencies, or the FBI. If these organizations are unwilling or unable to assist, the VS staff will advocate for the victim with ISPs or law enforcement. We do everything we can to make sure they get the help they need."

The NCVC, located in Arlington, Virginia, was founded in 1985 and is the nation's largest nonprofit advocacy and resource organization serving victims of all types of crime. It opened the Stalking Resource Center (SRC) in July 2000 to meet the newly recognized needs of online victims.

The SRC responds primarily to calls and technical assistance requests from victim service providers and criminal justice professionals seeking educational resources related to cyberstalking. The SRC mails out information packets and also makes referrals to online organizations that help victims—such as WHOA, SafetyEd International, Privacy Rights Clearinghouse, the American Prosecutors Research Institute, the FBI, U.S. Attorneys Office, National Cybercrime Training Partnership, the Federal Trade Commission (the identity theft case division), and other organizations.

What does Zeya feel is required to provide better help to online victims?

"Everything," Zeya says. "Law enforcement needs basic as well as specialized education and training. Many victims still report that law enforcement officers are not taking their complaints seriously. For the most part, law enforcement is unprepared when it comes to investigating and collecting evidence in cyberstalking cases."

Zeya would like to see:

- the general public getting more education to become more knowledgeable about online safety

- ISPs receiving training and education to become more sensitive and responsive to the needs of victims

- state and federal prosecutors receiving education and training on how to successfully prosecute cyberstalking cases

- colleges and universities taking cyberstalking more seriously and developing effective strategies to address both online and off-line stalking on their campuses. *(Note: the SRC has been working with universities across the country, encouraging them to address cyberstalking in their regular anti-stalking policies, practices, and procedures.)*

Zeya feels that law enforcement professionals are finally acknowledging cyberstalking as a serious and growing problem and that they need education and training to combat it.

"Most of the people who contact us readily admit they don't know a whole lot about how to handle these types of cases," Zeya says. "They are, however, very interested in improving their skills and investigative techniques. A few departments have established specialized computer crimes units with trained computer forensic investigators. That's a positive step in the right direction."

The U.S. Department of Justice

The United States Department of Justice (USDOJ) has several departments that handle online-related crimes, including Computer Crime and Intellectual Property Section (CCIPS, see Figure 15.3) (also see www. cybercrime.gov). Created in 1991, CCIPS began as the Computer Crime Unit of the former General Litigation and Legal Advice Section, and then became a section of the Criminal Division in 1996. Today, CCIPS works with the U.S. Attorneys Offices (USAO) in each of the districts to pursue cases of hacking, virus dissemination, and denial of service attacks.

CCIPS includes the following divisions:

- CCIPS, Criminal Division-Intellectual property/trade secret violations
- Child Exploitation and Obscenity Section, Criminal Division-Child pornography/luring
- Fraud Section, Criminal Division-Fraud
- Office of Consumer Litigation, Civil Division-Illegal sale of pharmaceuticals
- Civil Rights Division-Hate Crimes
- Organized Crime and Racketeering Section, Criminal Division-Illegal gambling
- Narcotics and Dangerous Drugs Section, Criminal Division-Illegal drugs
- The National Infrastructure Protection Center (NIPC, www.nipc.gov), an inter-agency center housed at the FBI, serves as a national critical infrastructure threat assessment, warning, vulnerability, and law enforcement investigation and response entity.

Figure 15.3   U.S. Department of Justice.

From Cop to Cybersnitch

It sounds worse than it actually is.

Thor Lundberg, a technological security specialist with the Raynham, Massachusetts, Police Department, had a plan in 1996. He and his brother, Eric, developed Cybersnitch (see Figure 15.4), a public service crime-fighting solution for Internet users. Their two goals:

1. To prevent crime from occurring on the Internet.
2. To network all law enforcement at all levels in the mission of fighting computer crime, patrolling, and securing the Internet.

Figure 15.4 Cybersnitch.

In March 1997, Cybersnitch made its debut at www.cybersnitch.
net, with law enforcement membership representation in more than
26 states in the US, plus some in Canada and the United Kingdom.

"Cybersnitch is designed for enabling the quick and aggressive
investigation and prosecution of virtually all computer crime occurring
on the Internet," Lundberg says. "And it eases the jurisdictional limitations inherent in the investigation of Internet-based computer crimes."

Cybersnitch has been responsible for shutting down hundreds of
sites displaying contraband. Cybersnitch is not only designed for law
enforcement; the site puts cybercitizens in direct communication with
law enforcement officials—it's a virtual 911 for victims of cybercrime.

"The online cases we've seen the most are those involving e-mail
and chat rooms equally," Lundberg says. "It typically starts with chat
rooms, then progresses to e-mail, and from there, in some cases, it
continues to phone calls, standard mail, or worse—real-life stalking."

When Cybersnitch receives a harassment report, it tries to resolve
the situation. If it can't, it helps the victim by putting him or her in
direct contact with a law enforcement agency that can.

"It's kind of a Catch-22 situation sometimes," Lundberg says.
"Online friendships occur, solidify, and then sour over time, resulting
in harassing situations. People need to be cautious about who they
consider a friend online, especially if that is the only way communication has occurred."

SamSpade.org

SamSpade.org (see Figure 15.5) is a tool that many law enforcement agencies and cybercitizens use to track suspects. Steve Atkins
initially created the SamSpade program in 1996 to combat spam.

Sam Spade.org

Figure 15.5   SamSpade.org.

"I used to be active in the technical aspects of theater—stage management, sound, and lighting design—and I maintained the FAQ for the newsgroups rec.arts.theatre.stagecraft and alt.stagecraft," Atkins says.

Since alt.stagecraft was next door, alphabetically, to alt.sex, Atkins found that his e-mail address was harvested by porn spammers who had targeted the alt.sex newsgroup. He saw his e-mailbox fill up with pornographic spam e-mail.

Atkins poked around the newsgroups and found news.admin. net-abuse.email, where others complained about the porno spam. He posted a few messages and found that most of the people in the newsgroup used the Windows operating system. An idea for a way to combat spam came to him and he soon devised a simple program that conducted a WHOIS query. This determined who owned the domain of the originating ISP of the e-mail/Usenet post and what the trace route was (tracking where the message came from, server by server).

That simple program grew into a full-fledged Windows program (a free one) that can be downloaded to use on your computer. Or you can go to SamSpade.org and use the more than 40 tools available on the Web site.

"I get quite a lot of fan mail both from individual users and a lot of ISP abuse desks," Atkins says.

But not everyone has been a fan. In addition to e-mail complaints, he's had spammers forging e-mail addresses he hosts and a few Denial of Service attacks (a program designed by hackers to try to cripple the SamSpade network so that people could no longer access the Web site), which have put the site out of commission for a day or two.

"But I know my provider well," Atkins says, "and there haven't been any problems. The site averages 100,000 hits a day, and sometimes I see as many as 1,000 downloads a day of the program. I must be doing something right."

16

Universities Catch Up with the Net

When universities fail ...

Nina attends a prominent university in the northeast and felt safe there the first two years she attended. She struck up a friendship with a fellow student, Jim, a sophomore. She considered him a friend, but eventually he began to have more feelings for her and started sending love poems via e-mail. At first she ignored the love poems, but when they continued to arrive she told him that even though at one time there may have been a possibility of more than a friendship, now she didn't think so.

Nina continued seeing Jim in class and around campus, and they chatted about inconsequential things like school and movies. One day, she found a new love poem in her e-mailbox calling her a "soft-spoken temptress." He began Instant Messaging (IMing) her, too. She always sent the same reply: "Please leave me alone."

She went home to Virginia for a week to visit her family and friends and checked her e-mail when she arrived. A message from Jim was waiting for her:

"I like you, but I'm going to kill you last."

Nina shrugged it off since she was so far away from the university—she knew he wasn't close enough to do anything. When she returned to school, nothing more happened. It was soon time for the holiday break and she went back home again. While there, she canceled the username that Jim knew and created a new one, even though he'd been quiet. Better to be safe than sorry, she thought.

When she returned to the university, Jim left a note under her door at the dormitory: "Why won't you talk to me online?"

He somehow found her new username and began IMing her again, asking her why she wouldn't reply. She wrote back that he should f—k off. He responded with threats. That's when Nina became frightened.

In early January, she received a Trojan Horse virus via e-mail that shut down her hard drive, essentially making her computer useless. Five days later, someone hacked into her e-mail account; Nina found this out was when she was talking to her sister in Virginia complaining about being without her computer. Her sister told her that Nina's username popped up on her IM buddy list as being online. Her sister sent an IM to Nina's username but there was no response, and the person quickly signed off.

This occurred a few more times while Nina's computer was being repaired. Each time her sister saw Nina's username on IM, she would send a message. There was never a reply and the person always signed off.

"I went to the campus police and told them what had been happening. But all they did was tell him to stop making threats and showing up at my door," Nina says. "Jim implied to the campus police that we were romantically involved when we weren't. They began to not believe me, even when I showed them copies of the IMs he sent me—even the one where he threatened to 'kill me last.'"

The campus police and judicial affairs office at the university told her that the IM logs weren't good evidence and the threats were indirect, even though the Massachusetts state law clearly indicated that any "Internet communications threatening someone is regarded as stalking."

Nina moved to a friend's apartment off-campus and stayed there for the rest of the school year. She doesn't know if she'll return to school in the fall. She's scared Jim might escalate his stalking off-line.

Nina's case may seem extreme, but it happens more often than not. The campus police often aren't any help—not because they don't want to be, but because they have no knowledge of how to handle online-related cases.

Many universities are taking stock of this new online threat and becoming proactive. George Mason University (GMU) in Fairfax, Virginia, is one of them.

Cyberstalking on Campus: How Prevalent Is It?

A questionnaire was distributed to 235 undergraduate communication college students at a large southwestern public university, including 130 females and 102 males (three respondents did not respond).*

When asked, "Has anyone ever undesirably and obsessively communicated with or pursued you through computer or other electronic means (at least once)," respondents answered as follows:

- 38 percent had someone expose private information about the respondent to others or attempt to sabotage their reputation
- 34 percent were sent tokens of affection via poems, songs, electronic greeting cards
- 32 percent were sent threatening or harassing messages or pictures/images
- 31 percent were sent messages implying a relationship where there was none
- 27 percent had their computers hacked into, information stolen from their computers, etc.
- 26 percent were sent messages disclosing private information about the respondent's life, sex life, family, hobbies, etc.
- 25 percent were sent messages that were needy, such as pressuring to see them, give them another chance, etc.
- 21 percent had someone pretend to be someone else or the respondent
- 19 percent were sent pornographic/obscene messages or images
- 9 percent first met online, then were threatened, stalked, or harmed off-line

A national-level study conducted during the 1996–1997 school year found that out of 581 women polled:**

- 13.1 percent were stalked; of these:

- 25 percent involved e-mail as one of the means of stalking
- 2 percent were stalked solely via e-mail
- 83 percent of the victims knew or had seen their online stalker
- 17 percent never knew their online stalker

In a case study of 241 students enrolled in an Introduction to Psychology course at the University of Pittsburgh:***
- 5 percent indicated the person who did not reciprocate their love was an e-mail correspondent
- 79 percent of males and 71 percent of females reported they had sent or delivered notes, e-mail, or other written communication to express their interest

*From Cyber Obsessional Pursuit, 2000, by Brian Spitzberg and Gregory Hoobler.

**From "The Sexual Victimization of College Women," 2000, by Bonnie S. Fisher, Francis T. Cullen, Michael G. Turner, U.S. Dept. of Justice study.

***From "Breaking Up Is Hard To Do: Unwanted Pursuit Behaviors," 2000, Violence & Victims. Vol. 15, No. 1, pp. 73–90 by J. Langhinrichsen-Rohling, R.E. Palarea, J. Cohen and M.L. Rohling.

GMU Has a Clue

"A father of a girl in her senior year of high school called me in 1998 because one of our GMU students put up a Web page dedicated to her," says Connie Kirkland, coordinator of Sexual Assault Services at GMU. "Though no nude or otherwise derogative information was posted, there were pictures and information about the girl. The father asked, 'Does this mean that someone in Thailand could be looking at my daughter's picture right now?' I answered that it could mean that. He was distraught and asked that I intervene."

Kirkland got in touch with WHOA, which contacted the Web host provider, which promptly removed the Web page. Kirkland worked with GMU's Judicial Dean, who brought in the university's counseling center's expertise to assist with this fragile young man in hopes that no further stalking—online or in person—would result. So far, so good.

GMU has seen an average of 30 similar cases a year since 1997, when it received its first case. GMU has worked with online organizations, such as WHOA, and with local and campus police to resolve situations. In spring 2001, GMU sponsored a training session for campus and police officers from around the state of Virginia. Called "Catching A Stalker—Hook, Line & Sinker," the session covered online and off-line stalking. In addition, Kirkland developed a student-friendly brochure that is handed out to as many students as possible either at information fairs or presentations on campus. It is also available on the GMU Web site.

Most GMU cases tend to involve IMs, such as Nina's, but many involve e-mail as well. In 1999 a female student came to Kirkland for help because she was receiving harassing e-mail from an acquaintance in a religious club on campus. She was upset because she was engaged to be married in a few months and didn't know why this club member was e-mailing her. He wrote that he loved her, that she should break up with her fiancé, that he was meant for her, and that he wanted her to have his baby.

"At first, she rebuffed his online advances, but then he became more aggressive and she became scared," Kirkland says. "I referred the case to the campus police, who believed there was enough of a threat from him and fear in her to arrest him for stalking."

Kirkland went to court with the victim. A plea agreement stating that the perpetrator would have no further contact with the victim was reached without hearing testimony. The case was dismissed. Kirkland was concerned about enforcement of this agreement and contacted the religious organization's faculty advisor for assistance.

"The identification of the harasser/stalker coupled with the inability to get a conviction on the cases that we've taken to court is the hardest for us to deal with," Kirkland says. "It seems the judges believe the victim and are ready to convict, but they don't believe that the prosecutors adequately prove intent or prove stalking has occurred. Training in this area for prosecutors seems crucial at this point."

Consider this information on the same subject from a study titled "Cyberaggression: Safety and Security Issues for Women Worldwide" by Sharon Levrant Miceli, Shannon A. Santana, and Bonnie S. Fisher of the University of Cincinnati:

"Cyberaggression laws distinguish illegal speech in the form of threats from constitutionally protected free speech. The first case to address First Amendment issues relative to cyberaggression is *United States vs. Jake Baker and Arthur Gonda.*[1] Jake Baker and Arthur Gonda exchanged e-mail messages with one another regarding sexual fantasies that they both had about harming young women. Baker, a University of Michigan student, was indicted for violation of 18 U.S.C. 875 that prohibits transmission through interstate or foreign commerce of any communication that threatens to kidnap or injure another person. The court's decision basically affirmed the Watts[2] 'true threat' standard for cyberaggression cases. Because there was no direct threat made to another person, Baker and Gonda's communication was constitutionally protected."

For an insightful article about the Jake Baker Scandal, visit www.trincoll.edu/zines/tj/tj4.6.95/articles/baker.html (warning: it is very graphic).

Jim Dempsey, deputy director of the Center for Democracy and Technology (CDT) discusses this complicated issue further. "In a way, there's a little more latitude for expression online," Dempsey says. "For example, when you stand in front of the White House and yell, 'It's time to take over the White House!' that may be a crime. But if you say the same thing online in a chat room, it's not a crime. Making threats against people online is roughly similar. The context is about the same."

UB Good

Since 1996, campus police at the University at Buffalo (UB) in New York have had reports of online auction fraud, stolen credit cards used online, soliciting obscenity from a minor, and hacking. But harassment in the form of e-mail and chat is much more prevalent.

"In one case, we received a report from a high school teacher in Arkansas that one of his 15-year-old female students was having some rather obscene e-mail exchanges with one of our older male students," recalls Harvey Axlerod, UB's Computer Discipline Officer. "Our university police department had to secure an affidavit from the minor's parent allowing us to investigate. We collected the original e-mails from the victim and then secured a search warrant for the suspect's emails, computers, disks, etc."

Axlerod and members of the university police expected to find e-mail originating from the UB servers. But there was nothing. Then they checked the UB system backups and found, according to Axlerod, "volumes of incriminating evidence."

Since New York state law for soliciting obscenities from a minor is a Class E felony, law enforcement officers arrested and prosecuted the student on that charge. However, the judge allowed the perpetrator to plead to a lesser charge.

"I can say with certainty that the number of cases reported increases constantly," Axlerod says. "I believe there are two reasons. First, the sheer volume increase in Internet connectivity guarantees that the number of creeps will increase as well. Second, since UB has a full-time person—me—to deal with such issues, it has become well-known that there is an office to take complaints, to investigate, and take appropriate action."

Axlerod finds that the anonymity of the Internet sometimes hampers his investigations.

"Some online harassers are very savvy at hiding their identities," Axlerod says. "The free e-mail services, such as Hotmail, Yahoo!, and Lycos, have a tough time keeping up with these folks, who often use phony personal data to open an account, then move on to establish new bogus usernames. The most difficult cases are those that use anonymous remailers. These sites often keep no records, so the e-mail is quite untraceable. In one case, a clever user had one remailer forward to another remailer, in effect double-dipping the anonymity."

This doesn't stop Axlerod from being a bulldog on cases, actively working with university police and local police when needed. He's found that a mutual working relationship usually results in seeing the case closed quickly.

Educating students and faculty at UB is a priority for Axlerod. "When dealing with minor infractions of university policy, this becomes an opportunity for individual counseling and training," he says. "Also, I encourage students to share their experiences with friends. The grapevine is a very effective means of communications. For example, after a flood of pyramid (for example, Ponzi[3]) schemes and chain e-mail several years ago, the word spread that this was unacceptable. I can't recall seeing a case of either since then."

UB publishes its university policies in print and online. Freshman orientation includes creative efforts at explaining what is acceptable and what is not. UB also provides lectures and student skits to show what dangers lurk online.

"It's a common misconception to regard the Internet as a virtual world," Axlerod says. "I'm always amazed at how much information people give online when the same requests in person would draw a rebuke. The Internet is different but hardly separate from the traditional world. Unfortunately, it often takes an unpleasant experience, such as harassment, stalking, or fraud, before the light goes on in one's head."

What Can Universities Do to Prevent Online-Related Incidents?

1. When giving a student a university/college e-mail address, let the student select his or her own username and make sure it's gender neutral. Too many universities and colleges automatically hand out e-mail addresses to students and faculty consisting of the first name initial and last name or partial last name, such as jhitchco@umuc.edu. If someone is harassing or stalking a student or faculty member, the victim's e-mail address can be very easy to figure out.

2. Do not post e-mail addresses, dorm room numbers, class schedules, telephone numbers, etc. on the university or college's Web site or in printed form. This information should remain private, as it only gives harassers and stalkers another tool to escalate online harassment to off-line.

3. Have a sign-in system for library or computer lab use. Make each student and faculty member sign in to a certain computer, the time they signed in, and the time they signed out. Then, if any harassment or fraudulent activity is found to originate from a certain computer, it can be traced back to the faculty member or student who used it at that time.

4. Create an acceptable use policy that clearly mentions what will not be tolerated online, such as harassment, stalking, or threats.

5. Publish online safety tips on the university or college's Web site and in brochure form, as GMU does. Distribute a printed brochure at rallies, information seminars, or other campus activities. Let students

and faculty know there are online organizations that can offer great advice and help if the victim doesn't want to approach campus police.

6. Hold an online safety lecture for students and faculty once a semester. Talk about what can happen online and encourage students and faculty to voice their concerns or their own experiences.

7. Make sure campus police are trained to handle online-related cases. Training costs are minimal. Police officers can either attend workshops sponsored by other universities or colleges or schedule one for themselves through groups such as WHOA (www.haltabuse.org). As long as campus police officers have a basic knowledge of the Internet and Web browsers, they can learn how to track down online harassers and stalkers and how to work with victims in a day's training.

CMU Cares

When Steve Johnson became Central Michigan University's (CMU) Sexual Assault Services Coordinator in 1996, he began to see online-related cases, mostly relating to chat and e-mail.

"One I remember clearly is a man allegedly from Florida who started chatting with one of our students," Johnson says. "After about a month of chatting, he showed up at her apartment, talked a bit—and raped her."

He understands that this was an extreme incident but feels he should have been able to prevent it. "We've had a few cases that involved e-mails where the offender would make comments and write things that were sexually explicit," Johnson says. "Some students ignored the letters and they went away. Two that I recall went to the local police, with one offender being caught."

Although online harassment and related issues are covered in student orientation, Johnson thinks more can be done to enlighten the students.

"I'm sure there are more cases happening here. However, students are not coming forward," Johnson says. "This leads me to believe that we must address it better so students recognize it for what it is, and that they—the students and the faculty—are aware there are people at the university who care and want to help."

A Distinct Challenge

Other universities and colleges find the Internet a distinct challenge.

"There actually have been very few reported cases at the University of Maryland University College (UMUC) involving online harassment, stalking, or identity appropriation," says David Freeman, vice president of communications at UMUC.

Those cases were handled swiftly and well, prompting UMUC to update its institutional policies to address online-related issues and other threats to the students, faculty, and staff. This included adding an article titled "How to Protect Yourself on the Net" to all CAPP (Computer Application) courses as required reading. The article, co-authored by UMUC Instructor Patti Wolf and me, is available to enrolled UMUC students online at the university's Web site.

"We are keenly aware that the combination of technological advances and increased populations here at the university certainly increases the probability of such situations," Freeman says. "Our Institutional Technology unit is constantly assessing technology that will enable us to provide the most effective protections to our faculty, staff, and students."

Although most students and faculty think their school-related e-mail accounts are private, they'd probably be surprised to know that the school usually monitors e-mail and other communications.

"Universities have the right to read your messages and discipline accordingly," says Howard Meyer, former trial lawyer, Senior Trustee Emeritus, and former instructor at the University at Buffalo. "If I was sent child pornography and I opened it, the university could likely be monitoring me. And if I solicited that child pornography, there could be consequences. Heck, 40 percent of corporations occasionally audit and review e-mail, so nothing is actually private, and if you think it is, think again."

Howard recalls an experience he had while teaching at UB. "I had a girl in my class, what I call a 'hair-flipper.' I never exchanged a word with her, which is rare for student/teacher interaction. She received a 'C' at the end of the semester and then sent me an e-mail asking why her grade wasn't higher. I replied, and in my message I mentioned that her being attractive was disconcerting—a joke that obviously didn't go over too well via e-mail. She went straight to the

Dean with that e-mail, claiming it was sexual harassment. I've learned to be careful when writing my e-mails."

Endnotes

1. United States vs. Jake Baker and Arthur Gonda—890 F. Supp. 1375 (1995).
2. Watts vs. United States—394 U.S. 705 (1969)—where a threat must be a "true threat" to be considered illegal speech.
3. A Ponzi scheme is a type of investment fraud. The person who runs it promises high returns/dividends that people wouldn't get with traditional investments. But, instead, the schemer uses money from subsequent investors to pay off the initial ones. This usually falls apart when the schemer either flees with the money he or she has collected or when no more victims take part and the "dividends" are no longer paid out.

   The scheme was named after Charles Ponzi of Boston, Massachusetts, who operated an investment scheme in the early 1900s. He guaranteed investors a huge return on their investments, but in the end could not pay the dividends. He was found guilty of mail fraud and imprisoned for five years. Thus the Ponzi scheme was born (http://home.nycap.rr.com/useless/ponzi).

Encryption Made Easy

> ## Encryption
> Encryption scrambles messages so that they are unreadable by anyone except the sender and the recipient. One of the most popular encryption programs is Pretty Good Privacy (PGP).

> ## Electronic Signatures
> A form of encryption that allows online users to sign documents, pay bills, bank, and shop online with an electronic or digital signature unique to only them.

You've probably heard about encryption and electronic signatures (also called e-signatures or digital signatures). In this chapter you'll become more familiar with their functions—and how they can help you.

Encryption Is Built into Your Web Browser

"Whenever people use an online commerce Web site that has a 'secure server' or they go to a site that begins 'https' instead of 'http,' they are using the encryption built into their browser," says Stanton McCandlish, technical director of the Electronic Frontier Foundation

(EFF). "But encryption is useful for a lot of other things, many of which most people don't think about."

For instance, you might want to think twice the next time you send an e-mail about a project you're working on for your company. Why? A competitor could be on the watch for anything new going on in the company you work for and could be intercepting your e-mail.

Or, you might be exchanging e-mail with someone you'd rather your spouse or another family member didn't know about. And what if you are planning a vacation—you might be e-mailing your credit card information to a travel agency.

"Your e-mail is being read by someone other than the intended recipient, guaranteed," says Neil Schwartzman, founder of PeteMoss Publications and publisher of the popular Spam e-newsletter. "Do not put anything on your computer that you would not share with your mother. If you must put it on your computer, then encrypt it."

Here's another scenario. Someone forges messages in your name on a message board, in newsgroups, or in e-mail sent to your family or employer. It may sound farfetched, but it can and does happen.

Checking Your Web Browser

Microsoft Internet Explorer (MSIE; v5.0 or higher, see Figure 17.1):
- Click on Tools in the top toolbar, then Internet Options.
- A separate window pops up, click on the Content tab.
- Click on Certificates and this shows what (if any) certificates you have acquired from your visits to Web sites. Clicking on Advanced Options allows you to change the settings so that you can send Secure E-mail with Outlook (the incorporated e-mail program with MSIE), among other settings.
- A "lock" graphic that appears in the bottom right of the browser lets you know when you're visiting a page or site that is secure or encrypted. If the lock is open, the site is insecure (usually a personal page or informational). If the lock is closed (or locked), the site is secured/encrypted (usually a site where you have to use a password to enter it, or a commerce site).

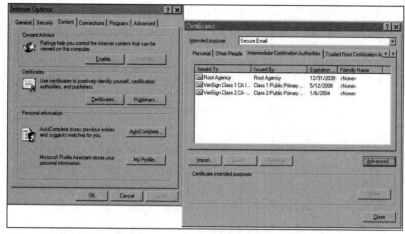

Figure 17.1 MSIE e-mail.

Netscape Communicator/Navigator (v4.75 or higher, see Figure 17.2):

(Note: Netscape is a little more comprehensive when it comes to privacy/security in its browser.)

- Click on Communicator in the top toolbar, then Tools, then Security Info.
- A separate browser window pops up with a menu on the left side.
- Security Info: Lets you know if the Web page you are currently visiting is encrypted or not; if it isn't (usually a personal Web page or informational site), you can click on Open Page Info to find out what other pages are on that particular site. If it is encrypted, that means you are most likely on a commerce or secured site, such as a shopping site or a site where you have to enter a username and password (the graphic of a "lock" is in the lower left-hand corner of the browser). On an encrypted page, a certificate will be associated with it.
- Passwords: If you use a password in Communicator, you can designate it to protect your certificates. This is especially useful if you share your computer with someone else.

- Navigator: Change any settings here if you want to be warned when you enter, leave, or view an encrypted page, etc.
- Messenger: This is Communicator's e-mail program and this is where you change security settings so that you can encrypt or sign e-mail or newsgroup messages.
- Java/JavaScript: The default is that no applet or script is allowed on your computer without your permission; if you accepted any, they are listed here and can be deleted or edited.
- Certificates: This allows you to create a certificate (or key—see info about PGP in the next section) so that if you do encrypt messages, others will know they came from you. You can also view certificates saved from others.
- Cryptographic Modules: This provides more information on the encryption Netscape offers.

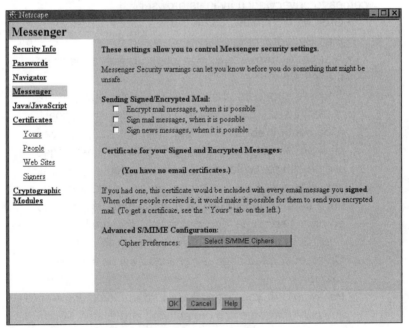

Figure 17.2   Netscape e-mail.

What's PGP?

PGP, for Pretty Good Privacy, is an encryption program developed by Philip Zimmermann in 1984.

"I began PGP as a human rights project back in 1984, although I'd had the idea floating in my head before then," Zimmerman says. "I was involved with a grassroots political movement and I felt it would be useful to have something that would protect their communications."

A paper he wrote about PGP was published in 1986 in *IEEE* magazine, but he didn't officially release the program until June 1991. At that time, the need for encryption wasn't a necessity, but there were Bulletin Board Systems (BBS) that utilized it. Also using it were people who encrypted files on their computer hard drives or who wanted to send and receive files safely from one computer to another.

It has only been in recent years that PGP and similar encryption programs have become more popular. People are realizing that what they think is private online just isn't.

"Before the Information Age, we had privacy. Every conversation was private because it was face to face or over the telephone," says Zimmerman. "Now all communications technology has undermined privacy and we need to get it back. Encryption helps do this."

Stanton McCandlish, technical director of the Electronic Frontier Foundation (EFF) agrees. "*Everyone* should use encryption," he stresses. "There is a slight learning curve to use the program but most mass market encryption software, like PGP, have easy graphical interfaces and pretty simple 'quick-start' documentation."

So, how does PGP work? The easiest way to find out is to download an encryption program and follow the instructions, but basically, PGP works like this:

1. During installation, you designate your full name and the e-mail address you will be using so that a "key pair" (a key is essentially encrypted information, such as the message you are sending or receiving, a signature file, your passphrase, etc.) can be assigned to you. The pair consists of a private key and a public key. The public key is what you use when sending a message so that the recipient—or anyone who reads it, such as when it is broadcast on a newsgroup—will know that you are the real author of that message.

2. Now you need to create a passphrase, which will protect your private key. Make sure you write down your passphrase somewhere, preferably on a piece of paper and kept someplace

secure. You don't want to save it in a file on your computer. Usually, a passphrase is at least eight characters long with a combination of letters and numbers. Your key pair will then be generated.

3. You can then "publish" your public key, and store your private key in a safe place, such as on a ZIP disk, diskette, or CD. Remember, if you lose the original private key, you can't decrypt anything encrypted to that key. Depending on the program you install, you should be able to publish your public key to a Web site called a keyserver. People who then want to send you private e-mail can download your public key from one of these key-servers, or you can send your public key to them directly. Some people also place their public key on their personal Web site or in their signature file. The caveat to using encryption is that both the sender and the recipient need to be using the same encryption program, although just about all versions of PGP, free or commercial, are compatible with each other.

4. To send encrypted messages to someone, you need his or her public key, from the person or from a keyserver. You encrypt your message to the public key, copy, and then paste it into the text of an e-mail message, or, if you are using a program that incorporates encryption by way of a plug in, such as Qualcomm's Eudora, the message will be automatically encrypted for you without copying and pasting. The same thing goes with decrypting the message. The recipient then decrypts the message with his or her private key. To receive an encrypted message, the sender uses your public key to encrypt the message, e-mails it to you, then you decrypt it with your private key.

Once you exchange public keys with one or more people, you can add their public keys to a "keyring" in your encryption program so that you have them handy instead of having to go back to the keyserver each time you want to send an encrypted message. To encrypt a file on your hard disk, use your private key.

Cynthia went online one day and found someone was forging messages in her name on a newsgroup. The messages were intended to get others in the newsgroup mad at her—and it almost worked. After explaining to the newsgroup that she hadn't posted those messages, she found an encryption program, began using it, and hasn't had a problem since.

"Now I PGP-sign all of my real messages so that they can be verified as having come from me. This person who impersonated me cannot forge the PGP signature," Cynthia says. "Sometimes people get confused by the PGP signature, but I simply post an explanation and the URL of my Web site, where there is an introduction to PGP."

Examples of Encryption

A Public Key will look something like this sample:
Cynthia's Public Key:
-----BEGIN PGP PUBLIC KEY BLOCK-----
Version: 5.0
Comment: PGP Key Server 0.9.2

```
mQCNAzJLTZUAAAEEANDW3sS9W3TaxNtQ9GROA
ooL7yKg6nMgBYSWlGlrQi5bkuUvYjVgcYV5pMpnxp92S
GbKC7Rka1asj/fnA8hp5kAKnQDg/PhQwaRv6l6XUH
QLINJyVC0KYqfVurk6Q+pvlruQfQgOdxa7LnzbF5Pm
WlGp7VHqP2ltWB1LUpdZB1XtAAURtC5DeW50aGlhlEF
ybWlzdGVhZCBTbWF0aGVycyAoY3luQHRlY2hub21vbS
5jb20ptB1UZWNobm9Nb20gPGN5bkB0ZWNobm9tb20u
Y29tPokAlQMFEDJLTpQdS1KXWQdV7QEBSeoD/3l/nTo
7oA1kluwjrYkbTUOv81odX5CnG99UCa3sqRfjeSyc80Yh
A2Spom8ZgiNEQCl5OQtUmifvZLCNm7U6OcjWipyXNzlh
MMtAcJW1k2R8MU8pqoZsf25hOQyTgFmSGmdeOoczU
7BmolUak4f/2rsxzPgC4mDrTRNDwTEh7u//tDJDeW50a
GlhlEFybWlzdGVhZCBTbWF0aGVycyA8Y3ludGhpYUB0
ZWNobm9tb20uY29tPrQzQ3ludGhpYSBBcm1pc3RlYW
QgU21hdGhlcnMgPGN5bnRoaWFAbWluZHNwcmluZy5j
b20+tDVDeW50aGlhlEFybWlzdGVhZCBTbWF0aGVycyA
8dGVjaG5vbW9tQG1pbmRzcHJpbmcuY29tPg===hXyP
-----END PGP PUBLIC KEY BLOCK-----
```

Cynthia mentions that she PGP-signs all her messages. This is, in effect, her electronic or digital "signature." If you received a message from her and wanted to verify that it did indeed come from Cynthia, you could do so by checking the signature using her public key. Yes, it sounds confusing, but once you begin using an encryption program, you'll find it easy to understand.

A sample message from Cynthia is shown below:
-----BEGIN PGP SIGNED MESSAGE-----
This is a PGP-signed message. The signature will be longer for longer messages.
Cyn
(See www.technomom.com/pgp.html for further info on PGP)
-----BEGIN PGP SIGNATURE-----
Version: PGP Personal Privacy 6.5.8

iQCVAwUBOfNHEB1LUpdZB1XtAQGcvAQAxr9NOOQ
YovebGwv28aheAnUIAJjsRYXPbU+0QeUBwf3MRFUxPo
6X26donmHmoofLalabjaIFEvnEmAWfrQkKZ+xvNSCvR
WBt9s8EHSTm/5ARzL89xV4QUUkimgj2cG9xe9b7liPyN
CTW6Rg4cbPDmnpEbu2FT4qvzjxoZMAseU==Tbam
-----END PGP SIGNATURE-----

Then there are PGP Fingerprints (see Figure 17.3), which are shorter versions of public keys. People sometimes use a PGP Fingerprint because it is not only easier to add onto the end of every message sent out, but the more often the Fingerprint is sent out, the more likely someone will notice if another person is trying to forge your key(s). Eudora, a popular e-mail program from Qualcomm, offers encryption capabilities such as these.

This is an example of a PGP Fingerprint:
703A C3CA AFF2 1D7B 97A6 839D 7A80 DE98 0550 E8F2
Here is an example of a PGP encrypted message:
-----BEGIN PGP MESSAGE-----
VersionPGPfreeware 7.0.3 for non-commercial use <www.pgpi.com>
17-7
qANQR1DBwU4Dh0YjJERFJwcQB/94APRAEG8DZq5
zKluo1kNa1xg+u5l9eE6l+3ZcXDKERHrTyeXwmfjOwAGr
zaVbUreZXKgKKNnWbXT6bH2LffGuujwGoKS0wos+yxC
OOMrVaCQy5zoLaeZ88ZoRr1Wlld1d5rl5J1ew8m9NRPt
nzjGxfZgcbVdbO4eDJ8Bl+FZXmlnFlFdqisnPcXxQZTks2
oJ/0NfLVaR6oa2J3LHDRrrAxPfUjQyRhjlrnhQ4
30eruNTVY1SpKDxMyoeXU0KFmYyoJz4wQZUfWqV
cnwEAwqeN3O/QT99f9ffgMXpZh68PM23HSwPBKS4jAX

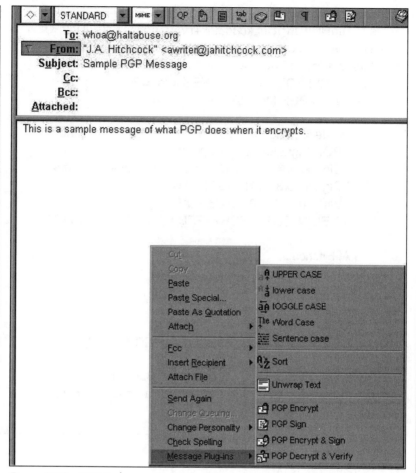

Figure 17.3   PGP Eudora.

8sZxgOV/L0i7CvFI5AAKtGehbMrDneCACpbfsi6/tdXAFu4
9ppYVLFYOYWrLpW1hTxUpKjpTJavloadmBzHzCPIFqg
GzStYRTYWLYscgKBiCOGt7RPEMR5I0c4oEHh8KnuzjZ
uGGGe1Rr6Spd9UE7V8xids5ZVdZucks0LKuIm5B5vZVU
6C6rxMtM5zOhyCOskVG6mC6vIz2F+U4KoKhlly/17w25
RYAdjo1oiXLNPEgKrNRr023yG7H/gpJAzxHHsdq6B2IIU
EljzzkoWASJDhSOlOCoatQoUu9NWqP2XJh2kv4azTTK
Bq6tSObd1G7nnBPdqp4Qob+CgPfKPKhKC/QtgtTg+Bt2
52c1b42k5ZAKZBF9cuidTycAmnqbxEXR3TEVQNbHPE
KiR0YCGEwkQMHPK78MK2JMjyAGeM+ZkxVEtePJw3w
4RY/WWxMdtjKTf+jzmwRKJVDgH1xpQcyeq3ie+AA5xY

W6vRyNhb+sMI7MS3YFBLRbf6h2nd5/IXw2eca40UpPP7
s04i1uaHBVUwuQcLkc8d69lk+rVyu2bgtjcn+RGwDdl/FU
5+tgUWmlot7QjnU+ftNTQcXZnEvLx30KUIxzbFhCDumh
1U59JhMnzt457wG2HGxYdWWfOVUBujzftJvjxd1HYc3z
51NaNS3KLPODJB9ABhgUfVSyNPjg==PcTv
    -----END PGP MESSAGE-----

After decrypting the message, this is what was sent:
*** PGP Signature Status: good
*** Signer: J.A. Hitchcock <awriter@jahitchcock.com>
*** Signed: 5/3/2001 113521 AM
*** Verified: 5/3/2001 113809 AM
*** BEGIN PGP DECRYPTED/VERIFIED MESSAGE
***

J.A. Hitchcock
Author & Lecturer
http://www.jahitchcock.com

*** END PGP DECRYPTED/VERIFIED MESSAGE ***

All that for such a short message! But if privacy really concerns you, then PGP—or a similar encryption program—is the right thing for you.

Electronic or Digital Signatures

Wouldn't it be great to get a loan online, open a bank account, or have funds transferred without waiting for paperwork to arrive in the mail for a signature, or going to the bank in person? Electronic (otherwise known as "digital") signatures may help you avoid those inconveniences.

With the passage of the Federal Electronic Signatures in Global and National Commerce Act in 2000, online "digital contracts" that consumers agree to have the same legal status as pen-and-paper contracts (see http://thomas.loc.gov/cgi-bin/bdquery/z?d106:s.00761:). You can purchase a car, buy an insurance policy, get a new or second mortgage, receive credit card and other bills electronically, and much more—either on the company's Web site or via e-mail.

"Read the fine print before you enter into an online contract," says Gail Hillebrand, senior attorney with Consumers Union's West Coast Regional Office. "As consumers turn to the Internet to handle more of their business transactions, they need to be vigilant to avoid unwittingly sacrificing their legal rights in the process."

This means that if you decide to use an electronic signature and then change your mind, you should be able to do so without paying a fee. If you don't carefully read the agreement on the Web site you're dealing with, you could end up with more trouble than the service is worth. Another caution: if you decide to conduct business transactions online or receive legal papers via e-mail, make sure you check your e-mail regularly or you could miss a deadline and end up paying late fees or other fees.

An electronic or digital signature is set up with you and the online business you choose. Ideally, in the future there should be one standard electronic signature, no matter which software or hardware you use. But now you must check with the online business to see what they prefer as a signature standard. The electronic signature is a unique key, much like a PGP public key, and thus impossible to forge (in theory).

The Consumers Union offers these additional tips when considering using electronic signatures:

- Use only one e-mail address for all your personal business.
- Read the description of what software and hardware you will need to access future electronic notices.
- As with any contract, read the fine print. Don't agree to a contract you don't understand.
- Print your order, confirmation screen, and any electronic notices you receive, and save the hard copies for later use.
- Keep a list of the businesses with whom you have consented to receive electronic notices, and notify those businesses if your e-mail address changes.

Protect Your Computer!

Trojan

Much like the fabled Trojan Horse the Greeks built to gain entrance into the city of Troy, a Trojan in computerese is a program designed to perform functions on a computer without the computer user knowing it's there.

Virus

A program that "infects" your computer. Some computer viruses are a mere nuisance (snow or dancing animals may appear on your screen for a few minutes, then disappear), but others can cause serious damage, such as corrupting or deleting computer files. Some—like the Melissa virus, which appeared on computers worldwide in 1999—can wipe a hard drive clean.

Hackers

You've seen them in the movies and on TV. Most hackers are people who want to test a Web site or Internet connection just to see if they can break in, sometimes for the fun of it, sometimes at the owner's request. Some are called "crackers," people who are out to cause trouble and possibly fraud by doing something such as breaking into the computer systems of banks to transfer money to hidden bank accounts in their names. They are also known to wreak havoc at a former employer's Web site or LAN,[1] steal someone's Internet account to spam or harass someone, copy files from hard drives, wipe a computer hard drive clean, and more.

We may think about protecting ourselves when we go online, but most of the time we forget our computer is vulnerable, too. This chapter covers computer viruses, firewall/Internet security, hackers, passwords, and cookies (not the kind you eat).

Viruses

Most computer systems—desktop, laptop, or notebook—come packaged with anti-virus software, such as McAfee VirusScan or Norton Antivirus. What you probably don't know is that unless you use your anti-virus software properly, your computer won't actually be protected.

What are viruses? There are four types to date:

1. *Boot virus*: This virus places its code in your computer hard drive so that when you start or "boot up" your computer, the boot virus loads and runs first. After the virus finishes its run, the original boot code loads and you're none the wiser.

2. *File virus*: Attaches itself to executable programs—usually with an .exe extension, such as runme.exe—so that when you run the infected program, first the virus code executes and then the program loads and executes, and the computer is infected.

3. *Macro virus*: Attaches its macros—quick commands that can be created in programs such as WordPerfect and MS Word—to templates and other files so that when you execute the program, the first invisible instruction is to execute the virus.

4. *Companion virus*: Attaches to the operating system (OS), such as Windows, Linux, and DOS. So, if you were in DOS and gave the command to run a file called runme, instead of looking for runme.exe (usually the default when running a file), a companion virus places its code in another file with a .com extension that matches the existing .exe file. Then, the infected file named runme.com runs instead of runme.exe.

To avoid virus infection, learn how to update your virus definitions. Do this at least once a month, though many experts recommend weekly, if not more often. Virus definitions are a database of viruses for which your anti-virus software scans. A scan can be set to run automatically on a daily, weekly, or monthly schedule, or you can manually start a scan. Many anti-virus programs come with automatic updates so that every time you go online, the anti-virus program automatically checks for updates. If there are any, the program will automatically download and install the updates. This is a highly recommended option if it's available in your anti-virus program.

If you forget to update the virus definitions, don't be surprised if your computer gets hit by a new virus—and you might not be safe even if you don't open that e-mail attachment.

Speaking of attachments, the ground rule is to never open an attachment that comes with an e-mail message. Period. The exception is when someone lets you know ahead of time that he or she is sending an attachment.

You may have heard the stories of people who have clicked on cute attachment names, expecting to see a fun program, but get a virus introduced into their computer instead. As previously defined, viruses can range from simply annoying to very destructive.

A worm—such as Sircam, which proliferated in the summer of 2001—is similar to a virus, but it doesn't need to attach itself to a certain file or sector on your hard drive. Once a worm is executed, it seeks other people's systems instead of part of your system to infect. Then it copies its code to the other systems. An example is an infamous worm that discusses Snow White and the Seven Dwarfs. It usually arrives in your e-mailbox looking like this (misspellings and all):

```
To:   your e-mail address
From: hahaha@sexyfun.net
 Subject:    Snowhite and the Seven Dwarfs
- The REAL story!
 Attachment: DWARF4YOU.EXE  (or  JOKE.EXE,
GIRL.EXE, or MIDGETS.SCR)
 Today, Snowhite was turning 18. The 7
Dwarfs always where very educated and
polite with Snowhite. When they go out work
at mornign, they promissed a *huge* sur-
prise. Snowhite was anxious. Suddlently,
the door open, and the Seven Dwarfs enter..
```

Your first reaction is likely to be to open the attachment, which in this case would be DWARF4YOU.EXE. You open it, expecting something cute that finishes the "joke." Instead of something cute, you get a worm. This type is called a W32/Hybris, which overwrites certain files on your hard drive and then sends out a copy of itself via e-mail by utilizing the address book in your e-mail program. The copies of the Hybris virus e-mail are sent by the infected user (you) without your knowledge to everyone in your address book.

With the Sircam worm, you would receive what looks like a legiti-mate e-mail from someone you know. It would look something like this:

```
From : "Michael Kearns"<mmkearns@
       worldnet.att.net>
To : anotherwriter@hotmail.com
Subject : Inn Creek Commentary
Date : Wed, 8 Aug 2001 21:58:29 -0600
Attachments :
InnCreekCommentary.doc.lnk (209k)

Hi! How are you?
I send you this file in order to have your
advice
See you later. Thanks
```

"The subject line may seem appropriate for you because these are people you are communicating with who are working on similar top-ics," says Jose Nazario, a researcher at Crimelabs (www.crimelabs. net). "Sircam goes through the address book in Outlook (Microsoft's Web browser e-mail program), sends e-mails to the people listed there with a subject line that is actually the title of a document on the victim's computer. It uses that title as its payload, so to speak. So the attachment has an appropriate-sounding name."

If you open the attachment, you may be in for a world of trouble, says Doug Muth, technical director of WHOA. "Under certain condi-tions, Sircam may attempt to delete all files and folders on the hard drive," he says. "That's why regularly maintaining backups of your hard drive is important."

A virus doesn't have to come as an attachment to infect your com-puter's hard drive. If you download a shareware or freeware program or even a retail program from a secure site, sometimes a virus will be attached. There have also been reports of commercial software—pur-chased in retail stores, boxed, and shrink-wrapped—that have viruses in them. Sometimes these viruses are activated by a triggered event, meaning the virus may launch on a certain date, by a specific series of keystrokes, or when a simple DOS function is performed.

This is what happened when the Code Red virus came on the scene in 2001.

"In a nutshell, Code Red is a common 'buffer overflow,'" Nazario says. "What this means is an attacker attempts to place more data into a storage space than has been allocated, only because the software on the attacked computer system wasn't coded to do any checks on the size of the input. This means the computer receives arbitrary instructions, in this case 'download and execute this software,' which is part of the worm package."

The good news is that Code Red only affected computers and systems running Windows 2000 and NT operating systems. Reports claimed that more than 500,000 computers were hit by Code Red. Since most consumers use Windows 3.x/95/98 or Me, it didn't affect the average online user, although it did create problems for many Web sites, often shutting them down for hours.

"The only thing that is assured in the anti-virus markets is change," says Beau Roberts, director of product marketing for McAfee.com. "New viruses are discovered every day. While the operating systems, devices, and types of viruses may change over time, the need to protect your computing devices and data is always going to be there."

Here are some anti-virus programs mentioned in this chapter, plus a freebie:

Norton Antivirus
www.symantec.com/nav

- Automatic update of virus definitions while connected to the Internet.
- Worldwide network of LiveUpdate servers ensures fast, reliable downloads of virus definitions.
- Automatic scanning of e-mail attachments for standard POP3 clients including Microsoft Outlook, Eudora, MSN Mail, and Netscape Mail.
- Protection against viruses, Trojan horses, and malicious ActiveX code and Java applets.
- Detection of viruses in compressed files.
- Alert windows with detailed information and recommendations whenever a virus is detected.
- Quarantines infected files until they can be repaired, protecting your other data and files.
- Step-by-step Scan and Deliver Wizard for sending infected files to the Symantec AntiVirus Research Center (SARC) for prompt assistance with eliminating viruses.
- Protection against newly created macro, file, and boot-sector viruses.

McAfee VirusScan
www.mcafee.com/anti-virus

- Detection of destructive ActiveX and Java applets.
- Advanced e-mail X-Ray feature catches viruses in e-mails before new messages have been opened.
- Quarantines infected and suspicious files.
- AVERT Labs (Anti-Virus Emergency Response Team), the world's largest anti-virus research group, based in eight locations around the world, works to find the latest virus threats and distribute their cures 24 hours a day.

Freebie List
www.freebielist.com/antivirus.htm
Offers a list of several free anti-virus programs and tools.

Firewall, Internet Security, and Hackers

Even if you're using a regular modem, whether it's 24kbps,[2] 33.6kbps, or 56kbps, your computer is open for attack. Computers most at risk are those using cable or a digital subscriber line (DSL, available through telephone lines) modems because their Internet connections are on 24 hours a day. According to Ovum, a research company, the worldwide residential broadband[3]-installed base grew more than 500 percent in 2000.

Firewall or Internet security software will protect your computer from attacks, whether someone is trying to hack in, send viruses or Trojans, or commit some other mischief.

Consider what happened to Maurice, who lives in South Carolina.

Maurice, a software beta tester, had a company credit card that he used only for business expenses. He thought nothing of making purchases online, unaware that someone had hacked into his computer and stolen the credit card number. The hacker ran up charges of $1,000, including visits to porn and auto parts sites, and even a pizza-ordering site.

"I used the card online to purchase video camera batteries for an upcoming business trip," Maurice says. "My employer was ready to fire me for misuse of the card and I had no idea what he was talking about. I had to personally contact the merchants where the charges had been made to get them removed. Most of the merchants were very cooperative and provided information about who had stolen the credit card number."

That information was given to Maurice's employer, who ended up getting restitution from the credit card company for the charges that weren't removed by the merchants. Maurice never found out what happened to the hacker and never asked. But he made sure he put firewall protection on his computer right away.

"I actually purchased Norton Internet Security [NIS] the same day my boss almost fired me," Maurice says.

When Maurice first ran NIS, he discovered that his Internet connection was getting "hit" by people probing it to see if his connection was vulnerable to an attack. He was getting hit a lot more than he'd ever imagined—144 times in just the first seven days he used the program.

"What surprised me was the intensity of the attacks," Maurice says, still amazed. "It's not just once in a while but at least a dozen a day with every type of nasty Trojan you could think about."

Since Maurice was hooked up to cable for his Internet connection, he called the cable company and asked why they didn't provide better protection for their customers.

"They claimed it wasn't their policy or within their capability to protect their subscribers from attack," Maurice says. "They immediately suggested I purchase a software or hardware firewall because 'It's not our problem.'"

The "It's not our problem" reply is common. Cable and telephone companies are in the cable and telephone business—not the Internet business. When the opportunity to provide Internet service came about, they jumped on it, but many apparently don't care enough to offer adequate, or sometimes any, firewall protection. And typically they don't advise customers to use firewall protection on their own.

That's where a company like Symantec comes in—to provide reasonably priced and sometimes free firewall and anti-virus protection for your computer.

"We began working on Norton Internet Security in early 1999," says Tom Powledge, group product manager for Symantec's NIS. "The idea for the product stemmed from our analysis of Internet connectivity around the world—particularly DSL or cable. We found that with an increasing number of always-on connections, home computer users were becoming more susceptible to hacking."

Powledge's group surveyed online users to determine their level of concern for security and privacy issues. The researchers discovered that online users were concerned about protection of their personal, confidential information and viewed hacking as a threat on par with virus invasion. Powledge and his group concluded there was a good market for a security suite that included a personal firewall and anti-virus capability. They were right. When NIS was introduced in December 1999, the U.S. retail market for Internet security software grew more than 140 percent.

But before NIS, there was ZoneAlarm, from Zone Labs.

In 1997, Zone Labs founders Gregor Freund, Marie Bourget, and Conrad Herrmann realized that fast, big "pipes" connecting people to the Internet (i.e., DSL and cable modems—the always-on connections) would mean that a new type of threat could emerge. Viruses, mutations of viruses, and spyware could spread more quickly than ever, since more and more people were connected.

"They realized that the only way to truly protect a machine would be to ensure that the machine itself was fortified. You could no longer rely on the corporate network or your ISP," says Te Smith of Zone Labs. "They developed a core technology, called TrueVector,[4] which could monitor an Internet connection and, among other things, alert the user whenever a program wished to 'speak' to the Internet. That put the user in control of their Internet connection."

The first product based on this technology was ZoneAlarm, which shipped in July 1999. Free for downloading from the Zone Labs' Web site, the product has proven to be a very popular and effective program. Later that year, Zone Labs added a firewall feature, then continued to expand the product, and, finally, in August 2000, shipped ZoneAlarmPro. ZoneAlarmPro added support for local area networks, and enhanced MailSafe E-mail Attachment Protection, passwords, and advanced utilities for the techie users. The extra features in ZoneAlarmPro don't come free, although the program is fairly inexpensive and competitive with the other programs mentioned in this chapter.

"ZoneAlarm has kept my data secure and has logged all kinds of illegal attempts to either gain access to my system or to flood my ports," says Nancy, a devout ZoneAlarm user. "There were attempts to overwhelm the firewall with activity in order to bypass it. So far, no one has been able to beat ZoneAlarm, and I'm happy with my choice."

For some people, intrusions into their computer systems happen on a more personal level, as it did to Lorian.

"I was being hunted by an online predator who had fixated on me and had just enough computer skills so that I knew I needed to protect myself," Lorian says. "I was right. Shortly after installing BlackICE Defender, I caught him scanning my ports attempting to gain access. BlackICE logged his illegal activity and I forwarded that information to his ISP."

BlackICE Defender, a firewall program designed for personal computers, comes from NetworkICE, which provides firewall and other programs for businesses as well as consumers.

Greg Gilliom, CEO of NetworkICE, notes that Lorian's experience is hardly surprising. When NetworkICE first introduced BlackICE Defender, the company showed it to the biggest skeptics—journalists from magazines such as *TIME, U.S. News & World Report*, and *Business Week.*

"Most of them said, 'Hackers don't look at home computers,'" Gilliom says, laughing. "So we offered them a free copy to install on their home computers. After running it for a couple of days, the writers were amazed to see that their systems were being scanned from countries such as Israel, Poland, France, China, or Australia."

When you're connected to the Internet, your computer is part of a worldwide network and anyone can try to connect to your system. The best way to describe it is by contrasting it to your television, a one-way communication mechanism. The Internet is a two-way communication mechanism. While you're connected and accessing Web servers, your computer is listening for incoming traffic. And this is what hackers, crackers, and viruses are looking for.

Stephen Gibson, founder of Gibson Research Corporation, explains the phenomenon further:

"The Internet allows multiple simultaneous data 'connections,' and unless the computer is running a firewall program, those connections can be completely hidden and occurring without our knowledge or permission. Thus, malicious software called 'Spyware,' with its own agenda, running quietly and secretly inside our computers, can silently connect to remote computers located anywhere in the world while we're innocently exchanging e-mail, surfing the Web, or doing anything with our Internet-connected computers."

Even savvy consumers find the attacks troubling. Cynthia and her husband had a LAN set up for the home business.

"When we got a DSL connection, we installed a firewall program right away because we knew we'd be more attractive targets for hackers," Cynthia says. "We didn't think twice about it. But then when we saw the sheer number of hack attempts, we were shocked."

Cynthia realized that someone who'd been harassing her online found her new connection information and was trying to break into her computer—the IP address matched the harasser's perfectly. She knew it wasn't a coincidence. But there were other attacks not from the harasser and these attacks were not what are called a false/positive, or the firewall program thinking the user's ISP is attacking them (which does happen when the program first runs—the program has to learn the user's IP addresses to prevent hits in the future).

Cynthia says that in an average day she sees at least five attempts per hour. Most are apparently coming from people who are randomly scanning blocks of IP addresses owned by companies that provide DSL service, like the one Cynthia and her husband use. Her husband likes to chat occasionally on IRC (Internet Relay Chat), and when he does, the hack attempts go up to 20 or more an hour, because chatters tend to be on for long periods of time, allowing a hacker a lot of time to probe the chatter's computer or attack it with a virus/Trojan if there is no firewall program in place.

If you think using regular old dial-up modems is safer, think again. Trojan Horse programs have been around for quite some time, but one in particular caught the attention of Mikhail Zakhryapin, director of Agnitum Ltd., a software development company located in Cyprus.

"In 1999, one of my friends downloaded a program called Back-Orifice 1.2 and called me to say that this program would change the Internet," Zakhryapin says. "It allowed stealth installation and powerful remote administration—a real Trojan horse."

Zakhryapin went to a Web site that offered the program for free and was shocked to see how many people were downloading it. He decided to check his network at Agnitum to see if someone had infected it.

"The results were amazing!" Zakhryapin says. "From the 255 computers with dial-up modems, at least five were infected. I realized that BackOrifice and other Trojans were a very dangerous tool and a great number of people were probably infected without knowing it."

Zakhryapin spent his free time trying to come up with a solution. He installed a packet[5]-capturing program on his personal computer and dialed in to his ISP. He waited. After several hours, he discovered that someone tried to access two ports. He looked through the packets and found it was a typical BackOrifice scan. This led Zakhryapin to write a simple program he called Jammer.

"It was basically a utility that captured all the incoming packets and tried to find BackOrifice packets in the traffic, then send a message back, such as, 'Got you, hacker!'" Zakhryapin says, laughing. "After some time, a friend wrote a user-friendly interface, but it wasn't for sale; it was just for us and our friends to share. We put it on a shareware site for free downloading and found it became a popular program."

Zakhryapin and his friend worked full-time to produce a commercial version of Jammer, which is now available at their Web site. They also produced other programs that help protect your computer. Jammer kept the feature that sends a warning to the hacker and also offers the user the option of sending an e-mail with logging information about the hacking attempt to the hacker's ISP. This is consumers' revenge at its best.

Firewall Protection Programs Mentioned in This Chapter

(Note: Many of these Web sites offer free 30-day trial versions so that you can decide which program suits both your needs and your pocketbook.)

BlackICE Defender (see Figure 18.1)
www.networkice.com/products/blackice_defender.html

- Analyzes, in real time, all the communications from the Internet to your computer.
- Stops attacks while leaving normal Internet communications unaffected.
- Comprehensive "Back Tracing" identifies origination of attacks.
- Audio and visual alerts let you know when hackers are attacking.
- Manually customize BlackICE Defender to block or accept any IP address or TCP/UDP port.
- Logs malicious packets and hacking attempts into a central database for internal, civil, or criminal investigations.
- Can trust any IP address or TCP/UDP port to reduce false positives or insure compatibility with other security systems.

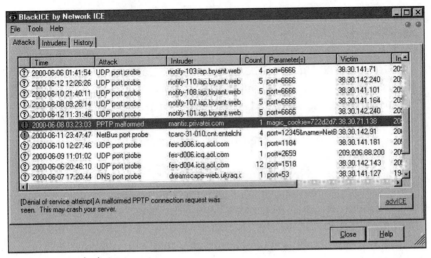

Figure 18.1   BlackICE.

Norton Internet Security (see Figure 18.2)
www.symantec.com/consumer_products/home-is.html
(includes Norton Antivirus)

- Script blocking proactively protects against certain known and unknown threats without the need for virus definitions.

- Keeps itself updated automatically.

- Intrusion Protection with AutoBlock automatically blocks systems from trying to probe your PC's ports.

- Security Assistant helps you quickly and easily configure product settings.

- Internet Access Control stops spyware and Trojan horse programs from spying on you or retrieving private information.

- Internet Zone Control simplifies firewall protection for home networks by allowing you to assign computers to a trusted zone behind the firewall.

- Alert Tracker informs you of important activities such as port scanning attempts and security alerts.

- Norton Privacy Control can prevent Web sites from tracking your activities with cookies.

- Ad blocking keeps banner ads, pop-up windows, and other Web clutter off your screen.

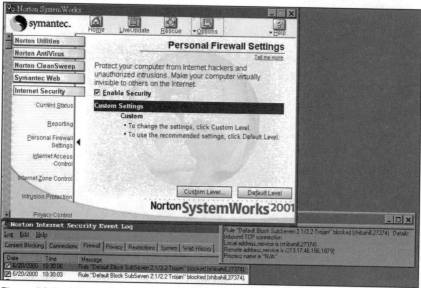

Figure 18.2   Norton Internet Security.

- 24-hour protection provides vital Internet security for dial-up, DSL, and cable modem users.
- One year of free virus definitions and firewall updates included.

Jammer (see Figure 18.3)
www.agnitum.com/products/jammer

- Multibarrier system blocks each step an intruder takes, monitors applications, and inspects both incoming and outgoing connections.
- AppWall™ technology controls any application's access to the Internet, eliminating the threat of adware, spyware, and all kinds and classes of Trojans.
- Allows specific applications to access the Internet and to deny access to others, per your instructions.
- Scanning detection modules discover intruders when they first probe your connection.
- Sends a message to the hacker's ISP warning them that their service is being used for unauthorized purposes.
- Monitors the Windows Registry for any attempt to modify critical sections.

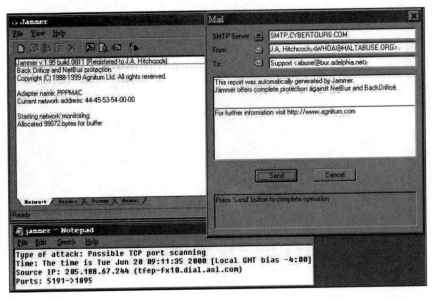

Figure 18.3   Jammer.

• Includes an advanced viewer so that you can see the hidden processes, which describes each running application and what it's doing.

• Monitors network connections and shows you which ports are active and who is connected to your computer.

McAfee Firewall (see Figure 18.4)
www.mcafee.com/myapps/firewall

• Filters inbound and outbound communications between your computer and the outside world.

• Provides comprehensive Log and Tracking.

• Integrates smoothly and transparently with the existing desktop environment while monitoring your system for security threats.

• Filters all applications, system services, and protocols including file and printer shares (i.e., NetBIOS); IP protocols (i.e., TCP/IP, UDP/IP); service-based protocols (i.e., FTP, Telnet); ARP/RARP and DHCP.

• Blocks IPX and NetBEUI on a per-device basis.

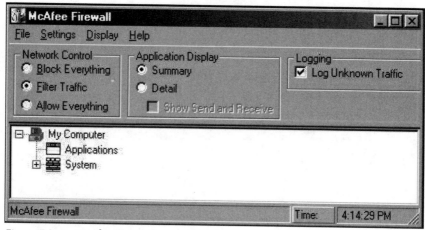

Figure 18.4   McAfee Firewall.

ZoneAlarm (see Figure 18.5)
(free)
www.zonelabs.com/products/za

- Sends immediate alerts when there is any new activity, giving you the opportunity to stop it instantly.
- Simple "yes" or "no" control over which applications can access the Internet.
- Runs in stealth mode so hackers can't find your computer(s).
- Simple and easy displays and controls.
- Customize the firewall or run it preconfigured.

GRC Net Filter (see Figure 18.6)
http://grc.com/nf/netfilter.htm

- An "abuse aware" filter that monitors all of the data flowing across Internet connections to "filter out" anything that should not be allowed.
- Monitors Internet activity to selectively block malicious and annoying content.

Putting a Spin on It

Some online users have taken matters into their own hands. Neil Schwartzman, founder of Pete Moss Productions at Petemoss.com,

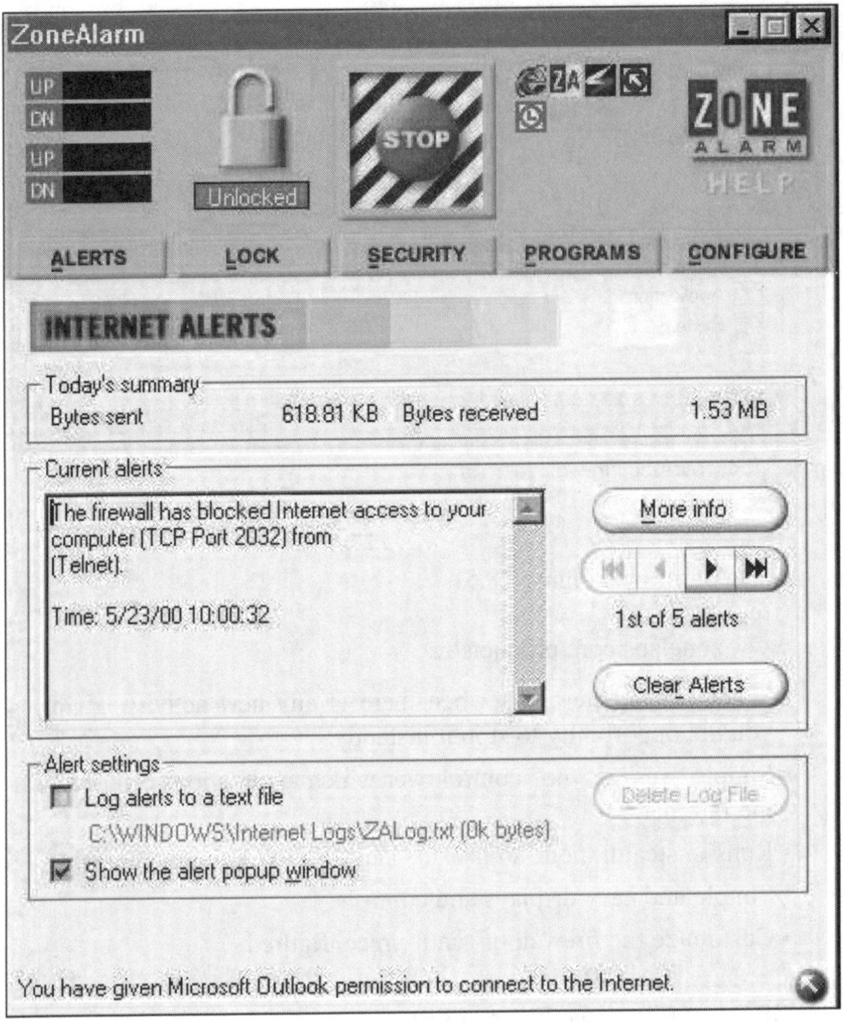

Figure 18.5   ZoneAlarm.

distributes weekly e-newsletters about spam and security. How he got to that point is an interesting story.

"Pete Moss Productions was my record company in the 1980s when I was producing independent albums for local bands," Schwartzman says. "That line of work dried up and the company remained dormant for a while. In 1992 I went online after a mass murder at the university where I worked, mostly because of my morbid curiosity about postings the killer had made to Usenet."

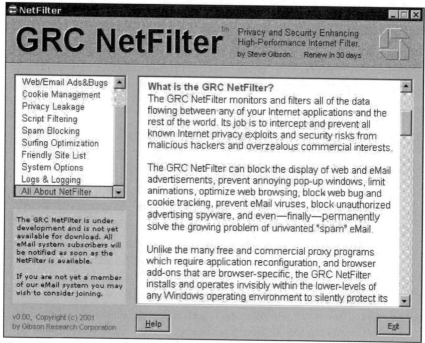

Figure 18.6   GRC NetFilter.

Schwartzman saw how fast spam proliferated not only on newsgroups but also via e-mail. Although he doesn't consider himself a techie, he began to collate and post news clippings about spam to a mailing list he participated in called SPAM-1. Not everyone on the list liked his frequent postings, so he began his own mailing list in 1996 and called it Spam News.

"One day I realized that to gain a modicum of legitimacy I needed to have a company under whose aegis I would publish," Schwartzman says. "I chose petemoss.com, harkening back to my old record company. I never quit my day job, and did this as a hobby."

Petemoss.com has grown over the years, as has his subscriber list. Although he's tried a few other weekly e-newsletters, Spam News and Security News are the only newsletters that remain. Their popularity hasn't waned.

As a result of his collating of news stories, Schwartzman has become something of a spam and security expert. He can see the potential for big problems for the future—and the present.

"Off-shore spammers and crackers, obviously operating not only outside the law, but oftentimes in places outside the reach of international law, are what we need to be aware of," Schwartzman says. "As hacktivism and cracking become more commonplace as methods of protesting government and business, crackers living in those regions will become freelance guns for hire. Indeed, this is happening to a certain extent now."

With the rise in online crimes, Schwartzman sees a future that many online users fear. It's what they refer to as "Big Brother."

"I think we will see legislation eventually, with bilateral agreements to deal with such things as advertising or spam, security, and privacy, as lawmakers become more savvy to the fact that the Net is indeed borderless," Schwartzman says. "Thus, the only effective way to deal with such problems is in tandem with international partners. Perhaps we will see an Interpol computer division stake its claim."

Schwartzman doesn't see the Internet, as a whole, being regulated.

"I'm not sure we want to," he says. "Regulate some of the activities, sure—that's happening now. Legislators will remain in a reactive rather than a proactive stance, as millions of new ideas are played out on the Net."

Rhode Island's Lieutenant Governor Charles J. Fogarty agrees to a certain extent.

"In the early 1990s, most of us didn't know what the Internet was. Then you look at it today and you see the advances and changes. You know we'll see problems and challenges that our laws need to keep up with, whether on a state or federal level," Fogarty says. "The laws have to keep up with these changes in technology because people want the same basic protections they have in the rest of their lives. I can tell you that Rhode Island, for one state, is going to make sure we keep on top of this."

An aside: Rhode Island became the 31st state to pass a cyberstalking law, in June 2001. A first offense is a misdemeanor and/or a fine; a second offense is a felony.

Common Home Computer Intrusions

The most common intrusion is still a good old virus, although the two most common traditional hacking activities that home users with cable or DSL modems experience are port scans and Trojan Horse access attempts. Tom Powledge of Symantec's Norton Internet Security notes the more common intrusions:

- Ping Sweeps: Ping is a diagnostic function generally used for network troubleshooting that reports whether a computer is online. A hacker can use ping to determine if your computer can be accessed without your knowledge.
- Port Scans: The hacker makes connection requests to selected ports on your computer to see if any of the connection requests are accepted. If the port being scanned is not in use (no listening service), the computer typically refuses the connection. Although the connection is refused, the message indicates that there is a computer at that IP address, encouraging the hacker to probe further.
- Trojan Horse Programs: Remote Access Trojans (RATs) are small servers that are installed on your computer without your permission, typically with a benign or seemingly useful program. Once installed, RATs let the attacker take complete control of your computer. Examples are Back Orifice and NetBus.
- Fragmented Packets: A Denial of Service (DoS) attack sends incomplete or fragmented packets to your computer. These packets cause your computer to request a resend or to hold the packets, waiting for the rest of the information to arrive. Enough of these requests can overload your computer and cause it to quit responding.
- Zombies: Zombies are small programs installed on your computer without your knowledge. Once installed, they let the attacker use your computer to launch a coordinated DoS attack against a third party. These are called Distributed Denial of Service (DDoS) attacks. The attacks against Yahoo! in February 2000 are examples of this type of attack.
- File Sharing Over the Internet: One of the more common and potentially most dangerous ways your computer can be hacked is if you inadvertently turn on File and Print Sharing over TCP/IP, which many home

users with networks and small businesses enable. However, if you then install a broadband Internet connection such as a cable modem, your networks are exposed to neighbors—or everyone on the Internet.

Passwords

Passwords ensure that your online connection, credit card information, various accounts, and Web site registrations are for your eyes only. But if you don't choose a password that is truly unique, a hacker or someone who is Net-knowledgeable and wants to create havoc can easily take over your online life.

The most common mistake people make when creating a password is to use something they won't easily forget, usually a pet's name, their birth date, an anniversary date, child's name, etc. If you won't forget it then it's likely that someone trying to break into your account will be able to guess your password.

The best way to create a password is to use a combination of letters and numerals, such as 1xp4u8m4. Yes, it will be harder to remember, but it's less likely to be guessed by someone else. If you insist on using something more familiar and easier to remember, then change your password once a month or more often. This keeps your private and confidential information a bit safer.

Several of the firewall/security programs mentioned offer alerts if confidential information is being accessed when you're online. You can input what confidential information you want to get alerts about, such as credit card numbers, your birth date, social security number, etc. If someone tries to use that information, the program will let you know and you can avert an undesirable situation.

Tips to Help Keep Your Passwords Confidential

1. Secure all pin numbers and password at all times. This means do not keep them in a file on your hard disk. If you want to keep them in a text file, save them

to a diskette, ZIP disk, or CD-ROM and then keep that in a safe place. Or you can write or print out the words and put them away for safekeeping.

2. Write your password on something—such as the back of a picture on your wall—but don't include any explanation for what it is. The point here is to keep others from knowing what it is.

3. Don't share passwords or pin numbers with others or use someone else's password to log onto the Internet. This sounds like simple advice, but you'd be amazed how many people are too trusting. For an example of what could happen, let's say a friend is visiting and wants to send an e-mail. You give him or her the password to your AOL account, and a week later you find out someone is using your AOL account and running up a big bill.

4. If you have a lot of passwords and find them hard to remember, consider using password management software such as Robo Form, www.roboform.com; Password Manager, www.password-manager.com; or EZ Password Manager, www.northwind-tech.com. These programs allow you to securely keep all your passwords in one place in case you forget them.

Cookies

Cookies are small text files created when you visit certain Web sites and stored on your hard drive. These files contain information about you and what you've done online. So the next time you visit the same Web site, the cookie tells that site what you did on your previous visit.

Some Web sites are just trying to keep track of how often you visit; others want to get as much information as possible, such as your buying habits at their online store, which photos or graphics you clicked on or saved to your hard drive, and your personal information—which they might share with others.

Sometimes cookies can be helpful, especially if you have to log onto a particular Web site and would rather not have to fill in that tedious information each time. The cookie file will keep your logon information so that the next time you go to the site, you're already signed in.

Stephen Gibson, the founder of Gibson Research Corporation, makes this comment:

> Cookies are not inherently evil but they are prone to abuse. If cookies were *only* used to track a person around a single, local, Web site—as they were intended—there would not be a problem. But cookies can be used to track individuals across the entire Internet, and that's a problem. When coupled with several insecurities in the way Web browsers accept input data through forms, comprehensive third-party databases can be created to assemble profiles of individual users.

The solution is not to simply kill all the cookies but to take proactive measures to tame the Web's browser cookies.

Do you have cookies?

How can you tell what cookies are on your computer and what information they have on you?

Usually, there is a file called cookies.txt in the same directory as the Web browser you use. Here's an example of what a cookie will look like:

audiobookclub.com   TRUE /   FALSE 2051222359 SITE-SERVER ID=3e0f44675cf50ea462eaf24adf12469e

tripod.com   TRUE /   FALSE 1019405226   CookieStatus COOKIE_OK

network54.com FALSE /   FALSE 1145689162   Apache bac2010d844cd74261dbbdbb1bb5488c

Looks like a bunch of gobbledy-gook, right? Believe it or not, these files give the Web site information such as whether or not you've disabled cookies on your computer, which site you visited before theirs, and your username (encrypted, such as the one for network54.com shown in the example).

How can you get rid of the darned things? If you're worried about cookies, you should get one of the firewall/security programs mentioned in this chapter and follow the instructions to clean the cookies off your hard drive. You could also open the cookies.txt file in

Notepad (or other word processing programs), select all the information, then delete it and save the file with no information in it. However, many experts warn against this, as it may cause problems when running your Web browser (although personally I've never had a problem with it).

Another option is to make your cookies.txt file a read-only document. This means you can view the document, but not make changes to it, which means that any new sites you visit that create cookies won't be added to the file. To do this:

- Find the cookies.txt file for Microsoft Internet Explorer and/or Netscape Navigator/Communicator.
- Place the mouse cursor on the file and right-click (the right button on your mouse).
- A mini menu pops up; select Properties.
- Click the Read-Only box under Attributes; then click OK.

If you don't feel comfortable going through these steps, you can reduce the number of cookies stored by turning cookies off in your Web browser. But, this does mean you'll be limited as to the number of Web sites you can visit. Many sites demand you keep your cookies turned on or you'll get a blank page or a "site not found" or similar error message.

To turn off cookies/change cookies preferences in your Web browser:

For Microsoft Internet Explorer 4.x/5.x:

- From the top toolbar menu, Tools, Advanced Options.
- A new window pops up.
- Select the Security tab.
- Click on the Internet "globe" graphic, then CUSTOM LEVEL.
- Scroll down to the Cookies options and select from:

  Allow cookies that are stored on your computer:
  - Disable
  - Enable (default)
  - Prompt

  Then Allow per-session cookies (not stored):
  - Disable

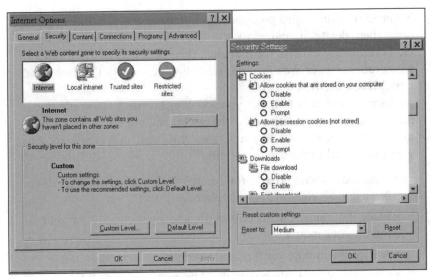

Figure 18.7   MSIE cookie.

- Enable (default)
- Prompt

If you select Prompt, be aware that you may be getting pop-up window alerts more often than you'd like. But give it a shot to try it out.

For Microsoft Internet Explorer 3.x (see Figure 18.7):

The steps are the same as above, but the only option given is Warn Before Accepting Cookies, the same as the Prompt option.

For Netscape Communicator/Navigator 4.x (see Figure 18.8):

- Top toolbar, click on EDIT, then PREFERENCES
- A separate window pops up

Click on ADVANCED, then select the option you want:

- Accept all cookies (the default)
- Accept only cookies that get sent back to the originating server (recommended)
- Disable cookies
- And/or check the "Warn me before accepting a cookie"

You can install software programs that kill or reduce the incidence of cookies. Some examples include:

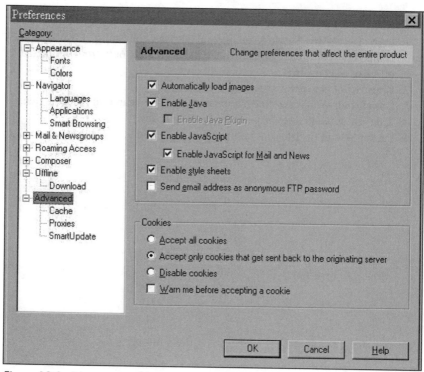

Figure 18.8 Netscape cookie.

Cookie Pal
www.kburra.com/cpal.html

AdSubtract
www.adsubtract.com

Cookie Crusher
www.thelimitsoft.com/cookie.html

Cookie Jar
www.lne.com/ericm/cookie_jar

Endnotes

1. LAN: Local Area Network; an internal network consisting of two or more computers "connected" to each other and accessible only from within that office or organization.
2. Kbps: Kilobytes per second; the modem speed.
3. Broadband: Word used to describe both DSL and cable Internet service.
4. TrueVector technology is patented by Zone Labs.
5. Packet: A unit of data sent between an origin and a destination online.

Is It Spam—or Harassment?

You've received an e-mail message that disturbs you. The subject line is something like "I Missed You Last Night" or "You Are So Hot." You open the message and find sexually explicit text. Is it spam? Or is it harassment? If the message doesn't have your e-mail address in the To: line, or if there are many other e-mail addresses in the To: line in addition to yours, then it's spam. If the message was sent only to your e-mail address, you need to determine whether it's harassment.

It is considered harassment if:

- the message contains any kind of threat
- the sender claims he or she will post your personal info online
- the sender claims he or she wants to harm or kill you
- you receive e-mail from people responding to an ad or message "you" supposedly posted

It is not considered harassment if someone:

- disagrees with something you said online, however strongly or unpleasantly
- sends you a single e-mail message that isn't overtly threatening

It's important to remember that spam is annoying, but it is not harassment. Messages posted to any open venue, such as a newsgroup, a Web-based board, an AOL discussion forum, or a chat room, or even posted on someone else's Web site, are seldom truly harassing unless they're forged to appear to come from you or contain direct threats or libelous statements.

Harassment involves repeated communications via e-mail, instant messaging, newsgroups, or other forums after the harasser has clearly been told to go away. The legal definition of harassment, according to *Black's Law Dictionary*,[1] is "a course of conduct directed at a specific person that causes substantial emotional distress in such person and serves no legitimate purpose; words, gestures, and actions which tend to annoy, alarm and abuse (verbally) another person."

This is a broad definition, which state and federal legislation and common law have narrowed and refined in various ways. You may want to check your local laws to see if they specify harassment in another way.

First Step: Full Headers

If you are the recipient of online harassment or spam, you have to find out first who sent the message and where it originated. I do want to urge you to use SpamCop (www.spamcop.net), which is a free service that does most of the work for you if what you've received is spam.

More than likely, the return address will be forged or the sender used a free e-mail account. This is where full headers come in. If you don't use an e-mail program that has the ability to show full headers, it's highly recommended you switch to one that does. (See the end of this chapter for examples of programs or services that show full headers.) Without full headers, there's not much you can do, legally or otherwise.

Here's an example of what you usually see when receiving an e-mail or reading a post on a newsgroup or forum:

```
From: Jason (sluzeinc@aol.com)
To:   money makers
Subject:    make money
Date: Thu, 31 May 01 18:42:17 EST
```

It looks like this message originated from AOL, but how can you tell if the From: line is false? After activating the "full headers," the message will look something like this:

```
From Jason Thu May 31 11:02:10 2001
  Received:    from [24.150.161.136] by hot-
mail.com (3.2) with ESMTP id MHotMailBCDFD
  1080064400431601896A18809900;  Thu  May  31
  11:00:35 2001
```

```
From: Jason (sluzeinc@aol.com)
To:    money makers
Subject:   make money
X-Reply-To: Jason (sluzeinc@aol.com)
Content-Type:   t e x t / p l a i n ;
charset=ISO-8859-1
Content-Transfer-Encoding:   7bit
```

Now, if the message you receive is spam, you can report it to the ISP(s) involved by using a free service such as SpamCop, mentioned earlier. Just highlight the entire message, with the full headers, copy, then paste it into the text box, as shown on Figure 19.1, at SpamCop's site and click on the Process Spam button.

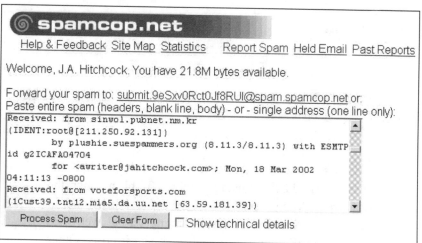

Figure 19.1 SpamCop.

You'll then get a "results" page, as shown in Figure 19.2, where SpamCop has determined whether this is really spam, and if it is, shows you which ISP(s) the complaint will go to. Then all you do is click on the Send Spam Reports Now button. SpamCop takes care of sending the e-mails for you.

Looking at the headers above, the second line is what we're interested in. It contains the IP address: 24.150.161.136. This IP address is the numerical equivalent of a Web site URL (address).

Steve Atkins, creator of SamSpade (a great resource when looking up IP addresses and other information at www.samspade.org) expands on this for us:

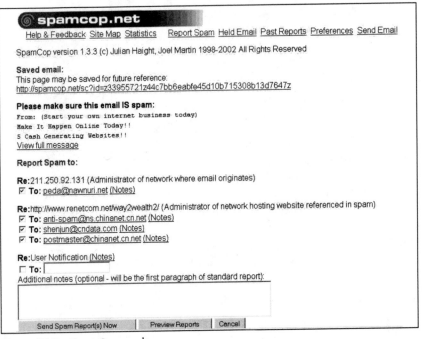

Figure 19.2   SpamCop results.

Each server connected to an IP network—such as the Internet—is addressed using a unique 32-bit number, the IP address. Many servers will have more than one IP address. For example, a server running virtual Web sites will have an IP address for each Web site it hosts. Other times, a pool of IP addresses is shared between a number of servers. For example, on a dynamic-IP dialup connection your machine will be allocated a different IP address each time you connect.

This is why full headers are so important. They tell the ISP involved who was using that IP address, right down to the second, such as 11:05:35 (see the full headers example above).

To find out who owns the IP address in our example, we just go to SamSpade, type in the IP address—or copy and paste it—in the top text box, then click on the DO STUFF button (see Figure 19.3).

We find that the WHOIS results (see Figure 19.4) show CGOCA-BLE.NET, Cablenet, a Division of Cogico Cable Inc. located in Canada, is the ISP.

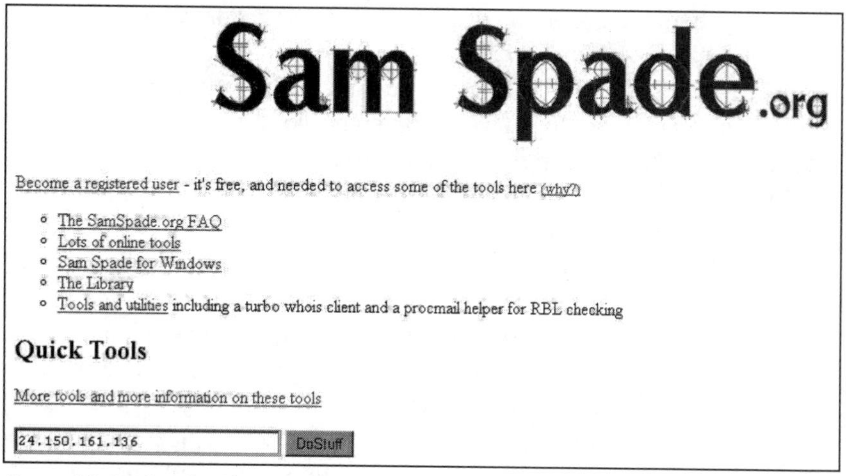

Figure 19.3 SamSpade.

WHOIS is a database of domain names and who registered that domain, with contact information that sometimes includes a mailing address, telephone and fax numbers, and e-mail addresses. If there is an e-mail address listed for the technical contact, you could forward the spam or abusive message to that person with the full headers so that the administrator can handle it from there.

If there is no technical contact or your complaint comes back as undeliverable, go to the ISP's Web site. The site usually has a page devoted to its guidelines[2] regarding spam, abuse, and harassing messages, and will provide an e-mail address where you can send complaints. Most sites use the same e-mail username, such as

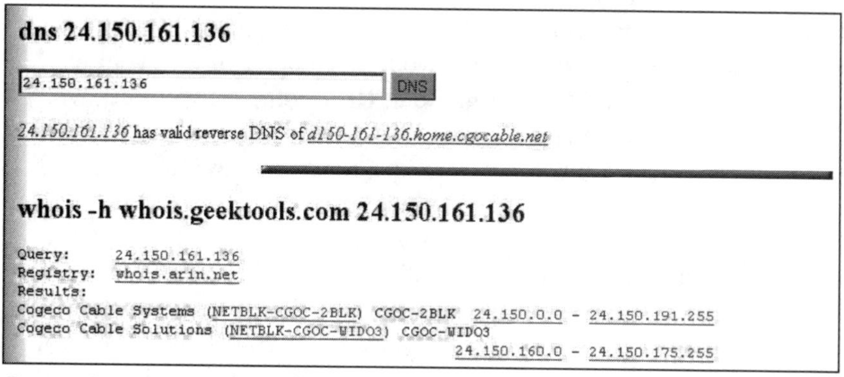

Figure 19.4 SamSpade results.

abuse@yahoo.com, so if you don't find an e-mail address on WHOIS or the ISP's Web site, try abuse@ispname and also postmaster@ ispname—the latter is the normal default e-mail address for most Web sites. Remember to send the complaint not only to the originating ISP, but also to any free e-mail services or remailers used.

In a sidebar in this chapter, you'll find a list of how to find full headers in e-mail and newsreader programs.

Now, if you've determined that you are being harassed online, follow these steps:

1. *Clearly tell the harasser to stop.* Usually, it's unwise to communicate with a harasser. However, as soon as you determine you're truly being harassed, you must very clearly tell them to stop. Send an e-mail or chat/IM message with something simple, such as, "Do not contact me in any way in the future." You don't need to explain why, just state that you don't want the person to contact you. If you want to, copy (cc) the message to the harasser's ISP or forward a copy to his or her ISP along with copies of the harassment you've been receiving (don't forget those full headers!). Do not respond to any further messages from the harasser. It is common for the harasser to claim you are harassing him. But if you aren't contacting the person after your initial request to stop, it's clear you aren't the harasser. This is valuable if you end up going to court or getting law enforcement involved.

2. *Save everything.* One of the first things many harassment victims want to do is delete all communications they've received, especially if vulgar or obscene language is involved. Don't. It's important to save absolutely every communication you have had with the harasser—e-mail, chat logs, instant messaging histories, anything—no matter how embarrassing it is. If the harasser has created a Web site about you, save copies of it to your hard drive or on a disk and print it out. Have someone you trust, who would testify in court for you if necessary, do the same. If you receive telephone calls from the harasser, have them traced immediately (call your local phone company for help with this). If you receive any kind of postal mail or other off-line communications, save them along with the envelopes, boxes, etc. Do not destroy any evidence.

3. *Complain to the appropriate parties.* If you're harassed in a chat room, contact whoever runs the Web site or server you were on. If you're harassed on an instant messaging service,

read the terms of service and harassment policies they've provided and use any contact e-mail address given there. If someone has created a Web page to harass you, complain to the owners who host that page. The best way to find out where to complain is to put the URL, such as disney.com, into SamSpade (like the IP address in the example at the beginning of the chapter) and you'll find out who owns the site and who administrates it. That's the person you'll want to e-mail. Or look on the Web site for contact information. Many sites have e-mail addresses specifically for harassment and abuse complaints. If you're being harassed via e-mail, complain to the sender's ISP plus any e-mail service (like Hotmail) used to send the messages. If the ISP(s) involved won't handle the matter appropriately by either canceling the harasser's account or warning them to stop, your next step is to call your local or county police. Make sure you ask to speak to the Computer Crimes Unit or, if they don't have one, to an officer or detective who is Net-knowledgeable. If local officers can't help, call your state police—many have Computer Crimes Units. If they can't help you, call your county District Attorney (DA) or the state Attorney General's (AG) Office. If you feel you can't go to law enforcement agencies, consider contacting an online agency, such as WHOA, SafetyEd, Operation Blue Ridge Thunder, or Cybersnitch (descriptions of each follow this list). Visit their Web sites and make sure they handle cases such as yours. Some specialize in handling online child pornography or pedophile cases, others only adult harassment or stalking cases, and others a combination.

4. *Determine your desired result.* You need to be realistic about the situation. It's reasonable to expect that you can get the harasser to stop contacting and harassing you. It's reasonable to expect that you can increase your safety online and off-line and also the safety of your family. It's not realistic to expect an apology from the harasser or any kind of payback or revenge. If you want to file a lawsuit because of something the harasser said about you, find a lawyer who will take the suit. To do this, you need to locate a lawyer who specializes in Internet-related cases, or is Net-literate and willing to take you on as a client. You do have to be realistic about this avenue, though. You'll probably have to pay significant legal and court costs, the case could drag on for months or years, and you may never get any kind of satisfaction.

Your goal should be to stop the harassment. If that means you need to change your username, e-mail address or chat handle, or stop going to a certain newsgroup, forum, or chat room, then do it. Your safety should be your primary concern. Once things calm down, you can probably go back to your old haunts. And you'll go back a much wiser and more careful person.

Some Tips for Contacting the Police, DA, or AG

- Use the telephone; do not e-mail them. Better yet, go in person. Provide them with copies of the most harassing messages you have received, not everything you've kept. Give them as much information as possible. If you've traced the messages back to a certain ISP, let them know. Anything you can provide will only make it easier for them. Be as clear, concise, and calm as possible.
- Do not contact the FBI, Secret Service, CIA, ATF, or other federal agency unless there has been a death threat directed at you, you have been physically harmed, or there is a threat of physical harm. They will refer you to the police or attorney general's office if you contact them for any other reason.

Where to Go for Help Online

Following is a partial list of the many online safety organizations available. These sites were mentioned throughout the book and are recapped here for your convenience. Do a search through your favorite search engine to see what other choices may be available.

WHOA
www.haltabuse.org

WHOA was created in February 1997 by Lynda Hinkle, a victim of cyberstalking. She initially called the organization Women Halting Online Abuse because the majority of online victims at that time were women. When I took over as president in June 1999, a vote from the Board of Directors changed the name to Working to Halt Online Abuse. More men were coming forward for help, so our new name described us better. WHOA works primarily with adults; we refer child-related cases to other organizations.

Since its inception, WHOA has grown and so has its Web site. Included on the site are a page listing every state and whether they have a cyberstalking or related law on the books, with links to the pending or current law; instructions on how to show full headers in most e-mail and newsreader programs; and explicit instructions on what to do if you've been harassed.

All board members are volunteers, and most are former victims of cyberstalking and online harassment. Victims who come to WHOA for help won't be told, "Stay off your computer" or "I don't understand what a newsgroup is."

WHOA works with law enforcement agencies around the world. We not only help enforcement officers with cases but provide training as well. Although WHOA members aren't cybercops, we are able to resolve more than 80 percent of the cases without involving law enforcement officials.

SafetyEd International
www.safetyed.org

SafetyEd International was founded in August 1998 by Colin Gabriel Hatcher (current president and CEO) as a nonprofit organization devoted to cyberspace safety education.

Hatcher, a world-renowned expert in this field, has spent more than 10,000 hours online teaching, researching, and otherwise working in the field of cyberspace safety.

SafetyEd works in many areas of Internet safety including proactive educational programs and resources and child protection and child advocacy. SafetyEd's Web site has many resources aimed at helping you enjoy cyberspace safely, with both original research and links to other useful Web sites and organizations.

Operation Blue Ridge Thunder
www.blueridgethunder.com

In 1998 the Bedford County Sheriff's Office (BCSO) in Virginia unveiled Operation Blue Ridge Thunder, the code name for the undercover cyberspace patrol that cracks down on child pornography distributed over the Internet and other computer-related crimes. Its successes have garnered the attention of local, national, and international media and of the U.S. Dept. of Justice which, in October 1998, awarded the BCSO a $200,000 grant to continue its efforts.

The people behind Operation Blue Ridge Thunder include a supervisor, two full-time investigators, an analyst, and a capable, comprehensive task force who blend their talents and resources to fight child exploitation on the Internet. They work diligently to apprehend perpetrators, protect potential victims, and educate parents, teachers, and children all over the country.

Cybersnitch
www.cybersnitch.net

Cybersnitch was developed in 1997 as a voluntary online crime reporting system enabling the public to take action against all crimes that occur using computer technology and the Internet.

Reports go directly to members of the Cybersnitch Investigators Network. The Network consists of law enforcement officers and agencies and experts in high-tech criminal investigation.

National Center for Missing and Exploited Children (NCMEC)
www.ncmec.org

NCMEC was created in 1984 as a public-private partnership and serves as the national clearinghouse for information on missing children and the prevention of child victimization online and off-line. NCMEC works in partnership with the Office of Juvenile Justice and Delinquency Prevention of the Office of Justice programs at the U.S. Department of Justice. NCMEC's state-of-the-art Web site at www.missingkids.com brings images and information about missing children and a wealth of child protection information to a global audience.

National Center for Victims of Crime
www.ncvc.org

The National Center for Victims of Crime (NCVC) is the nation's leading resource and advocacy organization for crime victims. It is dedicated to forging a national commitment to help victims of crime rebuild their lives. The National Center's toll-free help line, 1-800-FYI-CALL, offers crime victims, criminal justice officials, attorneys, and concerned individuals practical information on appropriate community resources for crime victims. It also offers information on how to find supportive counseling and skilled advocacy in the criminal justice and social service systems.

The NCVC Stalking Resource Center provides resources, training, and technical assistance to victim advocacy organizations and criminal justice professionals in an effort to promote a shared national understanding of stalking.

How to Find Full Headers in E-Mail and Newsgroup Programs

Following are instructions for showing full headers in various e-mail and newsreader programs. Unless otherwise noted, forward or send the message with full headers to the ISP(s) involved. An updated list can be found at www.haltabuse.org/help/headers.

AOL E-Mail

Before you can forward the message, you need to save it with the full headers intact:

1. Open the e-mail message you want to save, as if you were reading it.
2. Click on File.
3. Click on Save as ....
4. Identify which directory you would like to save the file in. This is done using the normal save function of Windows. If you're not comfortable with directories, save the file in Desktop. This will have the file icon visible on your regular desktop screen and be very easy to find later on.
5. Provide a name of the file in the File Name box.
6. Select the "type" as "html" if possible. If your browser does not show "html" type, just select the type as "All Files" and add ".html" to the file name generated, such as e-mail.html. The dot before the html extension is important. The objective of this step is to have the extension of the file as an "html" type file.
7. Press Save.

To forward the file:

1. Click on Write.

2. Insert the e-mail address you want to forward the file to.

3. Type any information in the body of the message, if needed.

4. To add the html file you just generated in the above steps, click on Attachments.

5. When the Attachments Window opens, click on Attach.

6. Find the file in the directory window and highlight the file name. If you followed the "Desktop" instructions, the directory name is c:\desktop. If there are too many files that appear, type "*.html" in the file name. The use of the asterisk (*) lists all files that are html.

7. Click on Open.

8. Click on OK.

9. Click on Send Now.

Please be aware that AOL only keeps messages in your INBOX for two weeks unless you save it as NEW or save it in a separate folder in your AOL directory on your computer. Additionally, a screen name of tose-mail1 has been identified as a source of help for unacceptable e-mail in the AOL system. Just enter tose-mail1 in the Send To screen. If you are outside of the AOL environment, the address is tose-mail1@aol.com.

CompuServe

The default option is that full headers appear at the BOTTOM of each received message.

Eudora Pro

1. When reading an e-mail message, look at the toolbar just above the message itself. There should be a button that reads:

   BLAH
   BLAH
   BLAH

in black and white. Click on this and the full headers will appear.

2. Select All, copy, and paste into a new message to send to the ISP, or click the forward button and the full headers will automatically be placed in the new e-mail message.

Excite Webmail

1. View the message.
2. Use the Save to Disk option.
3. Open the message's text file with your favorite text editor (notepad).
4. Copy the message from the text editor.

Free Agent/Agent (newsgroup program)

1. Click on Message, then Show Full Headers.
2. Go to the message, click inside the message pane.
3. Copy, then paste to a text file or forward the message.

Hotmail

1. Go to Options.
2. Go to Other Preferences.
3. Scroll down to Headers, then click on Advanced Headers.
4. Open the message, then forward.

Juno Version 4+

1. On the Options pull-down menu, select E-mail Options (or press ctrl-E).
2. Under Show Message Headers, select the Full option.
3. Click the OK button to save the setting.

Juno version 4+ can display MIME and HTML e-mail, but does not provide a way of viewing the HTML source for the message within Juno. To get the full source, including HTML codes:

1. Click File and then Save Message as Text File (or ctrl-T).
2. Give the file a name you'll remember.
3. Double-click on the resulting file.
4. Copy, then paste into an e-mail message and forward.

Lotus Notes 4.6 (Win 9x client)

1. Open the Properties box on the message (in the default installation of the Notes Client, it will be the first smart icon on the left, but you can also right-click on the document and choose Properties from that menu).
2. Choose the second tab on the Properties box, which is a list of fields and their contents.
3. Scroll down to the field "$additionalheaders."
4. Select the contents of the field and hit Ctrl+C to copy them to your clipboard.
5. Open a new e-mail message, put your cursor in the body of the message, and hit Ctrl+V to paste the headers there.
6. If Notes will not permit you to select the contents of the field, you'll have to manually copy them to a new message. Be very careful in doing so.

Microsoft Exchange

1. Open the message in Exchange to view it.
2. Choose File, then Properties, then Internet.
3. The header will be visible and will be highlighted.
4. Right-click, copy it, then paste into a new e-mail message.

Microsoft Internet Explorer

1. Choose Properties under File.
2. Click on the Details tab. This will show the full headers.
3. Right click and choose Select All, then copy the headers.
4. Start a new e-mail message, paste the headers into this new (and temporary) message.
5. Copy the header from the new message and paste it back onto the original, then send. The paste command doesn't work directly on the original message.

Microsoft Internet News

1. While viewing the message, click on File, Properties, then the Details tab.

2. Forward the message.

Microsoft Outlook 98 and Outlook 2000

1. Open the message and select View, then Options from the pull-down menu.

2. Near the bottom of the screen you'll see a section titled INTER-NET HEADERS.

3. Copy the headers and paste them into a new e-mail message.

Microsoft Outlook Express 5

1. Right-click on the message and select Properties.

2. Choose the Details tab and select the Message Source Button.

3. Select All and Copy.

4. Close the Message Source window and the Properties window.

5. Select New Mail and position your cursor in the body of the e-mail.

6. Paste the copied information.

Netscape Messenger

1. Select the message, then press Ctrl-U.

2. A new window opens with the full message, including the complete header.

3. Copy, then paste into a new message.

Netscape News

1. Simply click View Document Source and copy and paste or forward the message.

Newswatcher

1. Go to File, choose Preferences, and check the Show Article Headers box.

Operamail

1. Choose Options and enable [x] Show Message Headers in Body of Message.

Pegasus

1. Hit Ctrl-H (or the backspace key) while reading a message.
2. Do this *before* hitting "F" (for Forward) so that the full headers are forwarded, too.

Pine

1. From the main Pine menu, type S for Setup, then C for Configure.
2. Use the spacebar and down arrow to scroll until you reach the option [] enable-full-header-cmd.
3. Type X in the box to toggle the option on.
4. Type E to exit Configure, and Y to save changes.
5. The next time you read a message, type H and the full headers will be displayed at the top of the message. Type H again to hide the headers.

Unix

There are two ways to show full headers in Unix:

1. Save the message in a directory, then use the Type command or print it out; *or,*
2. a. Exit your current mail program and look at the mail message using mail or mailx.
   b. Show a message with the Print or P command to display all of the header lines. Note the capital P—it's important.
   c. Save the current message with the save-retain command to save all of the header lines (on some systems, Save or S— does this too).

WebTV

1. While viewing the message, hit Forward on the sidebar.

2. Address the document to yourself.

3. Completely erase the subject line.

4. Put your cursor on the first line of the body (text area).

5. Hit Return (Enter) twice. Your cursor should now be on the third line of the text area.

6. Type any Alt character on this line; DO NOT HIT "RETURN."

7. Cut and Paste the Alt character onto the subject line: (CMD+"A"), (CMD+"X"), (CMD+"V"). The Alt character should "jump" down to the message text area.

8. Hit Send. Open the Received Mail; full headers should appear.

Yahoo!

1. Go to Options.

2. Go to Mail Preferences.

3. Under Mail Viewing Preferences, go to Message Headers, then select ALL.

Endnotes

1. *Black's Law Dictionary: Definitions of the Terms and Phrases of American and English Jurisprudence, Ancient and Modern*, p. 717 (6th ed. 1991), ISBN: 0314228640, West Group.
2. Guidelines: Many Web sites also call these their Terms of Service (TOS).

A Recap: The Basics of Staying Safe Online

In this chapter, I'll present you with general advice on how to protect yourself online.

We'll start with some basic guidelines, and then get into more specific information.

Use a Gender-Neutral Username

Always select a gender-neutral username for the first part of your e-mail address or for chat or discussion forums. Don't pick something cute, such as misskitty@someisp.com or use your first name if it is obviously female. The majority of online victims are female, and this is whom harassers generally seek.

Also, don't select something that will distinguish where you live, such as dovernh, hollywood, or ImInIowa.

A combination of letters and numerals is a good bet for two reasons: it's more likely someone won't already have that username, and no one will know whether you are male or female.

In the set-up of your e-mail or newsgroup program, where you add your e-mail address, use your initials for your real name so that when you send a message the FROM line will read something like:

```
FROM: "JAH" <anotherwriter@hotmail.com>
```

Of course, you don't have to put anything in. You can have it so that just your e-mail address shows up in the FROM line.

Keep Your E-Mail Address Private

Keep your primary e-mail address private and use it only for people you know and trust. Once you get to know someone, you can then give that person your real e-mail address (see the next tip below). You'll also notice you won't get spam, or at least not as much of it, because not using your primary e-mail address everywhere online means it's less likely that spammers will find it.

Get a Free E-Mail Account

Establish a secondary, free e-mail account and use it for all your "other" online activity, including chatting, IM, newsgroups, forums, shopping, and communicating with people you do not really know. Make sure you select a gender-neutral username that is like nothing you've had before. There are many free e-mail providers, such as Hotmail, Juno, Yahoo!, and Hushmail. Perform a search using your favorite search engine and choose the e-mail provider that best suits your needs. Many free e-mail providers have built-in filtering for spam or bulk e-mail so that the majority of junk you get in your e-mailbox will go into a separate folder. However, they won't be able to filter out all the spam. For help in eliminating spam refer to Chapter 19.

Don't Defend; Don't React

It's a natural impulse to defend yourself, and that's why it's the most common reaction when someone taunts you online. But a reaction from you is just what harassers want. They are "fishing." When you reply, whether in a chat room, via IM, e-mail, newsgroups, message boards, or anywhere else online, you've taken the bait. No matter how difficult it is, ignore these people. When they realize they can't get you to react, they'll move on.

Lurk First

Lurk—meaning don't post, chat, or reply—on newsgroups, message boards, mailing lists, and chat rooms before posting messages. This gives you a chance to read what everyone else is posting before joining in. Go somewhere else if you find it's not exactly what you wanted.

Read FAQs

If you do join a newsgroup, mailing list, message board, or forum, check to see if it has a Frequently Asked Questions (FAQ) page or file. Many do. Read it before asking any questions or making comments. If you don't and start asking questions without reading the FAQ, you'll mostly likely be told to read the FAQ and you could get rude replies.

Go to Moderated Forums

Moderated forums are better than nonmoderated because they tend to weed out people who are looking to cause trouble—whether it's a troll going from forum to forum to start arguments or a run-of-the-mill harasser. Moderated forums are also more likely to take action and ban someone from the group.

Watch What You Say Online

Don't be too bold or aggressive—only write what you would say to someone's face. Many people tend to divulge things online they wouldn't dream of saying in person. This happens most often in chat rooms, where two chatters forget there are other people in the room who can read what they're saying. And if it's something very personal, it could come back to haunt them or be used against them. The other chatters could be as far away as another country, but they could also be down the street. Why take the chance? Remember: If you wouldn't say it to a stranger in an elevator, don't say it online.

Write Simple Signature Files

Signature files are a few lines of text that are added to the end of your messages, whether for e-mail, newsgroup posts, or forums. If you use a signature file, make sure it doesn't contain your full name, address, and phone number. Most signature files are set to be automatically added to the end of every message sent out; some have to be manually added—it depends on the options in your programs. A simple and short one is always best. I personally use:

J.A. Hitchcock
www.jahitchcock.com

If you must have an address and phone number in your signature file, consider the next two pieces of advice.

Get a Free Fax/Voicemail Number

If you need a contact phone number anywhere online—in your signature file or in your profile—get a free fax/voicemail number. Quite a few Web sites offer this service and yes, it's really free. You register, get a free telephone number (not always in your area code, but you can pay a nominal monthly fee for that, usually as little as $4.95/month), and then you can post it on your Web site or put it in your signature file. It can also be used to give to someone you're not quite sure you trust. If someone calls this number, he will get a pre-recorded message stating you're unavailable. First, they'll hear a short ad; that's why it's free. They can then leave a voicemail message or send a fax. You'll receive notification via e-mail that a voice-mail message or fax has arrived. You can play the voicemail message on your computer (you need speakers and a sound card for this) or open up the fax and print it.

Get a P.O. Box

If you need a contact mailing address, spend the money and get a P.O. Box in your town or the next town over. It's better to be safe than sorry!

Get an Unlisted Telephone Number

If you currently have a telephone number that's listed in the White Pages, remember that in the Information Age it's available worldwide. If you don't believe me, go to The Ultimates at www. theultimates.com. Click on White Pages, input your information, and you'll see how many directories you're listed in. Try a reverse search, too (meaning input your telephone number).

If you want to be removed from these online directories, you have to go to each directory's Web site, find the link to get your name removed, and follow the instructions. An unlisted telephone number costs a bit more each month, but it may be better than being listed everywhere!

Get Caller ID

If you decide to keep a listed phone number, then get Caller ID so that if someone harasses you, you can figure out who it is (much of the time, anyway). Also think about using *69 (reverse call) and *57 (phone trace), if these services are available in your area.

Don't Give Out Your Password

Never give your password to anyone, especially if someone sends you an IM (instant message) or e-mail pretending to be your ISP asking for it. Your ISP will never, ever ask you for your password while you're online or via e-mail. In fact, they shouldn't ever contact you to ask you for your password, period. They can get it from their own records if they need it for any reason. If you call them for support, there are a few—rather rare—instances in which the support person might ask you for your password. There's no legitimate reason for anyone to ever contact you to ask for your password.

Don't Give Out Your Credit Card Number

Don't provide your credit card number or other identifying information as proof of your age to access or subscribe to a Web site run by a company you're unfamiliar with.

Don't Let Your Children Give Out Information

Explain to your children that they should never, ever give out personal information such as their real name, address, or phone number without your permission.

Monitor a Child's Internet Use

You have to monitor what your child is doing online, even if you feel you've trained him or her to be safe online. And there's no software in the world that can replace the involvement of a concerned parent.

Be Cautious About Posting Photos

Be very cautious about putting any pictures of yourself or your children online anywhere, or allowing anyone else—relatives, schools, dance academies, sports associations—to publish any photos. Some stalkers become obsessed because of an image. There are some wonderful secure Web sites that allow you to put photos up of your newborn, wedding, anniversary, etc. You send the URL to the people you want to view the photo(s) and they're given a password to receive access to that page.

Install Anti-Virus Software

Not only install an anti-virus program on your computer, but remember to keep it updated at least once a week so that your computer is inoculated against new viruses that crop up.

Install a Firewall Program

A firewall program will protect your computer and Internet connection from hackers and Trojan viruses. Whether you have a regular modem or are using DSL or cable, everyone should have a firewall program installed. Make sure to keep it updated. If you don't, then your computer won't be protected from new Trojans and new ways to hack into your system.

An Ego Surf

How much information is there online about you? How about your family members? The best thing to do is ego surf. In other words, look for yourself online.

A good place to start is a search engine. Why? Search engines keep a list of Web pages and sites available online. They don't have every page or site available, but depending on the search engine, they can have literally hundreds of thousands listed.

How does this work? Programs called "bots" go out and search for new or updated pages, sometimes looking for specific keywords. If a page or site matches the keyword(s), it will be added to the search engine's directory.

Here's how to search for yourself online (we'll use Yahoo! for this example):

1. Go to Yahoo! at www.yahoo.com and type your name in quotes, such as "john smith," then click the Search button. You'll either get no results or a listing of Web pages related to your name. The more common your name, the more Web pages there will be. But if you take the time to go through some of them, you may be surprised to find you're on Web pages you didn't know about.

   For instance, if you signed a guestbook at a Web site, there's a good chance that guestbook is listed in a search engine. If you went to a message board located at the Web site of your favorite

TV show and posted a message, it might show up in a search. If you purchased a home or property and your town or state has a Web site, it's very likely your purchase is listed on the site. If your employer has a Web site, you may be listed as an employee. Local newspapers are putting their archives online, so if you won an award, got married, had a baby, got a divorce, got into a car accident, or were arrested for DUI, it just might be online.

Besides finding legitimate listings of your name, if someone has put up a Web site about you or forged your name in newsgroups, forums, in personal ads, or somewhere else, there's a good chance you can catch it and get it taken down or removed before any damage is done.

A nice feature at Yahoo! is that if you go Back to the first Results page and scroll down to the bottom, you'll see Other Search Engines listed. Since you already input your name in Yahoo!, if you click on one of these you'll get any results in the other search engine. Each search engine may offer different results, so it's always good to go to more than one to see what results are there.

2. Go to a metasearch engine such as Metacrawler (www.metacrawler.com), Copernic (www.copernic.com), or DogPile (www.dogpile.com). Type your name in quotes and click the Search button. A metasearch engine compiles results from several different search engines to come up with a more compact list of results (most of the time). It's a good idea to also do searches for the names of your spouse, significant other, and children. Remember to put their names in quotes to refine the search results.

Profiles

Don't fill out profiles! When you sign up for an e-mail account, for chat, IM programs, message boards, forums, or Web sites, fill out as little information about yourself as possible. You do not need to fill out everything they request. When you hit the Submit button, you will be told what information is absolutely necessary to get your account opened or to enter the chat room, Web site, etc.

Preferences

Do block or ignore unwanted users. Whether you are in a chat room or using IM, you should always check out what options and

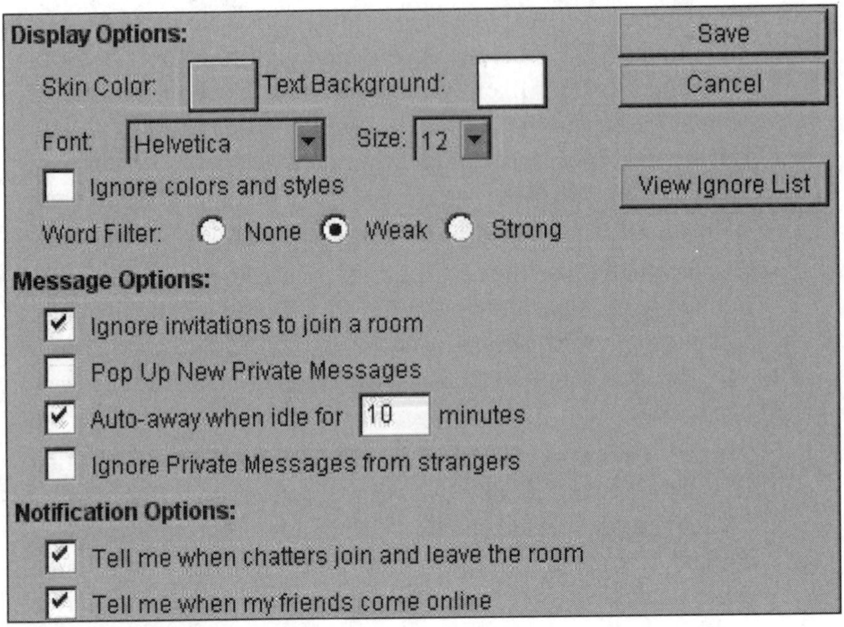

Display Options:

Skin Color: [ ]   Text Background: [ ]

Font: [Helvetica ▼]   Size: [12 ▼]

[ ] Ignore colors and styles

Word Filter: ○ None   ◉ Weak   ○ Strong

Message Options:

[✔] Ignore invitations to join a room

[ ] Pop Up New Private Messages

[✔] Auto-away when idle for [10] minutes

[ ] Ignore Private Messages from strangers

Notification Options:

[✔] Tell me when chatters join and leave the room

[✔] Tell me when my friends come online

[Save]
[Cancel]
[View Ignore List]

Figure 20.1   Yahoo! chat.

preferences are available to you and take advantage of them (see Figure 20.1).

Following are instructions for some of the more popular chat and IM programs:

Yahoo! Chat Preferences

1. When you go into the chat room of your choice, click on the pencil graphic in the toolbar just above the text box.

2. Click on the Preferences you want. It's highly recommended to check the boxes next to Ignore Invitations to Join a Room and Ignore Private Messages from Strangers.

3. Go back to the main chat window and right-click on your username.

4. A small window pops up.

5. Check the Preferences there. If you filled out your profile, click on Edit Your Profile and change or delete any information that someone could use against you, such as your real name, your age, location, and personal Web page. If you clicked on female, change it to male to be safe.

6. If anyone bothers you in a chat room, right-click on their username, then click on Ignore Permanently so you will no longer see them or their chat in the chat room, and/or check the box next to Ignore.

7. If someone continues to bother you by signing on under a different username, contact chat-abuse@yahoo.com or fill out their feedback form at http://add.yahoo.com/fast/help/us/chat/cgi_feedback.

CompuServe Chat Preferences

1. Choose the chat room of your choice, then click on the Options tab, as shown in Figure 20.2.

2. There are boxes that have been prechecked. The only ones that should be left checked are:

   • Accept incoming text styles.

   • Record room transcript. (Click on the Browse button to see which folder the log file is in for future reference.)

   • Record group transcript (same as above).

   • Track member actions. (This brings up a separate window so that you can see who's going to what rooms; click this only if you're already being harassed and need to keep track of the harasser. This pop-up window stays up even when you leave chat, so it can become annoying.)

3. If you click on the Members tab, you can highlight a name and click on Ignore so that they won't appear in any chat room you go into. You can also do the same thing once you enter a chat room.

4. Click on Enter or Eavesdrop. If you're new to the room or chatting in general, Eavesdrop is the best choice so that you can "lurk" and get to know the room before chatting.

ICQ—(Instant Messaging Program)

1. Switch to Advanced Mode.

2. Click on View/Change My Details and make sure the information there is correct. If your real name is listed, change it to initials or something else that is nonidentifying.

3. Click on Preferences.

4. Click on Security/Privacy.

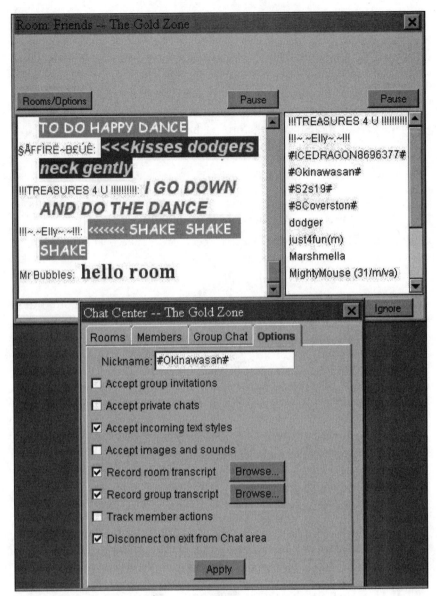

Figure 20.2   Compuserve chat.

5.   Click on the Security tab, as shown in Figure 20.3.

6.   Check the boxes for:

    • My authorization is required before Users add me to their Contact List.

Figure 20.3 ICQ security.

- Do not publish IP address.
- Security Level—High.

7. Make sure Web Aware is unchecked.

8. Take advantage of the Ignore, Invisible, and Visible Lists when someone bothers you.

To view a saved ICQ chat:

1. Click on the System Notice button in the ICQ Window and select History & OutBox or double-click on System Notice, click on My ICQ and select History, then select History & OutBox.

2. Click the System tab to display a list of events received.

3. Click the OutBox tab to show the events that you sent (see Figure 20.4). Events are stored in the OutBox until you connect to an ICQ server and if necessary, until the recipient goes online.

4. Double-click on a message to get a dialog to display the contents of that message.

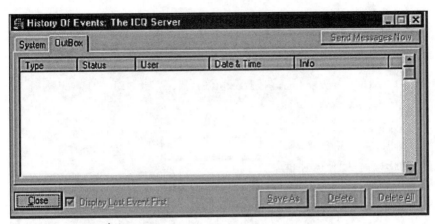

Figure 20.4   ICQ chat.

5. Right-click on System Message for options regarding the selected message.

AIM (AOL Instant Messenger)

1. Click on File, My Profile and make sure your profile is unchecked and not filled out. If it is checked and filled out, people can search for you by the information you've put in there.

2. Click on File, My Options, then Edit Preferences; a separate window pops up.

3. Click on the General tab, look at your preferences, make any changes, and check the Always View Time Stamp box.

4. Click on the Controls tab (see Figure 20.5), then check either Allow Only Users on My Buddy List or Allow Only the Users Below (then add users to the list).

5. If someone has been bothering you, check the box and add their username(s) in the Block All Users Below.

6. Click on Only That I Have An Account underneath the Allow Users Who Know My E-mail Address to Find.

7. To save a chat on AIM, highlight the chat, copy, then paste it into a document using something like Notepad or Wordpad and save the file.

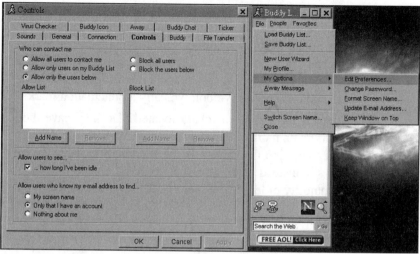

Figure 20.5   AIM.

Shopping and Banking Online

Here are some important rules of thumb for conducting financial transactions online:

1. Use one credit card for all your online purchases or trans-actions and use it only for that purpose. Then, when you get your monthly statement, you can tell if it was used illegally. It's much easier to cancel one credit card instead of several.

2. For auctions, use a service such as Paypal or Billpoint, which allow payment with a major credit card. Then, if something happens, you can dispute it through the bank issuing your credit card and file a complaint with PayPal or Billpoint. Many online merchants also use these services as a way to let you pay for items in their store if they don't accept credit cards directly.

3. Don't give out financial information, such as your checking account and credit card numbers and especially your SSN, to a Web site or anyone online unless you initiate the com-munication and know the person or organization.

4. Protect your passwords and Personal Identification Numbers (PINs) for your ATM, credit cards, and online accounts.

5. Be creative in selecting passwords and PINs for any ATM, credit card, or online account. Avoid using birth dates, part of your Social Security or driver's license number, address, or children's or spouse's names. Try using passwords that are at least eight characters in length and a mix of letters and numbers and one special symbol, typically a punctuation mark.

6. Where is the online merchant located? Do they have their own domain name or are they using a free Web site through someplace like Geocities? If the merchant is using a free Web site instead of its own, that could be a warning sign—the majority of legitimate merchants have their own domain or use a paid site, such as eBay Stores and Amazon.com Stores.

7. Does the Web site look professional? If it doesn't, you might want to steer clear.

8. If the merchant doesn't have physical contact information with the street address or telephone number, that's a warning sign.

9. Does the Web site have secure shopping? If it doesn't state so on the site and you go to the order page and your Web browser doesn't show it as being secure, don't shop there.

10. If you're buying an expensive "I have to have it" item, and the merchant doesn't have secure shopping, ask them if they'll go through an escrow service, such as Tradenable (formerly iEscrow). If they won't, you don't have to have it that badly.

11. Find out what information the merchant collects and what they do with it; most sites have privacy policies clearly stated.

12. Make sure you know everything about the product/offer—how much the item is, shipping and handling costs, taxes, insurance, guarantees or warranties, return and cancellation policies, and when and how fast will it be delivered.

13. If you're still unsure, check with the Better Business Bureau (BBB) online or in the state where the merchant is located.

14. Keep records of everything. Print your order form with payment information, product description, delivery information, privacy policy, warranties, and any confirmation notices that the seller sends you via e-mail.

15. For online banking, make sure it's legitimate and that your deposits are FDIC-insured.

16. Find out what fees are involved to switch to online banking; sometimes it's actually less expensive than keeping your regular checking account.

17. Are there fees to cancel the service? Is there a contract?

Online Auctions

Bidders can be auction-savvy if they follow this advice:

1. Check the feedback or comments on the seller. Even if there are only a few negative comments, they can guide you toward making a safe decision. If need be, contact the people who left negative feedback via e-mail to find out why they were dissatisfied with the transaction.

2. See what else the seller is currently selling. Check any past auctions by that seller. If you see more than one of the same item you want to bid on, be wary. If you see a large number of the item you want to bid on, DON'T bid on them.

3. Look at other auction items of the same type and see if their descriptions match word for word. Many fraudulent sellers use several IDs or usernames to get as many of the same products out as possible.

4. If you're having doubts, get the seller's user information, e-mail address, and mailing address and compare it to similar items up for sale. If more than one seller matches, you'd be wise not to bid on that item.

5. If the seller has only a few feedback comments and you really want an item they have up for auction, see if they take credit cards, PayPal, BidPay, Billpoint, or some other form of online payment. If they don't and only accept money orders to be sent to a P.O. Box, be wary. Many fraudulent sellers will put "ghost" items up for auction, then disappear once the money is sent. If you use a credit card, make sure it's one that will allow you to dispute a charge in case the seller does turn out to be fraudulent.

6. Read the description carefully. Make sure the item is really what you want before bidding on it or you may be stuck with a lemon (unless that's what you wanted, of course).

7. Don't get caught up in last-minute bidding at the end of an auction. Some bidders feverishly try to outbid someone who's trying to outbid them and then end up with an over-priced item.

8. Don't be afraid to e-mail questions to the seller. If the seller responds curtly or negatively, then it might not be a good idea to bid on the item.

Online Adoptions

Chapter 7 is devoted to this heart-wrenching area of fraud. But here's a quick run-down on the safest way to proceed:

1. Go through an official agency or attorney.

2. Don't give in to requests for immediate money.

3. Be leery of e-mail messages or chat rooms. Don't reveal too much about what kind of adoption you're hoping for—scam artists love to sound like what you're looking for.

4. Remove any time limits. You won't get a baby or child overnight.

5. Ask for information about the birth mother and father: for example, social, psychological, and medical.

6. Network online with other adoptive parents and parents-to-be.

7. Educate yourself before you adopt and while you're wait-ing. Adopting a child can take a while, but when you bring the child home, are you really ready?

8. Don't be rushed into a decision.

9. If you have a Web site that includes contact information and a description of the kind of child you want to adopt, use a toll-free number or have calls go to your attorney or an adoption agency.

Staying safe online requires the equivalent of the efforts you make to stay safe off-line. You use "street smarts" when you're driving, walking, shopping, banking, and playing off-line—use "cyber street smarts" whenever you're online.

Afterword

While interviewing the experts and victims whose stories and advice appear in this book, the same question was posed to me time and time again: Why do so many mature people act so immaturely when they're online?

I wish I had an easy answer, because it is a serious and growing problem. You've read here about victims who were harassed because of jealousy, rejection, or a perceived insult. You've read how some were harassed on a dare, or simply because someone did not care for their username. You've read how people paid money to complete strangers for services or items they never received, how their credit cards were stolen and misused, how their computers were broken into and hacked, and worse.

People are inherently trusting, and for some reason it seems this is even more true online. A person one would never trust or do business with off-line is often assumed to be honest and competent simply because he or she is online. This never ceases to amaze me.

I see an increasing number of situations where what would amount to a relatively minor disagreement at an off-line meeting or gathering manifests as an all-out battle online, with childish remarks and pranks too often escalating to threats, harassment, and even physical stalking.

One myth of the Internet is that users can remain anonymous. I think this explains why most of the spamming, scamming, and harassing occurs: People think they can get away with it. The average online user who gets caught up in an online fracas is *not* anonymous, even if he or she uses a free e-mail account or bogus return e-mail address. Even Net-savvy people almost always trip up in the end. The online criminal is clever, but not smart. There are some devious tricks that can be employed to thwart an investigation, but typically the trickster will slip up, doing something so obvious that it seems he or she is begging to be caught.

Admittedly, some of those who offend, cheat, or harass other people online are mentally ill. But most are sane, regular folks who, when caught, insist they never meant to harm anyone or let the situation get out of hand.

Then there are the career criminals for whom the Internet is a new and efficient tool. They learned quickly that most crimes that can be committed in person, over the telephone, by fax, or via postal mail can now be committed online.

Every Internet user should use common sense. Naturally, you wouldn't open your door to strangers and invite them in for long, private conversations about your personal life. Yet, online, too many people welcome strangers into their lives, frequently sharing their most intimate thoughts, fantasies, troubles, and dreams. Later, if one or more of these online acquaintances uses some of this personal information against them, they are inevitably shocked and puzzled.

You can't choose your family, but you can choose your friends. Remember this as you use the Internet and you will have taken the first step in outmaneuvering the spammers, stalkers, and swindlers who are targeting you online.

Resources: netcrimes.net

Here, organized by chapter, is a directory of Web resources mentioned in the book, plus a few bonus sites. It would be impossible to include all available resources, and Web pages come and go, so I am maintaining a linked (and periodically updated) version of the directory on the official *Net Crimes & Misdemeanors* Web site, www.netcrimes.net. (See page xxi for more information.)

If you have questions about any of the resources listed here, information about dead links, or suggestions for additional sites that would be useful to readers of *Net Crimes & Misdemeanors,* please send e-mail to jhitchcock@netcrimes.net.

Chapter 1:
Cyberstalking Happened to Me
   jahitchcock.com
   www.jahitchcock.com

   Abuse of Usenet
   www.jahitchcock.com/cyberstalked

   WHOA (Working to Halt Online Abuse)
   www.haltabuse.org

Chapter 2:
Words Can Hurt
   "Shut the Door" Online Safety Brochure by Taryn Pream
   www.trf.k12.mn.us/lhs/shutthedoor.html

How to Show Full Headers
www.haltabuse.org/help/headers

WHOIS
www.networksolutions.com/cgi-bin/whois/whois

Chapter 3:
Spam Not in a Can

Jon Postel's "On the Junk Mail Problem"
www.ietf.org/rfc/rfc0706.txt

The Green Card Spam
www.urbanlegends.com/legal/green_card_spam.html

The Infamous "Green Card" Lawyers
http://agents.www.media.mit.edu/people/foner/Essays/
Civil-Liberties/Project/green-card-lawyers.html

Ray Everett-Church
www.everett.org

CAUCE (Coalition Against Unsolicited Commercial E-mail)
www.cauce.org

SpamCop
www.spamcop.net

SpamCon
www.spamcon.org

SPAM is not Spam
www.spam.com/ci/ci_in.htm

Spam News
petemoss.com/spam

Sign the Spam Boycott Petition
www.madaboutspam.org

Fight Spam
spam.abuse.net

101 Things To Do With A Spammer
www.studio42.com/kill-the-spam/pages/101.html

C-Spam
www.cspam.com

I Want Spam
www.iwantspam.com

In Defense of Spam
www.provider.com/framesbulke.htm

Chapter 4:
Urban Legends and Hoaxes:
Can They Possibly Be True?

Urban Legends Reference Pages
www.snopes2.com

AFU and Urban Legends Archive
www.urbanlegends.com

Urban Legends Research Center
www.ulrc.com.au

TruthOrFiction.com
www.truthorfiction.com

Don't Spread That Hoax!
www.nonprofit.net/hoax

The Urban Legend Combat Kit
www.netsquirrel.com/combatkit

Myths and Legends of the Internet
www.myths.org

HoaxBusters
HoaxBusters.ciac.org

Break The Chain
www.breakthechain.org

Purportal.com—Your B.S. Detection Kit
purportal.com

USPS Response to "E-mail Tax Bill"
www.usps.com/news/2002/emailrumor.htm

Chapter 5:
Scams, Safe Shopping, and
Online Banking

The FBI's Internet Fraud Complaint Center
www.ifccfbi.gov

National Fraud Information Center Internet Fraud Watch
www.fraud.org/internet/intset.htm
1-800-876-7060

Frank Fiore's Online Shopping Tips
onlineshopping.about.com

Skiftelecom Credit Card Fraud
www.landmarkinv.com/cardfraud.htm

PayPal
www.paypal.com

Billpoint
www.billpoint.com
Guzoo Escrow
www.guzooescrow.com

Bidpay
www.bidpay.com

MasterCard International ShopSmart
www.mastercardintl.com/newtechnology/set

American Express Private Payments
www26.americanexpress.com/privatepayments/info_page.jsp

Discover Financial Services Shopping Guide
www2.discovercard.com/shopguide/sec03_safe.shtml

Visa International Internet Shopping Guide
www.usa.visa.com/personal/secure_with_visa/secure_
commerce_program.html

Privacy Foundation
www.privacyfoundation.org

U.S. Postal Inspection Service
www.usps.gov/postalinspectors

Banking and Investing Online Resources Group
www.bank-accounts-online.com

Free Online Banking in America
www.free-online-banking-internet-checking.com

Electronic Banker
www.electronicbanker.com/btn/m_btn2.shtml

Quicken Online Banking
www.quicken.com/banking_and_credit

MS Money Online Banking Page
www.msmoney.com/mm/banking/onlinebk/onlinebk_intro.htm

Scams, Frauds, Hoaxes, etc. on the Internet from A to Z
advocacy-net.com/scammks.htm

Scambusters
www.scambusters.com
This is one of the most comprehensive Web sites devoted to
online scams, including shopping and banking. The site offers a
monthly newsletter with the latest information, which can be
e-mailed to you.

Scamwatch
www.scamwatch.com

Internet Scams Ezine
inetscams.hypermart.net

WebAssured.com
www.webassured.com

Planet Feedback
www.planetfeedback.com

Ecomplaints.com
www.ecomplaints.com

Epinions.com
www.epinions.com

BizRate.com
www.bizrate.com

Rating Wonders
www.ratingwonders.com

ConsumerSearch
www.consumersearch.com

Productopia
www.productopia.com

PriceWatch (comparison shopping)
www.pricewatch.com

Copernic Shopper
www.copernic.com/products/shopper/index.html

How to Avoid Online Investment Scams
www.sec.gov/investor/pubs/cyberfraud.htm

BBB Shop Safely Online
www.bbb.org/library/shoponline.asp

BBB (Better Business Bureau Online Complaint System)
www.bbb.org/bbbcomplaints/Welcome.asp

BBB Locator (for the office nearest you)
www.bbb.org/BBBComplaints/lookup.asp

National Consumer Complaint Center
www.alexanderlaw.com/nccc/cb-ftc.html

The National Consumers League
www.natlconsumersleague.org
(202) 835-3323

CCIPS (Computer Crime and Intellectual Property Section,
USDOJ)
www.cybercrime.gov

National Infrastructure Protection Center
www.nipc.gov
(202) 323-3205

National Fraud Information Center
www.fraud.org
1-800-876-7060

FDIC Tips for Banking Safely Online
www.fdic.gov/bank/individual/online/safe.html

Chapter 6:
Auction Caution

eBay Community Life (Online auctions advice)
pages.ebay.com/community/life

BBB Online Auctions
www.bbb.org/library/shoponline.asp

The WebStore Online Auctions Guide
www.thewebstoreguide.com/auctions.html

UACC (Universal Autograph Collector's Club)
www.uacc.org

PADA (Professional Autograph Dealer's Association)
www.padaweb.org

Chapter 7:
Where the Heartache Is: Adoption Fraud

NCFA (National Council for Adoption)
www.ncfa-usa.org
(202) 328-1200

Adopting.com—Internet Adoption Resources
www.adopting.com

Adopt: Assistance Information Support
www.adopting.org
1-888-490-4600

The Adoption Guide
www.theadoptionguide.com

Adoption.about
adoption.about.com

Waiting Families: Family/Child Matching
www.waitingfamilies.com

Adoption Resource Directory
www.adopt-usa.org

Adoption Assistance
www.adoption-assist.com

Adoptshop
www.adoptshop.com
1-888-490-4600

National Association of Ethical Adoption Professionals
www.NAEAP.com
(540) 462-6159

Chapter 8:
Cases of Stolen Identity

FTC (Federal Trade Commission)
www.ftc.gov

SEC (U.S. Securities and Exchange Commission)
www.sec.gov

U.S. Secret Service
www.treas.gov/usss/index.html

U.S. Government's Official Site about Identity Theft
www.consumer.gov/idtheft

Identity Theft Resource Center
www.idtheftcenter.org

Cybersnitch
www.cybersnitch.net

Equifax Credit Information Services—Consumer Fraud Division
P.O. Box 105496
Atlanta, Georgia 30348-5496
1-800-997-2493
www.equifax.com

Experian
P.O. Box 2104
Allen, Texas 75013-2104
1-888-EXPERIAN (397-3742)
www.experian.com

Trans Union Fraud Victim Assistance Dept.
P.O. Box 390
Springfield, PA 19064-0390
1-800-680-7289
www.transunion.com

MasterCard International ShopSmart
www.mastercard.com/education/fraud/fraud.html

American Express Private Payments
www26.americanexpress.com/privatepayments/info_page.jsp

Discover Financial Services Shopping Guide
www2.discovercard.com/shopguide/sec03_safe.shtml

Visa International Internet Shopping Guide
www.usa.visa.com/personal/secure_with_visa/secure_
commerce_program.html

Chapter 9:
Your Personal Life Exposed

Amyboyer.org
www.amyboyer.org

SafetyEd International
www.safetyed.org

WHOA
www.haltabuse.org

CyberAngels
www.cyberangels.org

The Stalkers Home Page
www.glr.com/stalk.html

For the Love of Julie
www.creepysites.com

SafePlace
www.austin-safeplace.org

U.S. Dept. of Justice Office for Victims of Crime
www.ojp.usdoj.gov/ovc
1-800-627-6872 (resource center number)

Chapter 10:
Ugly Beasts Lurking Online

Google Groups
groups.google.com

Newsone.net
newsone.net

Forte Agent
www.forteinc.com/agent

Yahoo!
www.yahoo.com

AltaVista
www.altavista.com

Google
www.google.com

Metacrawler
www.metacrawler.com

Dogpile
www.dogpile.com

List of Online Harassment/Stalking Laws
www.haltabuse.org/resources/laws

Chapter 11:
A Little Harmful Chat

TheGuardianAngel.com
www.theguardianangel.com

Yahoo!Chat
chat.yahoo.com

Park Chat (easy-to-use interface)
www.the-park.com

TalkCity Chat
www.talkcity.com/chat

Excite Chat
www.excite.com/communities

Lycos Chat
clubs.lycos.com/live/ChatRooms/ChatHome.asp?Area=1

ParaChat (add a chat room to your Web site)
www.parachat.com

The Center for Online Addiction
www.netaddiction.com

Chatmag.com
www.chatmag.com

You May Be Addicted to IRC (Chat) If ... (a humorous look)
www.humorspace.com/humor/lists/lirc.htm

Tech Dictionary
www.techdictionary.com/chat.html

Chapter 12:
Other Ways They Can Get You

Guestbook.de
two.guestbook.de

Dreambook
www.dreambook.com

Guestworld
www.guestworld.com

Creation Center
www.creationcenter.com

SpotLife
www.spotlife.com/home.jhtml

CUSeeMe
www.cuseemeworld.com

CamCities
www.camcities.com

CamCentral
www.camcentral.com

MyCams
www.mycams.com

iCamMaster
www.icammaster.com

1-2-3 Web Tools
www.freeguestbooks.com

Chapter 13:
Protecting the Children

NCMEC
www.ncmec.org/cybertip
1-800-843-5678

SafetyEd International
www.safetyed.org

Operation Blue Ridge Thunder
www.blueridgethunder.com

TheGuardianAngel.com
www.theguardianangel.com

COPPA (Children's Online Privacy Protection Act)
www.coppa.org

CIPA (Children's Internet Protection Act)
www.ala.org/cipa

CCRC (Crimes Against Children Research Center)
www.unh.edu/ccrc/factsheet.html

McAfee.com Kids
kids.mcafee.com

FTC's KidzPrivacy Site
www.ftc.gov/bcp/conline/edcams/kidzprivacy

DOJ's Kids Page for Staying Safe Online
www.usdoj.gov/kidspage/do-dont/kidinternet.htm

FBI's Parents Guide to Protecting Children Online
www.fbi.gov/publications/pguide/pguide.htm

Kids Privacy
www.kidsprivacy.org

Safe Kids
www.safekids.com

Safe Surfin
www.safesurfin.com

McGruff the Crime Dog
www.mcgruff-safe-kids.com

Child Online Protection
www.coplaw.com

Consumer Reports
www.consumerreports.org

Filtering Software and Filtered Web Providers (see Chapter 13)

Lighthouse
www.guidinglightsoftware.com

CyberSitter
www.solidoak.com/cysitter.htm

Net Nanny
www.netnanny.com

Internet Guard Dog (McAfee)
www.mcafee.com

Norton Internet Security 2001 Family Filtering
www.symantec.com/sabu/nis/nis_fe

CyberPatrol
www.cyberpatrol.com

Familynet
www.family.net

Family Connect
www.familyconnect.com

Mayberry USA
www.mbusa.net

Safe Access
www.safeaccess.com

Internet4Families
www.net4fam.net

The List
thelist.internet.com
(type "filtered" in the search text box)

Chapter 14:
Office Know-How:
Stay Safe in the Workplace

Title VII—Civil Rights Act of 1964
www.dol.gov/dol/oasam/public/regs/statutes/2000e-16.htm

WinWhatWhere
www.winwhatwhere.com

AMA (American Management Association)
A not-for-profit management and training organization
www.amanet.org

Stroz Associates (Computer crimes consulting firm)
www.strozassociates.com

SurfControl
www.surfcontrol.com

Vault.com
www.vault.com

Online Guide to E-Mail and the Internet in the Workplace
By Susan E. Gindin

The Bureau of National Affairs
www.info-law.com/guide.html

Creating an Online Privacy Policy
www.info-law.com/create.html

Technology and Online Harassment in the Workplace
www.westbuslaw.com/blt/internet_employment.html

Chapter 15:
Police Duty: Our Nation's
Finest Boot Up

Kennebunk, Maine, Police Department
kennebunkpolice.maine.org

Maine Computer Crimes Task Force
www.mcctf.org

Nashua, New Hampshire, Police Department
www.ci.nashua.nh.us/police

Massachusetts Attorney General's Office
www.ago.state.ma.us
(617) 727-2200

High Technology and Computer Crimes Division
www.ago.state.ma.us/htdefault.asp#crime

Alexandria, Virginia, Police Department
ci.alexandria.va.us/police

Somerset, Kentucky, Police Department
www.somersetpd.com

San Diego County District Attorney
www.co.san-diego.ca.us/cnty/cntydepts/safety/da

NCVC (National Center for Victims of Crime)
www.ncvc.org
1-800-FYI-CALL (1-800-394-2255)

Stalking Resource Center
www.ncvc.org/SRC.htm

Cybersnitch
www.cybersnitch.net

SamSpade
www.samspade.org

Computer Crime and Intellectual Property Section (CCIPS)
www.cybercrime.gov

The National Infrastructure Protection Center (NIPC)
www.nipc.gov

Cops Online
www.copsonline.com

Chapter 16:
Universities Catch Up With the Net

George Mason University
www.gmu.edu

GMU's Web site offers a host of advice, including security on campus and what to do if something should happen to students, faculty, and staff.
www.gmu.edu/facstaff/sexual/online_telephone_harassment.
html#online

Jake Baker Scandal
www.trincoll.edu/zines/tj/tj4.6.95/articles/baker.html

Center for Democracy and Technology (CDT)
www.cdt.org

University at Buffalo
www.buffalo.edu

Central Michigan University
www.cmich.edu

University of Maryland University College
www.umuc.edu

Campus Security (includes campus crime statistics links)
www.ed.gov/offices/OPE/PPI/security.html

Security on Campus, Inc.
www.soconline.org

Campus Safety
campussafety.org

Chapter 17:
Encryption Made Easy

EFF (Electronic Frontier Foundation)
www.eff.org
(415) 436-9333

Pete Moss Publications—Security News
petemoss.com/security/issue.html

Philip Zimmermann's Site
web.mit.edu/prz

Federal Electronic Signatures in Global and National
Commerce Act
thomas.loc.gov/cgi-bin/bdquery/z?d106:s.00761:

Consumers Union
www.consumersunion.org
(914) 378-2000

PGP Freeware
web.mit.edu/network/pgp.html

PGPi (recommended for Internet beginners)
www.pgpi.org

Public Key Server
pgpkeys.mit.edu:11371

PGP FAQ
www.cam.ac.uk.pgp.net/pgpnet/pgp-faq

Privacyrights.org
www.privacyrights.org

CDT (Center for Democracy and Technology)
www.cdt.org
(202) 637-9800

EPIC (Electronic Privacy Information Center)
www.epic.org
(202) 483-1140

Privacy Foundation
www.privacyfoundation.org

U.S. Government Electronic Commerce Policy
www.ecommerce.gov

OnSign (free electronic signature creation)
www.onsign.com

Instructions on setting up an electronic signature in MS Outlook
internetsrvr.fullerton.edu/humanresources/forms/creating_
signature.htm

Digital Signature Guidelines
www.abanet.org/scitech/ec/isc/dsg-tutorial.html

Chapter 18:
Protect Your Computer!

Crimelabs
www.crimelabs.net

Norton Internet Security
www.symantec.com/consumer_products/home-is.html

Jammer
www.agnitum.com/products/jammer

BlackICE Defender
www.networkice.com/products/blackice_defender.html

ZoneAlarm
www.zonelabs.com/products/za

McAfee Firewall
www.mcafee.com/myapps/firewall

GRC Net Filter
grc.com/nf/netfilter.htm

Robo Form
www.roboform.com

Password Manager
www.password-manager.com

EZ Password Manager
www.northwind-tech.com

Cookie Pal
www.kburra.com/cpal.html

AdSubtract
www.adsubtract.com

Cookie Crusher
www.thelimitsoft.com/cookie.html

Cookie Jar
www.lne.com/ericm/cookie_jar

Norton AntiVirus
www.symantec.com/nav

McAfee VirusScan
www.mcafee.com/anti-virus

Freebie List
Offers a list of several free anti-virus programs and tools
www.freebielist.com/antivirus.htm

Virus Encyclopedia
www.vet.com.au/html/zoo

Virus Bulletin
www.virusbtn.com/index.html

Joe Wells' Wild Virus List
www.virusbtn.com/WildLists

Computer Associates Virus Information
www.ca.com/virusinfo

CERT Advisories
www.cert.org/advisories

Virus Myths
www.vmyths.com

Software Reviews of online security/anti-virus products such as
Jammer, BlackICE Defender, and Norton Internet Security
computeme.tripod.com

Chapter 19:
Is It Spam—or Harassment?

WHOA's Is It Harassment
www.haltabuse.org/help/isit.shtml

SpamCop
www.spamcop.net

SamSpade
www.samspade.org

What Are Full Headers?
www.haltabuse.org/help/header.shtml

How to Show Full Headers in E-mail/Newsreader Programs
www.haltabuse.org/help/headers

State-by-State Online Harassment/Stalking Laws
www.haltabuse.org/resources/laws

WHOA
www.haltabuse.org

SafetyEd International
www.safetyed.org

Operation Blue Ridge Thunder
www.blueridgethunder.com

Cybersnitch
www.cybersnitch.net

National Center for Missing and Exploited Children
www.ncmec.org
1-800-843-5678

National Center for Victims of Crime
www.ncvc.org
1-800-FYI-CALL (1-800-394-2255)

Chapter 20:
A Recap: The Basics of
Staying Safe Online

Online Safety Tips
www.haltabuse.org/resources/online.shtml

FAQ Central
www.faq-central.net

Internet FAQ Archives
www.faqs.org/faqs

eFax.com (free fax)
www.efax.com

Jfax (free voicemail and fax)
www.j2.com

Free Voicemail/Fax Web Site Listings
www.fecg.net/voicemail.asp

The Ultimates White Pages Directory
www.theultimates.com/white

The Ultimates E-Mail Directory
www.theultimates.com/email

Web Shots
www.webshots.com

Picture It
communities.msn.com/PictureIt

Club Photo
www.clubphoto.com

Off-line Safety Tips
www.haltabuse.org/resources/offline.shtml

Report-It
www.report-it.com

Reader Bonus

Here are some additional useful sites, not found in the book, to keep you surfing safely!

Learn the Net
www.learnthenet.com
How to find information, download files, master the basics, and more. Soon you'll be surfing the Net like a pro!

Family Friendly Sites
www.familyfriendlysites.com
Offers a search engine with family-oriented results (no worries about pornography or obscene language here), online safety resources, and tips.

Family Internet at About.com
http://familyinternet.about.com
Find out everything you need to know about your computer, the Internet, and more.

Netiquette

www.albion.com/netiquette

Be polite online—this is the place to learn the "rules" of cyber-space. Follow these rules and you can stay safe.

Spyware

www.cexx.org/problem.htm

Are there programs hiding on your computer that shouldn't be there? Scan your computer and remove them by using a free software program called Ad Aware at www.lavasoftusa.com.

What is…?

http://whatis.techtarget.com

Got questions about computers and the Internet? Whatis?com is one of the best sites for the answers.

Freeware/Shareware

www.tucows.com

Want to get software for free or almost-free? Tucows.com offers everything you can imagine, from anti-virus to firewall software, to games and screensavers, utility programs, cookie removers, and lots more.

TracerLock

www.tracerlock.com

One of the best ways to keep track of yourself online, see if some-one's impersonating you, or just for curiosity—and it's free! Submit your search parameters—your first and last name or your e-mail address—and TracerLock will e-mail you when it finds a match on a Web page/site, in newsgroups/forums/message boards, "for sale" and auction sites, employment listings, and personal ads.

Ask An Expert

www.askanexpert.com

Whether you have a question about something online or off-line, Pitsco's Ask An Expert Web site has hundreds of "real world experts" who will answer your questions for free!

Looking For a New ISP?

www.isps.com

If you're looking for a new Internet Service Provider (ISP), look no further than this site. Search by area code, price, name, national, or toll-free ISPs.

Glossary

Address. The location of an Internet resource. An e-mail address usually looks like johnsmith@nowhere.com; a Web address looks like www.jahitchcock.com.

Baud. Modem speeds are measured by their baud rate, which is the rate at which they send and receive information.

BBS (Bulletin Board System). Not used as often now, but was popular in the early days of the Internet. This was basically a virtual bulletin board. Users could post announcements, have discussions, upload/download files.

Bookmark. Marking and saving a favorite Web site URL or location within your Web browser. Lets you easily return to it without having to search for the URL in a search engine or try to remember the URL off the top of your head.

Broadband. A wide band of frequency used for telecommunications. Term is used when describing either DSL or cable connection to the Internet.

Browser. A program used to view sites/pages on the World Wide Web. Popular browsers are Netscape Communicator, Microsoft Internet Explorer, and Mosaic.

Cable. High-speed Internet access through your cable service line.

Cache. A folder/area on your hard drive where frequently accessed data is stored, such as the Web sites and pages you've visited plus the cookies and graphics associated with them. The info in your cache allows your Web browser to access a Web site faster if you have visited it in the past, unless you have deleted the cache.

Chat. Real-time or live conversation online. This happens in a virtual room with a few or even a hundred people. Or it can happen one-on-one in a private room. People chat about anything and

317

everything, whether or not it has to do with the name of the chat room. Examples of names are The TV Room, Adults 30+, and Los Angeles Teens.

Client. A program—like a Web browser—that connects to and requests information from a server.

Communities. Many Web hosts, such as Geocities, AOL, and Excite, have communities that contain Web pages created by users registered with that ISP or Web site. These users can interact with each other within their "community" via chat rooms, discussion boards, or forums.

Cookies. Information files stored on your hard drive by your Web browser when you visit certain Web sites. This information is then used to keep track of, for example, the last time you visited that Web site, what you ordered, or where it was mailed. Each cookie is different. Some may have basic information, such as your last visit, while others may have a lot more information, including what kind of computer you use, the name of your ISP, and your full name, address, and telephone number. Not all Web sites "set" cookies (save them to your hard drive). Most firewall/security programs allow you to delete these cookies if you wish.

Cracker. Usually more destructive than a hacker, this is a person who breaks into a Web site or system to sabotage, or otherwise damages or alters, the site or system.

Cross-post. Post a message to several newsgroups at one time. This is actually considered a big no-no, especially when you post the same message to more than two newsgroups at once.

Cyberspace. Coined by author William Gibson in his novel *Neuromancer*, it refers to the Internet or World Wide Web as we know it and the culture that has spawned from it.

Cyberstalking. When one form of online harassment leads to other forms, then to an obsession with the victim, sometimes culminating in real-life stalking and harassment.

DSL (Digital Subscriber Line). Available through the telephone company, it allows high-speed access to the Internet through your telephone line.

Dial-Up Service. A way to connect to the Internet through a modem and telephone line if you don't have DSL or cable. The modem dials into your Internet Service Provider (ISP) and connects you to the Net.

Digital Signature. Also called a digital ID or certificate, a secure way of identifying individuals on the Internet; often used to authenticate each user in a digital transaction. VeriSign is one provider of digital certification.

Discussion Group. Also called newsgroup or forum, where people can post and reply to messages on a variety of topics.

Domain. The Internet is divided into smaller sets known as domains, including .com (business), .gov (government), .edu (educational), .mil (military), .org (nonprofit organizations), .net (miscellaneous organizations), and more to come in the future.

Domain Name. This identifies the Web site and consists of two parts: the first is the registered name of the site, the second is the subdomain or category. Take, for example, the Web site address usmc.mil. The "usmc" is the United States Marine Corps Web site and ".mil" is the military category. Put together, they form the domain name.

DNS (Domain Name System). A database system that translates a domain name into an IP address. For example, a domain name such as www.comset.net converts to the numeric address 213.172. 9.119.

Ego Surf. To perform a search online for yourself as a safety precaution to make sure there isn't more information out there on you than you want. The best way to ego-surf is to put your name in quotes in a search engine, such as "jayne hitchcock," then check the results to see which sites/pages you may be listed on.

Electronic Signature. A form of encryption that allows online users to "sign" documents, pay bills, bank, and shop online with an electronic or digital signature unique to only them.

E-Mail. An e-mail address consists of the user name, then the "@" (called an "at" sign), the name of the Internet service provider (ISP), and the domain, or what designation the ISP has been assigned. In the e-mail address "Janice@hotmail.com," the breakdown is: "Janice" as the user name, "hotmail" as the ISP, and ".com" as the domain category of companies.

E-Mail Bomb. When hundreds of e-mail messages are sent to one e-mail address in an effort to overload the account and shut that e-mailbox down.

Emoticon. A combination of characters that form a facial expression, of sorts, when looked at sideways. For example, the characters :) make a smile or, in Net terms, a smiley. Often used in e-mail and newsgroup messages, as well as chat rooms.

Encryption. A way of making data such as credit card numbers unreadable to everyone except the recipient. *See* PGP.

FAQ (Frequently Asked Questions). A collection of the most frequently asked questions and answers on a particular subject or about a newsgroup or Web site.

Feedback. Found mostly in online auctions, the seller and winning bidder can leave feedback or comments for each other when an auction sale is completed. Feedback results can be viewed by anyone prior to making a bid to check whether the seller or bidder has had a positive, neutral, or negative experience.

Finger. A program that reports the name associated with an e-mail address and may also show the most recent logon information or even whether the person is currently connected to the Internet.

Filtering. *See* Killfiling/kill filter.

Firewall. Protection for computer systems and networks from attacks by hackers, viruses, Trojans, and more, in either hardware or software form.

Flame. When someone writes a message on a newsgroup, mailing list, chat room, or via e-mail that someone else either takes offense to or disagrees with and then writes a nasty reply, you have a flame. If the original writer responds just as nastily, a flame war ensues. Sometimes this can be stopped before it gets out of control.

FOAF. Acronym for Friend of a Friend, a term often used in urban legends.

Forged. A term used when someone uses an e-mail address that is obviously not a real one.

Forum. Can also be called a discussion group, message board, or newsgroup.

Full Headers. Additional information found in e-mail and Usenet messages that denotes where a message really originates, even if someone forges the return e-mail address or uses a free e-mail account such as Hotmail.

Gateway. Hardware or software set up to translate between two protocols that are not similar. AOL, for example, is a gateway to the Internet. You must use its software to connect to AOL first and then use its interface to access Web sites, chat, e-mail, etc., which are outside of its system.

Guestbook. Much like a guestbook seen at weddings and other events, a guestbook is on a Web page/site so that a visitor can enter comments about the Web page/site. When others visit the Web page/site, they can view the messages, which frequently list a guest's e-mail address and name, too.

Hacker/Hacking. You've seen them in the movies and on TV, or read about fictional ones and real ones in books, newspapers, and magazines. Most hackers want to test a Web site or Internet connection to see if it's as secure as the person/business who owns it thinks it is. But some hackers are out to cause trouble and possibly fraud by breaking into the computer systems of banks to transfer money to hidden bank accounts in their name or to wreak havoc at a former employer's Web site or LAN. Hackers have also borrowed someone's Internet account to spam or harass a person, stolen files from hard drives, and wiped a computer hard drive clean. *See* Cracker.

Harassment. Badgering, annoying, worrying, or tormenting another person, often through repeated unwelcome contact. Online harassment typically occurs when someone begins sending nasty messages via e-mail, chat, IM, or newsgroups. If not stopped at this stage, it could lead to cyberstalking.

Header. What you usually see in an e-mail message or Usenet post: the TO:, FROM:, DATE:, and SUBJECT: lines. *See* Full Headers.

Hoaxes. Similar to urban legends, these are the messages and posts that try to convince people that they really can get something for nothing or that a bad virus is coming their way, or some other nonsense. As P.T. Barnum supposedly said, "There's a sucker born every minute." In the online millieu, suckers continue to fall for these hoaxes even after previous ones were found to be false.

Home Page. The first page of a Web site. Or, the Web page/site that automatically loads each time you launch your browser.

Host. The name of a specific machine within a larger domain.

HTML (HyperText Markup Language). What Web pages are really made of. Tags that make what you see look "pretty." Example: I am here would make those words show up in bold type: **I am here.** If you're not familiar with HTML, go to a Web site/page, right-click your mouse, click on "View Source," and you'll see what looks like a different language. Anything in "arrows" is the HTML code.

HTTP (HyperText Transfer Protocol). Seen at the beginning of a URL, this is basically a set of instructions for communication between a server and a site.

HTTPS. This means you've gone to a Web site that is secure, allowing for safe online transactions, whether it's shopping, banking, or a protected site that only certain people can access.

Identity Theft. When someone steals your identity online, impersonates you, and wreaks havoc in your name—many times charging money to credit cards you never received, taking out loans, and ordering items.

IM (Instant Messaging). Similar to chat in that it is live but the conversation is one-on-one. You can do IM with programs such as AOL Instant Messenger, ICQ, and Yahoo! Messenger.

Internet. A worldwide set of computers using TCP/IP; the World Wide Web is a subset of these computers.

IRC (Internet Relay Chat). Similar to chat, a system that allows you to have text-based communication with one or more people, but without all the "pretty" graphics.

ISP (Internet Service Provider). Also called an IAP (Internet Access Provider), a company that provides access to the Internet.

IP (Internet Protocol). How data is sent from one computer (aka a "host") to another on the Internet. This is the most popular of protocols on which the Internet is based. Each host has at least one IP address that uniquely identifies it from all other hosts on the Internet. *See* IP Address.

IP Address (Internet Protocol Address). A set of four numbers that identify where you are located. Every computer/server has a unique number, so if you use a dial-up ISP, you may have a different IP address each time you dial in to the Internet, as ISPs run more than one server to accommodate their customers. The larger the ISP, the more servers, thus more IP addresses. So one day you may log in to an IP address of 204.52.190.0, the next day you might log in to an IP address of 204.52.191.2.

Intranet. Similar to a local area network (LAN). An internal Internet available only to those within that company or building.

IT. Acronym for Information Technology.

Kbps. Kilobits per second, or the speed of a modem. Most dial-up modems now run at 56kbps.

Killfile/Kill Filter. Many e-mail and newsreader programs offer this feature so that the e-mail program can automatically delete any e-mail or filter out any Usenet/newsgroup messages that the user doesn't want. Most people use this to avoid spam.

LAN (Local Area Network). An internal network consisting of two or more computers connected to each other and accessible only from within that office or organization.

Lurker. Someone who is present in a chat room, newsgroup, or other online forum, but doesn't chat or post, reads the conversation going on around them. This is called "lurking."

Mailing List. This is similar to a newsgroup except that all messages and replies are sent to your e-mail inbox. Most mailing lists are moderated, which means that someone reads the messages before sending them on, eliminating a lot of the spam and unwanted clutter. However, some mailing lists are so busy that members can receive 100 or more messages per day.

Message Boards. Similar to a newsgroup or mailing list, but located on a Web site. More than likely they are unmoderated, which opens the door for trolls and spoofers.

Metasearch. Conducting a search on the Web by using several search engines at once, with the results compiled and given to you so that there are no repeats.

Modem. It's usually inside your computer (some people like to use external modems). A modem helps connect you to the Internet, whether you're using an older dial-up modem, cable, or DSL.

Mirror Site. A Web site set up as an alternate to a busy site, with copies of all the files stored at the primary location.

Mung. As in "munging an e-mail address." To add numerals, letters, or characters to your e-mail address so that spammers can't harvest your e-mail address to send you spam. Example: Instead of using anotherwriter@hotmail.com, change the preferences and reply-to settings in your e-mail program to read "another-NOT-writer@ hotmail.com."

Netiquette. To be polite online. Basically it's Internet etiquette.

Netizens. Common nickname for online users.

Newbie. Someone new to the Internet.

Newsgroup. Also known as Usenet, a newsgroup is similar to a message board. It is topic-specific, such as misc.writing for writers, alt.beer for beer lovers, alt.fan.harrison-ford for fans of the actor. A message is posted on a newsgroup usually about a particular subject that is already being discussed. Others can reply to that post or start a new subject. Anyone who visits the newsgroup can read the messages and replies without posting anything. This is called lurking. There are thousands of newsgroups on the Net, with the number growing every day.

Newsreader. A software program that allows you to access and keep track of available newsgroups through your ISP (alphabetically) and which ones you subscribe to; it also helps organize the messages and replies received from any newsgroups you're subscribed to. Many people like to use a separate newsreader program, such as Forte Agent, instead of using the newsreader that comes with their Web browser or a Web-based newsgroup search engine such as Google Groups or Newsone.net.

Network. A system of connected computers exchanging information with each other. A LAN is a smaller form of a network. The Internet is a fantastically huge worldwide network of computers.

NSLookup. A software program where you enter a host name (for example, "disney.com") and see what the corresponding IP address is. NSLookup also does reverse name lookup to find the host name for an IP address you specify.

Online. When you connect to your ISP, whether it's AOL, CompuServe, Netcom, Earthlink, or a local bulletin board system, you are online. Anything you do related to this is considered being online, whether it's sending e-mail, surfing Web sites, chatting, or reading newsgroups.

Packet. A unit of data sent between an origin and a destination online. Example: When any file (e-mail message, graphic/photo, HTML file, Web site URL request) is sent from one place to another online, it's divided into packets so that these smaller "chunks" are easier to send. Each packet has its own unique number, which includes the Internet address of its destination. These packets may take different routes from each other, but they all arrive at the same destination where they are reassembled back into the original file that was sent.

PDA. Personal Digital Assistant, such as a Palm Pilot or other handheld "mini-computer" used for keeping track of appointments, to store phone numbers, and more.

Post. To send a message to a mailing list, newsgroup, or other online forum. You use links or click on graphical buttons that read something like "Post a new message/subject" or "Reply to this topic/subject." Each list, group, and forum has a different way to post.

Preference Settings (Options). Where you can select which options you want in your browser, e-mail, newsreader, and IM programs.

PGP (Pretty Good Privacy). A form of encryption, it scrambles messages so they are unreadable by anyone except the sender and the recipient. This is one of the most popular encryption programs available.

Profile. All about you, depending on how much information you input. Popular with chat programs and some ISPs, such as AOL. Remember, the less information you provide, the less likely you'll become an online victim. Don't give away too much.

Remailer. An online service that allows you to send e-mail messages through their Web site instead of through your e-mail program so that you retain a bit of anonymity.

SSL (Secure Socket Layer; also known as Secure Server). A form of encryption that scrambles your credit card and other information, allowing for safe transmission of the transaction.

Screen Name. *See* Username.

Scroll. When on a Web site, to scroll, place your mouse cursor on the bar on the far right or bottom of the screen and move the bar down or up to go to a different part of a Web page; the page up/page down or a scroll button on a mouse can be used to do this as well.

Search Engine. A tool for searching for information on the Internet by topic. Popular search engines include Yahoo!, Google, Ask Jeeves, and Excite. You type in your search query using one or more words.

Server. A computer connected to the Internet that stores and/or provides information, such as Web pages, e-mail messages, and newsgroup posts.

Shill Bidding. Found on auction Web sites, this refers to sellers with more than one User ID. These sellers use one ID for selling the item(s), then the other(s) to bid on the item(s) to drive the bid up, unbeknownst to legitimate bidders.

Signature. A line or two of words, usually a user's name and contact information, automatically added to the end of every e-mail or Usenet message sent out.

Site. A single page or collection of related Web pages at one domain.

Smiley. *See* Emoticons.

Snail Mail. The U.S. Postal Service delivers this to your house six days a week.

Sock Puppets. An e-mail address that goes nowhere when someone tries to send a message to it.

Spam. Unsolicited electronic junk mail, usually advertisements or offers, usually unwanted by the receiver. Sometimes used as a revenge tactic by pretending to be someone else and then spamming messages to hundreds, sometimes thousands of people at one time.

Spoofer. Someone who impersonates someone else, sometimes creating several e-mail accounts in the victim's name, then using those accounts to place (post) messages on Web sites, send offensive e-mail messages to various people (usually employers, family, and friends of the victim), pose as the victim in chat rooms, newsgroups, and mailing lists, sign guestbooks, and other online annoyances.

Subscribe. To become a member of a mailing list, newsgroup, or other online service.

Surf. Common term for going from site to site or page to page on the Web.

Techie. Someone who is a computer and/or Internet expert.

Thread. A group of messages that are replies to a subject or topic being discussed in an online forum, newsgroup, or message board.

TOS (Terms of Service). Basically the rules and regulations an ISP, Web site host, forum, etc. implements; its users must abide by the rules or risk being kicked off or denied access to the service.

Trash. Usually a function in e-mail programs that allows the user to delete unwanted e-mail, thus putting it in the trash; usually the trash empties when the user exits or ends use of the e-mail program.

Trojan. Much like the fabled Trojan horse the Greeks built to gain entrance into the city of Troy, a Trojan in computerese is a program designed to perform functions on a computer without the computer user knowing it's there.

Troll. Someone who visits a chat room, newsgroup, message board, or other online forum and writes messages meant to get the other people online upset. The action is called trolling.

UCE (Unsolicited Commerical E-mail). More commonly known as electronic junk mail or spam.

UDP (Usenet Death Penalty). When an ISP is "shut off" from newsgroups and other forums because of the lack of response to complaints about spammers using their service. A UDP means no one using that ISP can read or post messages to newsgroups and other forums until the ISP takes appropriate action against the spammers and revises its policies and/or terms to prohibit spammers from using them in the future.

UNIX. An operating system favored by many computer users. An operating system is the program that tells your computer what to do and how to interact with the keyboard, mouse, printer, and other peripherals. Other operating systems include Windows, LINUX, and DOS.

Urban Legend. Online, they're much like the ones heard from friends and family. Stories so incredibly unreal they're, well, unreal. The difference is that online legends seem to keep popping up, in e-mails, on Web sites, in newsgroups, and chat rooms, even after they've been debunked.

URL (Uniform Resource Locator). A Web address or location. For example, www.jahitchcock.com would be the URL for my personal Web site.

Usenet. Short for "User's Network," this is a list of thousands of discussions on just about any topic you can imagine. Broken down into several categories, you'll find everything from alt.sex.fetish to comp.microsoft to rec.bicycling to misc.writing.

Username (also user ID or screen name). What you select or are given to use as your ID online. Example: anotherwriter@hotmail.com—"anotherwriter" is my username/user ID for my Hotmail account. It's always good to select a gender-neutral username.

Virus. A program that infects your computer. Can range from being only a nuisance and cause things like "snow" to fall on your screen or "dancing animals" to appear to being a serious threat that damages your files and hard drive. Some viruses have been known to completely wipe a hard drive clean. The most famous virus was Melissa, which appeared on computers worldwide in 1999.

Virtual. Objects, activities, etc. that exist or are carried on in cyberspace. For example, you can shop at a virtual store on the Web.

Web Host. A site that allows users to join/subscribe and receive a host of services, such as personal Web page space, e-mail accounts, chat, message boards, and more, usually for free. Web hosts are available to people who already have online access through an ISP.

Whois. An Internet database that provides information on who owns a certain domain.

Worm. A type of virus. *See* Virus.

WWW. World Wide Web, or simply, the Web.

About the Author

Jayne A. Hitchcock is a nationally recognized Internet crime and security expert. She has helped pass laws related to online harassment in Maryland, Minnesota, Michigan, Maine, Rhode Island, and New Hampshire. As president of Working to Halt Online Abuse (WHOA, at www. haltabuse.org), Jayne helps victims of various Internet crimes fight back. She has taken her online harassment expertise to the lecture circuit throughout the country, providing messages of hope to victims and training workshops for law enforcement personnel. She also volunteers her time as a consultant on Internet crime cases for police departments nationwide, the U.S. Department of Justice Victims of Crime, and the National Center for Victims of Crime.

Jayne contributes articles and columns to several magazines, including *Link-Up, Cinescape, Naval History, Pipes & Tobaccos,* and *IT* (Information Technology), and is frequently quoted in media coverage of cyberstalking and related topics. She has been featured in *Time, Los Angeles Times, Boston Globe, Ladies Home Journal, Glamour, Family Circle's "The Web Made Easy,"* and on the Associated Press newswire. She has appeared on *48 Hours, A&E Investigative Reports, Inside Edition, Good Morning America,* and the *Montel Williams Show.*

Jayne is currently a teaching assistant at the University of Maryland University College for basic and advanced Internet courses. She lives in New England with her husband, Christopher, and their two Shiba dogs, Bandit and Guin. For more information about Jayne, visit her Web site: www.jahitchcock.com.

Index

attention, 120–121
definition, 326
resources, 300–301
TrueVector (Zone Labs), 236, 254
TruthOrFiction.com, 293
Turner, Michael G., 208

U

UACC. *See* Universal Autograph
Collector's Club
UB. *See* University at Buffalo
UCE. *See* Unsolicited Commercial
E-mail
UDP. *See* Usenet Death Penalty
UDP/IP, 242
Ugly beasts. *See* Flames; Spoofers;
Trolls
Ultimates E-Mail Directory, 313
Ultimates White Pages Directory,
313
UMUC. *See* University of
Maryland University College
Unencrypted information, sending,
66
Uniform Resource Locator (URL),
16, 65, 107
definition, 118, 327
investigation, 170
link, 149
obtaining, 147
providing, 149
sending, 277–278
United Parcel Service (UPS)
delivery, 105
usage, 86
*United States vs. Jake Baker and
Arthur Gonda,* 210, 215
Universal Autograph Collector's
Club (UACC), 88, 297
UACC3, 83
Universities
action, example, 213–214
challenge, 214–215
cyberstalking, 207–208
Internet usage, 205
examples, 208–212

online safety tips, publication,
212–213
online-related incidents, prevention, 212–213
resources, 307–308
University at Buffalo (UB),
210–212, 214, 307
servers, 210
University of Cincinnati, 209
University of Maryland University
College (UMUC), 8, 14,
214–215, 308, 330
Institutional Technology unit,
214
University of Michigan, 210
UNIX
definition, 326
Unix
usage, 270
Unlisted telephone number, obtaining, 276
Unsolicited Bulk E-mail, defense,
36
Unsolicited Commercial E-mail
(UCE)
definition, 326
usage, 30
UPS. *See* United Parcel Service
Urban legends, 43
archives, 293
combat kit, 293
definition, 326–327
education, 54–56
reference pages, 55, 293
resources, 293–294
top 10, 50–54
Urban Legends Research Center,
293
URL. *See* Uniform Resource
Locator
U.S. Attorneys Office (USAO), 200,
201
U.S. Bureau of the Census, 180
U.S. Department of Justice (U.S.
DOJ), 201–202, 264, 297